The Complete Encyclopedia of

CHINESE COOKING

The Complete Encyclopedia of CHINESE COOKING

Consultant Editor Kenneth Lo

Foreword by Madame Grace Zia Chu

CRESCENT BOOKS

Foreword
Madame Grace Zia Chu

When I began teaching Chinese cooking many years ago at the China Institute in New York City, there were very few people interested in learning to cook in the Chinese manner. Most of my students were school teachers who took the course in order to learn about another facet of a foreign culture.

Today it seems hard to believe that the world-wide popularity of this ancient cuisine is so recent; as one who was there at its onset, I can tell you that it has happened only in the last twenty-five years. I believe it was World War II that started this interest in Oriental food by bringing so many Westerners to the Orient. The cruel war had one good result, for when they returned home, the soldiers wanted to continue to eat the good things they had tasted in China, and so Chinese restaurants sprang up in the large cities of the Western World.

As soon as there was a body of sophisticated people who liked to eat Chinese food, it was inevitable that some of them would want to create the dishes themselves. And eventually a cuisine that had seemed so mysterious and impenetrable, so unlike the familiar cooking of their own countries, became available to Western cooks. The mystery was broken.

What is it that attracted so many people to a way of eating so different from their own? Chinese cooking has a tradition that goes back thousands of years. Since it originated in a vast country of extreme poverty combined with great wealth, and one which has widely different agricultural regions, it is by necessity extremely flexible. If you don't have one ingredient, you simply use another. You can be economical in your use of materials, so that a dish can be made cheaply from local vegetables and soy products. But with the addition of such expensive ingredients as steak, shark's fin and birds' nest, the same recipe becomes an exotic dish suitable for a banquet.

Furthermore, with very little knowledge of the science of nutrition, the Chinese have evolved a way of eating that is extraordinarily wholesome and nutritious. Carefully followed, a Chinese menu provides a balanced meal at low cost, with few calories and little cholesterol. The only change the modern nutritionist might make would be to substitute brown rice for white; but that is something no one has ever been able to do in China, where the people feel the same attachment to white rice as Westerners do to white bread.

Finally, I like to think that the Chinese way of eating is an expression of the best aspect of Chinese culture: the peacefulness and harmony of community life. By sitting about a round table and sharing our daily food with others, taking only as much as we need, and seeing that no one goes hungry, we learn from our earliest days how to get along with others.

This encyclopedia makes a valuable contribution to the subject of Chinese cooking that should interest both beginners and experienced cooks.

The authors are well known in their field. They deal with the very basic aspects of Chinese cooking – the utensils, techniques and ingredients – and present well-chosen recipes to illustrate every point. They describe the food served at various holidays and festivals and the characteristics of the different regional cuisines. A newcomer to Chinese cooking can begin with a careful study of the basic techniques and, once these are mastered, go on to cook any recipe in the book. An expert, on the other hand, could turn at once to one of the regional chapters to expand his mastery of this enormous subject.

Contents

Consultant Editor: Kenneth Lo
Foreword: Madame Grace Zia Chu
Consultants:
  Gloria Zimmerman
  Kitty Sham
  Anne Marshall
Authors:
  Kenneth Lo
  Deh-ta Hsiung
  Nancy Chih Ma
  Mary Ma Stavonhagen
  Julia Chih Cheng
  Kitty Sham

First English edition published 1979
by
Octopus Books Limited
59 Grosvenor Street
London W1

© MCMLXXIX Octopus Books
Limited
All rights reserved.

Library of Congress Catalog Card
Number: 7823748
ISBN 0-517-27337-3

This edition is published by
Crescent Books, a division of
Crown Publishers, Inc.

Produced by Mandarin Publishers
Limited
22a Westlands Road
Quarry Bay, Hong Kong

Printed in Singapore

Introduction
Kenneth Lo

As one travels around the world these days one cannot help being impressed by the extent to which Chinese food and cooking have become established in almost every corner of the continent. The growing appreciation of Chinese food may have been a gradual process during the 19th Century and first half of the 20th Century, but during the past couple of decades this popularization seems to have gathered sudden and overwhelming momentum. It is as if overnight there is Chinese food everywhere!

At one time there were no more than a dozen Chinese restaurants in London, and you could only get authentic Chinese food in the East End, along the West India Dock Road. But nowadays there is Chinese food not only in Birmingham, Manchester and Glasgow, but also in Carlisle, Inverness, Ipswich, Taunton and Truro.

In the U.S. the establishment of Chinese food has a longer history; initiated by early settlers in San Francisco, it became a part of the Wild West scene and lore during the Gold Rush. With Chinese working on the Pacific Railway, the tradition of Chinese cooking gradually spread eastwards towards the Eastern seaboard. Nowadays Szechuan and Hunnan cooking is all the rage in New York!

Looking further afield, one sees Chinese catering establishments opening not only in European cities – Stuttgart, Copenhagen and Vienna; but also in Sydney, Nairobi, Mombasa, Lagos, Sao Paulo, Lima and Santiago. It seems to have happened spontaneously – what is it that has caused the sudden success of Chinese food?

The answer lies in the tradition and techniques of Chinese cooking, and in the inherent appeal of Chinese food and flavours to the palate. In most areas of the world there has been a veering from sweet tastes to savoury foods in recent decades, and in the range of savoury dishes, Chinese cooking probably possesses a larger repertoire than any other cuisine. Much of Chinese cooking is based on the use of a small amount of savoury food (meat, fish or poultry) to flavour a large amount of bland, bulk food, such as rice. And, when only a small amount of savoury food is used, it has to be very savoury indeed.

This formula of savoury and bulk bland foods points to another aspect of Chinese cooking – its economy. Chinese food can be extremely economical, without reducing its appeal. It is also highly nutritious because ingredients are quickly cooked so as to retain all their natural goodness. A Chinese meal is never complete unless there is a large dish of quickly cooked and highly appealing vegetables on the table.

With the enormous variety of Chinese dishes, one would expect many unusual flavourings to be used. But the only type of flavouring ingredient used by the Chinese which is very different from those used in Western cooking is soy sauce, and other products derived from the salting or fermenting of soy beans: soy bean paste, dried (sunned) and salted soy beans, and fermented soy bean curd which is also called soy cheese. When these are used in conjunction with strong-tasting ingredients like onions, ginger and garlic; together with cooked meat, fish or poultry, and the usual seasonings of salt, pepper, paprika or chilli; the number of dishes and sauces which can be produced is countless. One American food writer put the number of Chinese recipes at 8,000 but if you went into all of the provincial variations, the number must exceed the round figure of 10,000!

Finally, the Chinese cooking tradition makes for a greater harmony of living, an aspect of Chinese cuisine which has often been overlooked. There is a great feeling of togetherness in the way the Chinese eat. They gather together, around a table, and partake of all the dishes which are placed on the table in communal style. Chopsticks are used, not only as eating implements, but also to help others to a choice piece – especially from a distant dish. This is an expression of respect and affection.

A Chinese family is usually larger than its Western equivalent, and there could easily be three or more generations dining together, all eating from the same dishes. When people are in good spirits, enjoying each other's company and the attractive and appealing food, a greater feeling of harmony is achieved. This eases any problems of communication between the different members of the family and helps to close the generation gap.

To conclude the factors which have made Chinese food so popular all over the world, it is the Chinese expertise in the production of savoury foods, their enormous repertoire of dishes, their ability to improvise and make use of every kind of ingredient and the inherent economy. Last but not least is the ability of the Chinese cooking tradition to promote a feeling of conviviality and togetherness. With these assets linked to the natural industry of the Chinese people, it may be that the latter half of the 20th Century and the first half of the 21st Century will become the 'Era of Chinese Food'. May I invite you to participate in the excitement of this appetizing 'Era', starting with this book.

Plateau of Tibet

Chinese Cooking Techniques and Utensils

Kenneth Lo

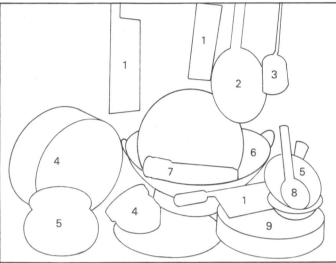

1. Chinese Cleavers; 2. Strainer; 3. Fish Slice; 4. Bamboo Steamers; 5. Clay Pots; 6. Wok; 7. Bamboo Whisk; 8. Ladle; 9. Chopping Board.

Cooking Techniques

Greater refinement in the use of heat for cooking has been achieved in China than in the West. This is probably because the Chinese often employ multi-phase heating for cooking. Hence, when one begins to learn about *He Hou*, or heat control, you will find there are 40 to 50 well-established methods. For example, in quick-frying, or quick-stir-frying, the heat used is so intense, and any increase or reduction of heat so rapid, that some 100 terms are required to denote the differentiation in heating pace.

By applying a term to each specific cooking technique, or sequence of preparation, or intensity of heating, the concept can be conveyed more easily. Take for instance, the term *Ch'eng* used in steaming. This indicates open-steaming, usually a quick process, in which the food to be cooked must be particularly fresh. The term *Tun* refers to closed-steaming, a long cooking process, effectively similar to slow-simmering. In this method, food is placed in a closed container, which in turn is placed in a steamer for a lengthy period of steaming. (This is similar to the Western use of a double-boiler.)

In quick-stir-frying, the term *Chow* (or *Ch'ao*) is used to denote simple stir-frying where several different foods, cut into similar-shaped pieces or shreds, are stir-fried together in a small amount of oil. Foods which require the longest cooking are added to the pan first. If the term *Pao* is used, only one or two ingredients are used for the initial stir-frying with a greater quantity of oil. This oil is drained away after frying and seasoning ingredients are added to make a thick sauce.

Chien indicates shallow-frying, in which the food is not stirred during frying so that it becomes crispy. *Cha* denotes simple deep-frying. The term *Ling* is used to describe a refined form of deep-frying, where the food is not wholly immersed in hot oil, but is suspended above it in a wire-basket and the hot oil is ladled over the food.

Lui denotes that food is poached in oil; the oil used is only moderately hot, and this initial poaching is followed by further cooking – in a thickened sauce, usually with wine as one of the ingredients. Food cooked in this way is intended to have a soft, rather than a crisp texture.

It is these refinements within the principal methods of cooking which create the enormous variety of Chinese cooking techniques.

Cooking in Water

The following methods show how variations in the temperature of the water and duration of cooking are used to achieve different results.

Quick-boiling

Quick-boiling or quick-poaching in broth or water kept at a rolling boil is a favourite form of cooking and serving food in North China in the winter. Although the cooking is plain and simple, the flavouring can be varied with dips.

A typical example of this type of cooking is Mongolian Hot Pot *(page 83)*, which is cooked at the table in fondue-style. Beef or lamb is cut into paper-thin slices and arranged on serving plates. The pot of boiling stock or clear broth is brought to a rolling boil and placed over a charcoal burner, methylated spirit stove or electric burner on the dining table. The diners pick up their pieces of meat with their chopsticks and drop them into the boiling stock or broth. The meat is quick-poached for not more than 2 minutes, then removed from the pot and dipped into a sauce or savoury dip before it is eaten.

Boiling Rice

Long-grain rice is the most suitable type to serve with Chinese food. Allow 0.5 kg/1 lb (2⅔ cups) rice for 4 to 6 people. Place in a heavy-based pan. Rinse once or twice under cold running water, then drain off the water. Add about 1¼ times of the rice's equivalent volume of cold water: about 500 ml/18 fl oz (2¼ cups). Bring to the boil and cover with a tight-fitting lid. Boil steadily for 1 minute then reduce the heat to low and simmer gently for 10 minutes. Turn off the heat and leave the rice to cook in its own heat for 10 to 12 minutes until quite dry.

Quick-boiling and cooking in the receding heat

This is a method which is frequently used for foods, including meat and poultry, which are very fresh and tender and can be cooked in large pieces in a relatively short time. In China, the food is cooked for a short time in boiling water on the stove; the heat is turned off and the remainder of the cooking is achieved by the receding heat. Modern cookers do not retain heat to the same extent. However, a similar effect can be obtained by lowering the heat after the initial period of rapid boiling, and simmering very gently until the food is just tender.

White-Cooked Boiled Chicken

METRIC/IMPERIAL

2.5 litres/4½ pints water
4 slices root ginger
1 × 1.5 kg/3 lb chicken
Dips
1 × 15 ml spoon/1 tablespoon shredded root ginger
1 × 15 ml spoon/1 tablespoon shredded spring onion (shallot)
1 × 15 ml spoon/1 tablespoon oil
2 × 15 ml spoons/2 tablespoons coarse sea salt
2 × 15 ml spoons/2 tablespoons soy sauce
1 × 15 ml spoon/1 tablespoon chilli sauce
1 × 15 ml spoon/1 tablespoon coarsely crushed black peppercorns

AMERICAN

5½ pints water
4 slices ginger root
1 × 3 lb chicken
Dips
1 tablespoon shredded ginger root
1 tablespoon shredded scallion
1 tablespoon oil
2 tablespoons coarse sea salt
2 tablespoons soy sauce
1 tablespoon chili sauce
1 tablespoon coarsely crushed black peppercorns

1. Pour the water into a large pan. Add the ginger and bring to the boil. Add the chicken, return to the boil and boil rapidly for 10 minutes. Reduce the heat to very low, cover and simmer for 20 minutes. Turn off the heat and leave the chicken to cool in the water.

2. When cold, drain the chicken and chop through the skin and bones into bite-size pieces. Arrange on a serving dish.

3. To make the dips, mix together the ginger, spring onion (shallot/scallion), oil and 1 × 5 ml spoon/1 teaspoon salt in a small bowl. Combine the soy sauce and chilli sauce in another bowl. Place the remaining salt and the pepper in a third bowl. Serve the dips with the chicken.

Quick-boiling, controlled by re-boiling

This cooking method is very similar to the previous one, except that the food requires more than one short period of boiling. In the following recipe, pork is cooked by three periods of vigorous boiling, in between periods of slow cooking in receding heat.

White-Cooked Boiled Pork

METRIC/IMPERIAL

2.5 litres/4½ pints water

1 × 1.5 kg/3 lb piece boned belly pork

Dips

4 cloves garlic, crushed

2 × 15 ml spoons/2 tablespoons sesame seed oil

2 × 15 ml spoons/2 tablespoons soy sauce

1 × 15 ml spoon/1 tablespoon shredded root ginger

2 × 15 ml spoons/2 tablespoons hoisin sauce

Garnish

1 chrysanthemum

AMERICAN

5½ pints water

1 × 3 lb piece boneless pork butt

Dips

4 cloves garlic, minced

2 tablespoons sesame oil

2 tablespoons soy sauce

1 tablespoon shredded ginger root

2 tablespoons hoisin sauce

Garnish

1 chrysanthemum

2. Boil steadily for 10 minutes then turn off the heat and leave for 10 minutes.

3. Repeat the boiling and resting process twice more. Leave the pork to cool in the water.

4. When cold, drain the pork and cut across the lean and fat into thin slices. Arrange the pork slices on a serving dish.
To make the dips, put the garlic and sesame oil in one bowl, the soy sauce and ginger in another, and the hoisin sauce in a third bowl. Serve the dips with the pork. Garnish the dish with the chrysanthemum.

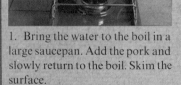

1. Bring the water to the boil in a large saucepan. Add the pork and slowly return to the boil. Skim the surface.

Clear-simmering

In China this technique is most frequently used to cook meat, fish and clear soups in an earthenware pot (called a sandpot) over a low charcoal heat. In the West, it can be achieved by cooking in a heavy flameproof casserole over a very low heat or in a cool oven. Clear-simmering differs from ordinary stewing in that few flavouring ingredients are used during cooking and the process is invariably a longer one – up to 4 hours using the lowest heat possible. Any additional ingredients are added during the last few minutes of cooking. Spicy dips are usually served at the table to counteract the blandness of clear-simmered food. Many people prefer this to heavy flavouring effected during cooking, as they can then flavour their portion to taste.

Sometimes clear-simmered food is deep-fried for a short period before serving.

Clear Broth

METRIC/IMPERIAL

1 meaty chicken carcass

0.75 kg/1½ lb pork spareribs

0.5 kg/1 lb ham, bacon or beef bones

2 litres/3½ pints water

2 × 5 ml spoons/2 teaspoons salt

2 × 5 ml spoons/2 teaspoons dried shrimps (optional)

AMERICAN

1 meaty chicken carcass

1½ lb pork spareribs

1 lb ham, bacon or beef bones

4½ pints water

2 teaspoons salt

2 teaspoons dried shrimp (optional)

Put all the ingredients into a large heavy pan or flameproof pot. Bring to the boil, cover and simmer gently for 1¾ hours, skimming frequently. Leave to cool. When cold, skim any fat from the surface. Reheat and serve as a soup or use as required.

White-Cooked Boiled Pork with assorted dips

Clear Broth (below)

Clear-Simmered Beef

METRIC/IMPERIAL

1–1.25 kg/2–2½ lb stewing beef

3 slices root ginger

2 × 5 ml spoons/2 teaspoons salt

1.75 litres/3 pints water

0.5 kg/1 lb spinach leaves, roughly chopped

1 × 15 ml spoon/1 tablespoon chopped coriander

Dips

4 × 15 ml spoons/4 tablespoons soy sauce

1 × 15 ml spoon/1 tablespoon shredded root ginger

2 × 15 ml spoons/2 tablespoons hoisin sauce

2 × 15 ml spoons/2 tablespoons English mustard

1 × 15 ml spoon/1 tablespoon chilli oil

1 × 5 ml spoon/1 teaspoon chilli sauce

AMERICAN

2–2½ lb stewing beef

3 slices ginger root

2 teaspoons salt

7½ cups water

1 lb spinach leaves, roughly chopped

1 tablespoon chopped Chinese parsley

Dips

4 tablespoons soy sauce

1 tablespoon shredded ginger root

2 tablespoons hoisin sauce

2 tablespoons English mustard

1 tablespoon chili oil

1 teaspoon chili sauce

2. Place the beef in a flameproof casserole or heavy pan with the ginger, salt and water. Bring to the boil and boil for 5 minutes; skim.

3. Lower the heat, cover and simmer very gently for 2½ to 3 hours.

Meanwhile, make the dips. Mix 2 × 15 ml spoons/2 tablespoons soy sauce with the ginger in one bowl. Put the hoisin sauce in a second dish, the mustard in a third, and mix the chilli oil, chilli sauce and remaining soy sauce in a fourth dish.

Add the spinach to the casserole and simmer gently for a further 1 to 2 minutes. Sprinkle with the coriander (Chinese parsley). Serve in individual soup bowls accompanied by rice. To eat this semi-soup, each diner lifts the meat out of the broth with chopsticks and flavours it with the dips. The broth is spooned into the rice bowls and eaten with the rice.

1. Cut the beef into 5 cm/2 inch cubes, using a Chinese cleaver or a sharp knife. Trim away any excess fat.

Clear-Simmered Beef with assorted dips

Twice-Cooked Pork

METRIC/IMPERIAL

2.25 litres/4 pints water

1 × 2 kg/4½ lb piece boned belly pork

3 slices root ginger

oil for deep-frying

Dips

2 × 15 ml spoons/2 tablespoons soy sauce

2 × 15 ml spoons/2 tablespoons chopped spring onions (shallots)

4 × 15 ml spoons/4 tablespoons wine vinegar

1 × 15 ml spoon/1 tablespoon shredded root ginger

4 cloves garlic, crushed

2 × 15 ml spoons/2 tablespoons sesame seed oil

AMERICAN

5 pints water

1 × 4½ lb piece boneless pork butt

3 slices ginger root

oil for deep-frying

Dips

2 tablespoons soy sauce

2 tablespoons chopped scallions

¼ cup wine vinegar

1 tablespoon shredded ginger root

4 garlic cloves, minced

2 tablespoons sesame oil

1. Bring the water to the boil in a large pan. Add the pork and ginger and bring to the boil, skimming off any scum that rises to the surface. Lower the heat, cover and simmer for 2½ hours.

2. Drain the pork and allow to cool, reserving the cooking liquor to make soup. When the pork is cold, cut into 4 equal pieces. To make the dips, combine the soy sauce and spring onions (shallots/scallions) in one bowl, the vinegar and ginger in another bowl, and mix the garlic with the oil in a third dish.

3. Heat the oil to 180°C/350°F. Deep-fry the pork, two pieces at a time, for 4 to 5 minutes. Drain well and cut, across the lean and fat, into 5 mm/¼ inch pieces. Serve hot, garnished with shredded spring onion (shallot/scallion), if liked, and accompanied by the dips.

4. To make Egg Drop Soup with the cooking liquor, soak 4 or 5 Chinese dried mushrooms for 20 minutes then drain, stem and shred them. Add the mushrooms to the cooking liquor and simmer for 5 to 6 minutes. Slowly pour in 1 or 2 beaten eggs along chopsticks, trailing the eggs over the surface of the soup. As soon as the eggs have set, sprinkle generously with chopped spring onions (shallots/scallions).

Twice-Cooked Pork with assorted dips (below left) Egg Drop Soup (below right)

Steaming

The food to be steamed is usually placed in a perforated container, which is held above the level of water contained in a wok or large pan. The water is kept at a constant boil to create steam, which enters the steamer and cooks the food.

Chinese bamboo steamers stack on top of each other, so that as many as four or five dishes can be steamed simultaneously. If you do not have a steamer, you can easily improvise. For example, the food can be steamed on a plate, placed on a rack inside a wok or large pan. The plate should be at least 5 cm (2 inches) above the water level and the pan should be covered during steaming to keep the food moist.

Quick-steaming

In quick-steaming, the food is first seasoned or marinated and then subjected to a short period of vigorous steaming. It is an ideal method for fresh small whole fish or fillets of larger fish, such as salmon, sea bream or striped bass.

Steamed Whole Fish

METRIC/IMPERIAL

3 slices root ginger, chopped

2 × 5 ml spoons/2 teaspoons salt

1 × 1.25 kg/2½ lb small fish (trout, sole, mackerel, etc.)

3 × 15 ml spoons/3 tablespoons soy sauce

1.5 × 5 ml spoons/1½ teaspoons sugar

1 × 15 ml spoon/1 tablespoon wine vinegar

2 × 15 ml spoons/2 tablespoons oil

2–3 rashers bacon, shredded

3–4 large dried Chinese mushrooms, soaked for 20 minutes, drained, stemmed and shredded

4 spring onions (shallots), cut into 5 cm/2 inch pieces

AMERICAN

3 slices ginger root, chopped

2 teaspoons salt

1 × 2½ lb small fish (trout, sole, mackerel, etc)

3 tablespoons soy sauce

1½ teaspoons sugar

1 tablespoon wine vinegar

2 tablespoons oil

2–3 slices bacon, shredded

3–4 large dried Chinese mushrooms, soaked for 20 minutes, drained, stemmed and shredded

4 scallions, cut into 2 inch pieces

2. Place the fish on an oval heatproof dish and spoon over the marinade. Sprinkle with the bacon, mushrooms and spring onions (shallots/scallions).

1. Mix together the chopped ginger and salt and rub over the fish, inside and out. Leave for 30 minutes. Mix together the soy sauce, sugar, vinegar and oil in a bowl. Pour this mixture over the fish and leave for 15 minutes.

3. Place the dish on a rack in a wok or large pan containing water. Cover and steam vigorously for 12 minutes. The fish should flake easily using chopsticks. Serve hot.

Long-steaming

For a long period of steaming, the food is enclosed in a wrapping, such as wonton skins or lotus leaves to retain flavour and prevent the food becoming dry.

Steamed Pork Wrapped in Lotus Leaves

METRIC/IMPERIAL

1.5–1.75 kg/3–4 lb boned belly pork

5 × 15 ml spoons/5 tablespoons coarsely ground rice

4 × 15 ml spoons/4 tablespoons soy sauce

2 × 15 ml spoons/2 tablespoons hoisin sauce

1.5 × 5 ml spoons/1½ teaspoons red bean curd cheese

2 × 5 ml spoons/2 teaspoons sugar

1 × 5 ml spoon/1 teaspoon chilli sauce

2 × 15 ml spoons/2 tablespoons dry sherry

pinch of 5-spice powder

2 large dried lotus leaves, soaked until soft and drained

AMERICAN

3–4 lb boneless pork butt

5 tablespoons coarsely ground rice

¼ cup soy sauce

2 tablespoons hoisin sauce

1½ teaspoons red bean curd

2 teaspoons sugar

1 teaspoon chili sauce

2 tablespoons pale dry sherry

pinch of 5-spice powder

2 large dried lotus leaves, soaked until soft and drained

1. Cut the pork into slices, approximately 6 × 15 cm × 5 mm/2½ × 6 × ¼ inch. Heat the ground rice in a dry frying-pan (skillet), stirring until aromatic.

2. Remove from the heat and mix in the soy sauce, hoisin sauce, bean curd cheese, sugar, chilli sauce, sherry and 5-spice powder. Add the pork slices and turn to coat with the mixture.

3. Lay the lotus leaves flat and place half of the pork mixture in the centre of each one.

4. Wrap carefully and tie into a secure parcel, using string.

5. Place each parcel in a steamer held over a wok or pan containing water, and steam for 2½ to 3 hours. To serve, unwrap each parcel with chopsticks and discard the lotus leaves. The pork should be very succulent and aromatic with the flavour of the lotus leaves.

Cooking in Sauce

This is a popular cooking method in China. In red-cooking soy sauce is the main flavouring ingredient, but it is never used in white-cooking.

Red-cooking

Red cooking is a unique Chinese method, used primarily for cooking larger cuts of meat and whole poultry. The soy sauce imparts a rich flavour and a reddish-brown colour to the food. In the following recipe, the rind should be left on the meat during cooking as it encourages the sauce to thicken and enhances the succulence of the meat.

Red-Cooked Pork with Eggs

Dark soy sauce should preferably be used for red-cooking.

METRIC/IMPERIAL

300 ml/½ pint oil

1 × 1.75 kg/4 lb piece knuckle end of pork or ham, with rind

5 × 15 ml spoons/5 tablespoons water

175 ml/6 fl oz soy sauce

2 × 5 ml spoons/2 teaspoons sugar

4 × 15 ml spoons/4 tablespoons dry sherry

4–6 hard-boiled eggs, shelled

AMERICAN

1¼ cups oil

1 × 4 lb piece fresh pork picnic shoulder or shank of ham, with rind

5 tablespoons water

¾ cup soy sauce

2 teaspoons sugar

4 tablespoons pale dry sherry

4–6 hard-cooked eggs, shelled

1. Heat the oil in a wok or pan. Add the pork or ham and fry for 4 to 5 minutes, turning, until lightly browned. Drain well.

2. Combine the water, 6 × 15 ml spoons/6 tablespoons of the soy sauce, the sugar and sherry in a heavy flameproof casserole or saucepan. Add the pork or ham and turn until it is well coated with sauce. Bring to the boil then reduce the heat to very low. Cover and simmer very gently for approximately 2 hours, turning the meat occasionally and adding a little hot water if it becomes too dry. Remove the meat from the pan and test for tenderness by piercing it through the centre with a chopstick or fork.

3. Add the shelled eggs to the sauce remaining in the pan, together with the rest of the soy sauce. Bring to the boil and simmer for 2 to 3 minutes, turning the eggs until they become quite brown.
Transfer the meat to a warmed tureen or bowl and surround with the brown 'soy eggs'; the meat should be tender enough to take off the bone with chopsticks. Serve with rice.

White-cooking

This method is frequently used for cooking vegetables, particularly leafy vegetables, such as cabbage and spinach.

White-Cooked Cabbage

METRIC/IMPERIAL

1 Savoy or Chinese cabbage, stemmed

300 ml/½ pint stock

1 chicken stock cube

25 g/1 oz lard

1 × 15 ml spoon/1 tablespoon dried shrimps, soaked in hot water for 10 minutes and drained

1 × 5 ml spoon/1 teaspoon sugar

salt

freshly ground black pepper

1.5 × 15 ml spoons/1½ tablespoons cooked chopped pork or ham

AMERICAN

1 Savoy or Chinese cabbage (bok choy), stemmed

1¼ cups stock

2 chicken stock cubes

2 tablespoons lard

1 tablespoon dried shrimp, soaked in hot water for 10 minutes and drained

1 teaspoon sugar

salt

freshly ground black pepper

1½ tablespoons cooked chopped pork or ham

1. Cut the cabbage lengthwise into quarters, then cut each section in half. Bring the stock to the boil in a wok or saucepan. Stir in the stock cube(s), lard, dried shrimps and sugar. Simmer, stirring, for 2 to 3 minutes.

2. Add the cabbage to the pan, turning the pieces to ensure they are well coated with sauce. Bring to the boil, lower the heat and simmer for 4 minutes. Toss the cabbage in the sauce, cover and simmer gently for a further 8 to 12 minutes.

3. Transfer the cabbage to a serving dish. Season the sauce with salt and pepper to taste and pour over the cabbage. Sprinkle with the pork or ham and serve hot, accompanied by a soy sauce dip, if liked.

White-Cooked Cabbage (above)
Red-Cooked Pork with Eggs (centre)

Roasting

Roasting is used to a lesser extent in China than in the West because the average Chinese kitchen is not equipped with an oven. However, it is a popular method of cooking in restaurant kitchens, particularly in Peking and Canton, and gives rise to such famous dishes as Peking Roast Duck *(page 96)*. The Chinese method of roasting involves hanging the meat or poultry on a rotisserie, or hook in the oven.

Cantonese Cha Shao roasting

Cha Shao is a method of quick-roasting meat or poultry at a high temperature for a short time. The meat is seasoned and marinated before roasting. The high heat causes the marinade to become encrusted onto the meat, forming a highly seasoned crisp outer layer, while the inside of the meat stays tender and juicy. Only tender cuts are suitable for *Cha Shao* roasting.

Cha Shao Quick-Roast Beef

METRIC/IMPERIAL

1 kg/2 lb beef fillet (in one piece)

4 cloves garlic, crushed

3 slices root ginger, shredded

Marinade

3 × 15 ml spoons/3 tablespoons soy sauce

1.5 × 5 ml spoons/1½ teaspoons red bean curd cheese

1.5 × 15 ml spoons/1½ tablespoons dry sherry

1 × 15 ml spoon/1 tablespoon soy bean paste

1.5 × 5 ml spoons/1½ teaspoons brown sugar

1 × 15 ml spoon/1 tablespoon oil

Dips

1 × 15 ml spoon/1 tablespoon English mustard

2 × 15 ml spoons/2 tablespoons chilli sauce

3 × 15 ml spoons/3 tablespoons plum sauce

AMERICAN

2 lb piece beef tenderloin

4 cloves garlic, minced

3 slices ginger root, shredded

Marinade

3 tablespoons soy sauce

1½ teaspoons red bean curd

1½ tablespoons pale dry sherry

1 tablespoon bean sauce

1½ teaspoons brown sugar

1 tablespoon oil

Dips

1 tablespoon English mustard

2 tablespoons chili sauce

3 tablespoons plum sauce

1. Place the beef in a shallow dish and sprinkle with the garlic and ginger. Combine the marinade ingredients and pour over the meat; baste well. Leave to marinate for 2 hours, turning the beef every 20 minutes. Meanwhile to prepare the dips, spoon the mustard and chilli sauce into one dish and place the plum sauce in another dish.

2. Put the beef on a rack in a roasting pan and baste with marinade. Roast in the top of a preheated hot oven (230 C/450 F, Gas Mark 8) for 10 to 12 minutes, turning the beef and basting with the marinade halfway through cooking.

3. Remove the beef from the oven and cut across the grain into 1 cm/½ inch thick slices. Arrange on a serving dish and serve hot or cold, accompanied by the dips.

Slow-roasting

Large pieces of meat and poultry, which are not suitable for *Cha Shao* cooking, can be roasted at a lower temperature. In the following recipe, the lamb is pre-cooked in a rich sauce which imparts a delicious flavour. Pre-cooking also reduces the required roasting time, thus ensuring the meat does not become dry.

Slow-Roast Spiced Leg of Lamb

The rich cooking sauce makes a delicious soup.

METRIC/IMPERIAL

1 × 1 kg/2 lb fillet end leg of lamb

Sauce

4–5 cloves garlic, crushed

4–5 slices root ginger, shredded

1 large onion, thinly sliced

1.2 litres/2 pints light stock or clear broth (see page 15)

4 × 15 ml spoons/4 tablespoons soy sauce

3 × 15 ml spoons/3 tablespoons soy bean paste

2 × 5 ml spoons/2 teaspoons chilli sauce

1 × 15 ml spoon/1 tablespoon whole 5-spice

2 × 15 ml spoons/2 tablespoons brown sugar

300 ml/½ pint red wine

Dips

3 × 15 ml spoons/3 tablespoons plum sauce

3 × 15 ml spoons/3 tablespoons hoisin sauce

2 × 15 ml spoons/2 tablespoons soy sauce

1 × 15 ml spoon/1 tablespoon wine vinegar

Garnish

shredded spring onion (shallot)

shredded root ginger

AMERICAN

1 × 2 lb sirloin half leg of lamb

Sauce

4–5 cloves garlic, minced

4–5 slices ginger root, shredded

1 large onion, thinly sliced

5 cups light stock or clear broth (see page 15)

4 tablespoons soy sauce

3 tablespoons bean sauce

2 teaspoons chili sauce

1 tablespoon whole 5-spice

2 tablespoons brown sugar

1¼ cups red wine

Dips

3 tablespoons plum sauce

3 tablespoons hoisin sauce

2 tablespoons soy sauce

1 tablespoon wine vinegar

Garnish

shredded scallion

shredded ginger root

1. Trim any excess fat from the lamb. Combine the sauce ingredients in a saucepan. Bring to the boil, cover and simmer for 20 minutes. Place the lamb in a heavy flameproof casserole or pan and pour over the sauce. Bring to the boil, cover and simmer gently for 1 to 1¼ hours, turning the meat halfway through cooking. Remove from the heat and allow the meat to cool in the sauce. When it is cold, set aside for a further 3 hours, or leave in the refrigerator overnight.

2. Lift the meat out of the sauce and place on a rack in a roasting pan. Roast in a preheated moderate oven (180 C/350 F, Gas Mark 4) for about 1 hour until the lamb is tender.

To prepare the dips, place the plum sauce and hoisin sauce in separate dishes. Mix the soy sauce with the wine vinegar in another dish. Slice the lamb and arrange on a serving dish. Serve, hot or cold, garnished with shredded spring onion (shallot/scallion) and ginger, with dips.

Cha-Shao Quick-Roast Beef (left)
Slow-Roast Spiced Leg of Lamb (right)

Cooking with Oil

The Chinese use oil for cooking more frequently than Westerners. Yet in most cases it is fairer to describe the technique as 'cooking with oil' rather than 'cooking in oil', because the quantity of oil used is minimal.

Quick-stir-frying

This simple technique involves frying a few ingredients together over high heat in a small amount of oil, stirring continuously and vigorously. The oil is heated in the wok or pan before the other ingredients are added. The food is usually evenly shredded, diced or cut into thin slices to ensure that it will be cooked through in the brief cooking time.

Stir-Fried Beef with Onions

METRIC/IMPERIAL

0.5 kg/1 lb rump steak

1 × 15 ml spoon/1 tablespoon dry sherry

1 × 2.5 ml spoon/½ teaspoon salt

freshly ground black pepper

2 × 15 ml spoons/2 tablespoons soy sauce

1 × 5 ml spoon/1 teaspoon sugar

4 × 15 ml spoons/4 tablespoons oil

2–3 slices root ginger, shredded

1 large onion, thinly sliced

3 garlic cloves, crushed

1.5 × 5 ml spoons/1½ teaspoons cornflour, dissolved in 3 × 15 ml spoons/3 tablespoons stock

AMERICAN

1 lb flank steak

1 tablespoon pale dry sherry

½ teaspoon salt

freshly ground black pepper

2 tablespoons soy sauce

1 teaspoon sugar

¼ cup oil

2–3 slices ginger root, shredded

1 large onion, thinly sliced

3 garlic cloves, minced

1½ teaspoons cornstarch, dissolved in 3 tablespoons stock

1. Cut the steak, against the grain, into thin shreds. Mix together the sherry, salt, pepper, soy sauce, sugar and 1.5 × 5 ml spoons/1½ teaspoons of the oil in a shallow dish. Add the steak shreds and leave to marinate for 15 minutes.

2. Heat 2.5 × 15 ml spoons/2½ tablespoons of the remaining oil in a wok or pan over high heat. Add the ginger and onion and stir-fry for 1½ minutes. Push them to one side and add the remaining oil to the other side of the pan. When it is very hot, add the steak and garlic.

3. Stir-fry the steak shreds and garlic in the oil for a few seconds until brown. Mix in the onion and ginger and stir-fry for a further 1 minute.

  Stir in the cornflour (cornstarch) mixture and cook, stirring for about 30 seconds or until thickened.

Double-stir-frying

In this method, the meat is subjected to two separate periods of quick-stir-frying. During the initial stir-frying the meat is sealed for maximum retention of juices and flavour. It is then drained and stir-fried once more this time with the flavouring ingredients added.

In the following recipe, the meat should be approximately three-quarters cooked after the initial stir-frying.

Double-Stir-Fried Pork in Soy Bean Paste (Sauce)

METRIC/IMPERIAL

0.75 kg/1½ lb lean pork, cut into 2 cm/¾ inch cubes

3 × 15 ml spoons/3 tablespoons oil

1 × 15 ml spoon/1 tablespoon hoisin sauce

1 × 15 ml spoon/1 tablespoon dry sherry

1.5 × 5 ml spoons/1½ teaspoons soy bean paste

1 × 15 ml spoon/1 tablespoon soy sauce

1 × 5 ml spoon/1 teaspoon sugar

15 g/½ oz lard

1 × 5 ml spoon/1 teaspoon cornflour, dissolved in 3 × 15 ml spoons/3 tablespoons stock or water

AMERICAN

1½ lb lean pork (loin), cut into ¾ inch cubes

3 tablespoons oil

1 tablespoon hoisin sauce

1 tablespoon pale dry sherry

1½ teaspoons bean sauce

1 tablespoon soy sauce

1 teaspoon sugar

1 tablespoon lard

1 teaspoon cornstarch, dissolved in 3 tablespoons stock or water

1. Rub the pork with 1.5 × 15 ml spoons/1½ tablespoons of the oil. Mix together the hoisin sauce, sherry, soy bean paste (sauce), soy sauce and sugar in a bowl. Heat the remaining oil in a wok or pan over high heat. Add the pork and stir-fry over high heat for 2 minutes. Drain the pork and set aside. Discard the cooking oil from the wok or pan.

2. Add the lard to the pan and melt over moderate heat. Add the soy bean paste (sauce) mixture and stir well. Add the cornflour (cornstarch) mixture and cook, stirring until thickened.

3. Return the pork to the pan and quick-fry, stirring, for 1 minute. Serve hot on a bed of shredded lettuce, if liked.

Stir-Fried Beef with Onions (above)
Double-Stir-Fried Pork in Soy Bean Paste (Sauce) (below)

Shallow-frying

This is a slower method of frying than stir-frying. More oil is required and the cooking is achieved over a moderate, rather than a high heat without stirring.

Soft-Fried Sole Fillets in Wine Sauce

METRIC/IMPERIAL

0.75 kg/1½ lb sole fillets (or any firm white fish), cut into small triangles

1.5 × 5 ml spoons/1½ teaspoons salt

1 × 15 ml spoon/1 tablespoon cornflour

2 egg whites, lightly beaten

300 ml/½ pint oil

2–3 × 15 ml spoons/2–3 tablespoons dried wood ears, soaked for 20 minutes, drained and stemmed

2 garlic cloves, crushed

Sauce

2 slices root ginger, crushed to extract the juice

4 × 15 ml spoons/4 tablespoons dry white wine

4 × 15 ml spoons/4 tablespoons chicken stock

1 × 5 ml spoon/1 teaspoon sugar

1 × 15 ml spoon/1 tablespoon cornflour, dissolved in 3 × 15 ml spoons/3 tablespoons water

Garnish

few spring onions (shallots), chopped

AMERICAN

1½ lb sole fillets (or any firm white fish), cut into small triangles

1½ teaspoons salt

1 tablespoon cornstarch

2 egg whites, lightly beaten

1¼ cups oil

2–3 tablespoons dried tree ears, soaked for 20 minutes, drained and stemmed

2 garlic cloves, minced

Sauce

2 slices ginger root, minced to extract the juice

¼ cup dry white wine

¼ cup chicken stock

1 teaspoon sugar

1 tablespoon cornstarch, dissolved in 3 tablespoons water

Garnish

few scallions, chopped

1. Sprinkle the fish pieces with the salt and coat with the cornflour (cornstarch). Mix the egg whites with 1.5 × 5 ml spoons/1½ teaspoons of the oil in a bowl; dip the fish into this mixture.

2. Heat the remaining oil in a wok or pan over moderate heat. When hot, fry the fish pieces, a few at a time, for about 2 minutes until crisp and golden. Lift the fish out of the oil, drain and keep warm while cooking the remaining pieces. Pour away all but 1 × 15 ml spoon/1 tablespoon of the oil.

3. Add the wood (tree) ears and garlic juice to the remaining oil and stir-fry for a few seconds.

4. Combine the sauce ingredients and pour into the pan. Cook, stirring, for about 1½ minutes until the sauce is thickened.

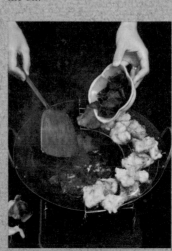

5. Return the fish to the pan, a piece at a time. When the sauce returns to the boil, lower the heat and simmer for 45 seconds. Serve hot, garnished with chopped spring onions (shallots/scallions).

Deep-frying

Deep-frying is used in Chinese cooking in the same way as it is in the West, to produce crisp-textured food. Occasionally it is used as the final stage in a multi-phase cooking process. The following recipe is a good example of this: the duckling is first boiled in water, then simmered in a master sauce and finally deep-fried. The master sauce can be re-used in another dish.

Crispy Duckling

METRIC/IMPERIAL

1 × 1.75 kg/4 lb duckling

oil for deep-frying

Master sauce

1.2 litres/2 pints stock

600 ml/1 pint yellow wine or dry sherry

7 × 15 ml spoons/7 tablespoons soy sauce

4 × 15 ml spoons/4 tablespoons soy bean paste

4 × 15 ml spoons/4 tablespoons hoisin sauce

4 onions, sliced

6 slices root ginger

1.5 × 15 ml spoons/1½ tablespoons sugar

6 garlic cloves, crushed

1 chicken stock cube

1 × 5 ml spoon/1 teaspoon 5-spice powder

1 kg/2 lb pork bones

0.5 kg/1 lb shin of beef, cubed

Accompaniments

10-12 Mandarin pancakes (see page 97)

5 × 15 ml spoons/5 tablespoons hoisin sauce

2 cucumbers, peeled and sliced lengthwise

4-5 spring onions (shallots), shredded

AMERICAN

1 × 4 lb duckling

oil for deep-frying

Master sauce

5 cups stock

2½ cups yellow wine or pale dry sherry

7 tablespoons soy sauce

¼ cup bean sauce

½ cup hoisin sauce

4 onions, sliced

6 slices ginger root

1½ tablespoons sugar

6 garlic cloves, minced

2 chicken stock cubes

1 teaspoon 5-spice powder

2 lb pork bones

1 lb shin of beef, cubed

Accompaniments

10-12 Mandarin pancakes (see page 97)

⅓ cup hoisin sauce

2 cucumbers, peeled and sliced lengthwise

4-5 scallions, shredded

1. Plunge the duckling into a wok or pan of boiling water. Boil for 10 minutes, then drain.

2. Combine the sauce ingredients in a large wok or saucepan. Bring to the boil, cover and simmer for 30 minutes; discard the bones. Add the duckling to the sauce and coat thoroughly. Bring to the boil, cover and simmer gently for 1½ hours, turning the duckling a few times during cooking. Lift the duckling out of the sauce and transfer to a wire rack to drain thoroughly while cooling.

3. When the duckling is thoroughly dry, heat the oil to 180°C/350°F. Lower the duckling into the oil and deep-fry for 8 to 10 minutes, spooning the oil over the exposed surface of the duckling. Drain and place on a serving dish. If liked, the duckling may be garnished with cucumber slices, strips of lemon rind and parsley sprigs. Serve hot with the accompaniments. The meat should be tender enough to be taken off the bone with chopsticks.

Paper-wrapped deep-frying

This is a popular Szechuan method of deep-frying. Small pieces of meat or fish are first marinated, then wrapped in greaseproof paper or non-stick parchment to form parcels, and deep-fried until tender. The wrapping helps to seal in the flavour and prevent the food absorbing oil. The food is served in its paper wrapping and opened by each diner, with chopsticks.

Deep-Fried Paper-Wrapped Meat

METRIC/IMPERIAL

1.5×15 ml spoons/$1\frac{1}{2}$ tablespoons soy sauce

1×15 ml spoon/1 tablespoon dry sherry

1×2.5 ml spoon/$\frac{1}{2}$ teaspoon sugar

2×5 ml spoons/2 teaspoons oyster sauce

1.5×5 ml spoons/$1\frac{1}{2}$ teaspoons sesame seed oil

225 g/8 oz lean beef, shredded

4 slices root ginger, shredded

2 spring onions (shallots), cut into 5 cm/2 inch pieces

2×5 ml spoons/2 teaspoons hoisin sauce

1×2.5 ml spoon/$\frac{1}{2}$ teaspoon chilli sauce

1.5×5 ml spoons/$1\frac{1}{2}$ teaspoons lard

225 g/8 oz boned chicken, shredded

2 large dried Chinese mushrooms, soaked for 20 minutes, drained, stemmed and shredded

1 large carrot, thinly sliced

oil for deep-frying

AMERICAN

$1\frac{1}{2}$ tablespoons soy sauce

1 tablespoon pale dry sherry

$\frac{1}{2}$ teaspoon sugar

2 teaspoons oyster sauce

$1\frac{1}{2}$ teaspoons sesame seed oil

$\frac{1}{2}$ lb flank steak, shredded

4 slices ginger root, shredded

2 scallions, cut into 2 inch pieces

2 teaspoons hoisin sauce

$\frac{1}{2}$ teaspoon chili sauce

$1\frac{1}{2}$ teaspoons lard

$\frac{1}{2}$ lb boneless chicken, shredded

2 large dried Chinese mushrooms, soaked for 20 minutes, drained, stemmed and shredded

1 large carrot, thinly sliced

oil for deep-frying

Place half of the soy sauce, sherry and sugar in a bowl. Stir in the oyster sauce and sesame seed oil. Add the shredded beef and half of the ginger and spring onions (shallots/scallions); mix thoroughly.

Place the remaining soy sauce, sherry and sugar in another bowl. Stir in the hoisin sauce, chilli sauce and lard. Add the chicken, mushrooms and remaining ginger and spring onions (shallots/scallions). Leave both dishes to marinate for 15 minutes.

1. Cut out 10 rectangular pieces of greaseproof paper or non-stick parchment, about 25×18 cm/10×7 inches. Divide both beef and chicken mixtures into 5 equal portions. Place each portion on a piece of greaseproof paper or non-stick parchment and top with a few carrot slices.

2. Fold each one, envelope-fashion, enclosing the filling and tucking in the flaps to secure.

3. Heat the oil to 180°C/350°F. Deep-fry about half of the paper envelopes for $2\frac{1}{2}$ minutes. Transfer this batch to a wok rack or strainer and allow to drain while cooking the remaining batch of envelopes.

4. When all the envelopes have been fried, return them to the hot oil and fry for a further 1 minute. Drain thoroughly. Transfer to a heated serving dish and garnish with shredded cucumber and cherries, if liked. Each diner takes his meat parcel and opens the paper with chopsticks.

Kitty Sham, Chinese consultant, opening paper-wrapped meat with chopsticks

Specialist Chinese Ingredients and Seasonings
Kenneth Lo

Although Chinese cooking is entirely different from cooking in the West, the basic materials used are almost identical. The Chinese use the same cereals and pastas, poultry and meat, fish and shellfish, and vegetables. The only difference lies in the treatment of these foods, whether in cutting, cooking or flavouring them.

In a good proportion of Chinese dishes, food is cut into small pieces (diced, shredded or thinly sliced) and cooked by quick-stir-frying, a method which is rarely used in the West. The ingredient the Chinese use for flavouring is soy sauce, which was hardly known in the West until Chinese food and cooking became popular, and other derivatives of the soy bean: salted or fermented black beans, soy-bean paste (sauce), sweet soy bean paste (sauce) and hoisin sauce. The importance of soy sauce in Chinese cooking can hardly be overlooked. With this one ingredient alone, you can embark upon cooking more than fifty per cent of Chinese food, which probably amounts to several thousand dishes.

Another product of the soy bean is bean curd. This is an important source of protein in both the Chinese and Japanese diet and should not be confused with other soy bean products, such as soy sauce, which are not eaten as food but are only added in small quantities to flavour food. Bean curd is quite tasteless and is a food which itself requires flavouring.

Apart from these basic ingredients, there are other specialist ingredients which contribute to the unique character of Chinese cuisine. They are important to Chinese cooking, but not to the extent that they cannot be replaced, or in some cases even eliminated. These ingredients are also described in this chapter, and in most cases, examples of their uses are given.

Soy sauce, salted or fermented black beans, soy bean paste (sauce), sweet soy bean paste (sauce) and hoisin sauce

Soy sauce is now a popular ingredient in the West, used in stewing, frying or to make sauces. It can be applied directly to meat, poultry, fish or vegetables, but as it is salty one should guard against using it excessively. In cooking, soy sauce is best used in conjunction with other ingredients, such as wine, sugar and stock. It can also add savouriness to cooked food. As a dip, it can be combined with other sauces, vinegar, and most of the strong-tasting aromatics, including onion, garlic and ginger. Soy sauce is available in different shades; the lighter brown varieties have a more delicate flavour and should be used in preference for dips. Dark brown soy sauce imparts a rich colour to food and is the most suitable type to use for red-stewing; it should be avoided in delicately flavoured dishes.

Salted or fermented black beans are available in polythene (plastic) bags and cans from Chinese food stores. They need to be soaked in cold water for 5 to 10 minutes to remove excess salt before use. The beans are always combined with other ingredients in cooking, such as fish, spare ribs and beef, often stir-fried over high heat. They impart a distinct flavour to food.

Soy bean paste (sauce), also known as 'brown-bean sauce', is sold in cans and jars in Chinese food stores. Being a paste (sauce) rather than a liquid, it is often used instead of soy sauce when a thicker sauce is required in stir-fry cooking. Because of its saltiness, soy bean paste acts as a preservative and is therefore often cooked with meat to be served cold later.

Sweet soy bean paste (sauce), also called 'red-bean paste (sauce)', is a thick paste (sauce), sold in cans. It is used as a dip, or to brush onto Mandarin pancakes when serving Peking Duck. It can also be used as a base for sweet sauces, or to accompany crispy dishes, like Prawn (shrimp) cutlets (*page 68*) or roast dishes, such as Cha Shao quick roast pork (*page 188*).

Hoisin sauce is a thick soy-based sauce, brownish-red in colour, with a slightly sweet, hot flavour. It can be served as a dip at the table, or used for cooking shellfish, spare ribs or duck. More often, it is used in conjunction with soy sauce in stir-frying.

Bean curd, dried bean curd, dried bean curd skin, fermented bean curd

Bean curd, fresh, also called 'tofu', is a rather tasteless substance made from puréed yellow soy beans. It has the appearance of an opaque junket and is sold in Chinese food stores in cakes about 7.5 cm/3 inches square, which can be cut to any shape. Bean curd is often cooked with other ingredients, such as meat, fish or vegetables. It should be stored in fresh water in a covered container until required.

Dried bean curd is sold in cake form. It can be cut into strips or slices, and stewed, braised or fried, generally with other ingredients.

Dried bean curd skin is available in thin, stiff sheets, It must be soaked, preferably in warm water, for about 30 minutes before use, and is usually braised or stewed with meat and vegetables.

Fermented bean curd, also called 'bean curd cheese', is made by fermenting small cubes of bean curd in wine and salt. It is available in two forms – the red Southern China variety and white fermented bean curd, both of which are available in jars and cans. Both are very salty and strong-tasting and are normally used for seasoning meats and vegetables or as a condiment. For breakfast in China, very small quantities of fermented bean curd are sometimes eaten with copious amounts of rice gruel.

Bean Curd with Fish Head

This is an inexpensive dish which is both nourishing and flavoursome.

METRIC/IMPERIAL

40 g/1½ oz lard

2–3 slices root ginger, shredded

1 large onion, thinly sliced

0.75–1.25 kg/1½–2½ lb fish head (carp, mullet or eel), cleaned and cut into chunks

750 ml/1¼ pints fish or chicken stock

3–4 dried Chinese mushrooms, soaked for 20 minutes, drained, stemmed and shredded

2 cakes fresh bean curd, diced

2–3 × 15 ml spoons/2–3 tablespoons dry sherry or yellow wine

salt

freshly ground black pepper

AMERICAN

3 tablespoons lard

2–3 slices ginger root, shredded

1 large onion, thinly sliced

1½–2½ lb fish head (carp, mullet or eel), cleaned and cut into chunks

3 cups fish or chicken stock

3–4 dried Chinese mushrooms, soaked for 20 minutes, drained, stemmed and shredded

2 cakes fresh bean curd, diced

2–3 tablespoons pale dry sherry or yellow wine

salt

freshly ground black pepper

Melt the lard in a pan. Add the ginger and onion and stir-fry for 1½ minutes. Add the fish head. Fry, turning, over high heat for 2½ to 3 minutes.

Pour in the fish or chicken stock and bring to the boil, then add the mushrooms and bean curd. Return to the boil, cover and simmer gently for 20 minutes.

Add the sherry or wine and salt and pepper to taste; simmer for a further 10 to 15 minutes. Serve hot.

Bamboo shoots

Western novices to Chinese food often confuse bamboo shoots with bean sprouts which are entirely different in substance, texture and appearance.

To prepare fresh bamboo shoots: remove the tough outer skin and cook in boiling water, with two red peppers added, for 40 minutes. (The red peppers help to remove the bitter taste from the bamboo shoots.) Canned bamboo shoots are more widely available than young fresh ones; these should be drained before use.

Braised Bamboo Shoots with Hot Meat Sauce

The pork should be just tender and there should be little liquid left when this dish is cooked.

METRIC/IMPERIAL

350 g/12 oz fresh or canned bamboo shoot (prepared as above)

3 × 15 ml spoons/3 tablespoons oil

1.5 × 15 ml spoons/1½ tablespoons lard

100 g/4 oz minced pork

2 garlic cloves, crushed

2 spring onions (shallots), finely chopped

2 × 15 ml spoons/2 tablespoons soy sauce

1.5 × 15 ml spoons/1½ tablespoons hoisin sauce

1 × 5 ml spoon/1 teaspoon chilli sauce

1 × 5 ml spoon/1 teaspoon sugar

1.5 × 15 ml spoons/1½ tablespoons tomato purée

4 × 15 ml spoons/4 tablespoons stock

2 × 15 ml spoons/2 tablespoons dry sherry

2 × 5 ml spoons/2 teaspoons sesame seed oil

AMERICAN

¾ lb fresh or canned bamboo shoot (prepared as above)

3 tablespoons oil

1½ tablespoons lard

¼ lb ground pork

2 garlic cloves, minced

2 scallions, finely chopped

2 tablespoons soy sauce

1½ tablespoons hoisin sauce

1 teaspoon chili sauce

1 teaspoon sugar

1½ tablespoons tomato paste

¼ cup stock

2 tablespoons pale dry sherry

2 teaspoons sesame oil

Cut the bamboo shoots into 3.5 cm/1½ inch triangular wedges. Heat the oil in a pan. Add the bamboo shoots and stir-fry for 2½ minutes. Remove from the pan. Add the lard to the pan. When it has melted, add the pork, garlic and spring onions (shallots/ scallions). Stir-fry for 4 minutes. Add the soy sauce, hoisin sauce, chilli sauce, sugar and tomato purée (paste) and mix well. Stir in the stock and sherry.

Return the bamboo shoots to the pan and turn them in the sauce until well coated. Cover the pan and simmer gently for 7 to 8 minutes. Add the sesame seed oil, stir and serve hot.

Bean sprouts

These are the sprouts of small mung beans, which are available fresh and canned. They can be grown indoors at any time of the year and, in properly controlled conditions, will sprout in a very few days. Because mung beans are such an inexpensive and convenient vegetable to grow, they seem to be a part of almost every other dish served in Chinese restaurants outside China. Bean sprouts are at their best when cooked for only a very short time to retain their crispness.

Quick-Stir-Fried Bean Sprouts

METRIC/IMPERIAL

3 × 15 ml spoons/3 tablespoons oil

2–3 garlic cloves, crushed

2 slices root ginger, shredded

0.5 kg/1 lb fresh bean sprouts

salt

freshly ground black pepper

15 g/½ oz lard

1.5 × 15 ml spoons/1½ tablespoons soy sauce

3 spring onions (shallots), cut into 2.5 cm/1 inch pieces

1.5 × 5 ml spoons/1½ teaspoons sesame seed oil

AMERICAN

3 tablespoons oil

2–3 garlic cloves, minced

2 slices ginger root, shredded

1 lb fresh bean sprouts

salt

freshly ground black pepper

1 tablespoon lard

1½ tablespoons soy sauce

3 scallions, cut into 1 inch pieces

1½ teaspoons sesame oil

Heat the oil in a pan. Add the garlic and ginger and stir-fry for a few seconds. Add the bean sprouts and sprinkle with salt and pepper to taste. Turn the bean sprouts quickly so that they become evenly coated with oil. Add the lard, soy sauce and spring onions (shallots/scallions) to the pan.

Continue to stir-fry over high heat for 2 minutes. Sprinkle with the sesame oil and serve hot.

Noodles

Many different varieties of noodles are eaten in China. Most are prepared from a hard flour, which is mixed to a paste with water, and sometimes eggs, like Italian pasta. Fresh plain and egg noodles are sold in Chinese food stores; these need only to be boiled for 7 to 8 minutes. Dried noodles, which are more widely available, require a longer cooking time – 10 to 15 minutes.

Allow at least 1.5 litres/2½ pints/6¼ cups water to every 100 g/ ¼ lb noodles. Cook in unsalted, boiling water until just tender, then drain in a colander and rinse under cold running water. Heat through in a pan of boiling water and drain thoroughly before serving.

Rice stick noodles are thread-like and white in colour. The sticks are about the same length as chopsticks and are sold in packages in Chinese food stores. They are used more extensively in South China than in the North, and are particularly suitable for cooking with seafood. Rice stick noodles do not require soaking before use.

Mixed Seafood Rice Stick Noodles

In China, this dish is usually served as a snack. Diners help themselves from a communal dish placed in the centre of the table.

METRIC/IMPERIAL

4–5 × 15 ml spoons/4–5 tablespoons fresh or canned clams

0.5 kg/1 lb rice stick noodles

3–4 × 15 ml spoons/3–4 tablespoons oil

2 onions, thinly sliced

3 slices root ginger, shredded

3 rashers bacon, shredded

2 × 15 ml spoons/2 tablespoons Chinese snow pickles

4 large dried Chinese mushrooms, soaked for 20 minutes, drained, stemmed and shredded

1.5 × 15 ml spoons/1½ tablespoons dried shrimps, soaked for 15 minutes and drained

6 × 15 ml spoons/6 tablespoons stock

3 × 15 ml spoons/3 tablespoons soy sauce

1 × 5 ml spoon/1 teaspoon salt

25 g/1 oz lard

100–225 g/4–8 oz broccoli, separated into florets

4–5 × 15 ml spoons/4–5 tablespoons shelled prawns

100 g/4 oz fresh squid, shredded

6 oysters (optional)

2 × 15 ml spoons/2 tablespoons dry sherry

AMERICAN

¼ cup fresh or canned clams

1 lb rice sticks

3–4 tablespoons oil

2 onions, thinly sliced

3 slices ginger root, shredded

3 slices bacon, shredded

2 tablespoons salted mustard greens

4 large dried Chinese mushrooms, soaked for 20 minutes, drained, stemmed and shredded

1½ tablespoons dried shrimp, soaked for 15 minutes and drained

6 tablespoons stock

3 tablespoons soy sauce

1 teaspoon salt

2 tablespoons lard

¼–½ lb broccoli, separated into florets

¼ cup shelled shrimp

¼ lb fresh squid, shredded

6 oysters (optional)

2 tablespoons pale dry sherry

If using fresh clams, remove from their shells; if using canned ones, drain. Cook the noodles (rice sticks) in boiling water for 7 to 8 minutes; drain and rinse in a colander under cold running water to wash away any excess starch.

Heat the oil in a large pan. Add the onions, ginger, bacon, pickles (mustard greens), mushrooms, dried shrimps and clams and stir-fry over moderate heat for 3 minutes. Add half of the stock, 2 × 15 ml spoons/2 tablespoons of the soy sauce and the salt; continue to stir-fry for a further 1½ minutes. Add the noodles and mix well. Increase the heat to high and cook, stirring, for a further 3 to 4 minutes. Remove from the heat.

Melt the lard in another pan. Add the broccoli and stir-fry over high heat for 2 minutes. Add the remaining soy sauce and stock, the fresh prawns (shrimp), squid and oysters if used; stir-fry for 2 minutes. Sprinkle in the sherry and remove from the heat. Keep hot.

Return the noodle mixture to the heat and stir-fry for 30 seconds until heated through, then transfer to a large serving dish. Garnish with the broccoli and fish mixture and serve hot.

Transparent pea-starch (cellophane) noodles, also called 'bean threads' and 'vermicelli' are opaque, white threads which become translucent and expand upon soaking. In Chinese food stores, they are sold in packets – in fluffy bundles which resemble candy floss (cotton candy). These noodles are never eaten on their own; they are usually added to soups or used in 'soup-type' dishes because they absorb quantities of stock which renders them highly savoury. Transparent (cellophane) noodles should be soaked in hot water for 5 minutes before use.

Chinese Cabbage Soup with Transparent (Cellophane) Noodles

METRIC/IMPERIAL

2 × 15 ml spoons/2 tablespoons oil

1.25 kg/2½ Chinese cabbage, cut into 2.5 cm/1 inch slices

6 large dried Chinese mushrooms, soaked for 20 minutes, drained, stemmed and shredded

225 g/8 oz boned belly pork, shredded

1.5 × 15 ml spoons/1½ tablespoons dried shrimps, soaked for 15 minutes and drained

1 litre/1¾ pints chicken stock

1 × 5 ml spoon/1 teaspoon salt

100 g/4 oz transparent pea-starch noodles, soaked for 5 minutes and drained

1 × 15 ml spoon/1 tablespoon soy sauce

1.5 × 15 ml spoons/1½ tablespoons red wine vinegar

2 spring onions (shallots), cut into 2.5 cm/1 inch pieces

1.5 × 5 ml spoons/1½ teaspoons sesame seed oil

freshly ground black pepper

AMERICAN

2 tablespoons oil

2½ lb Chinese cabbage (bok choy), cut into 1 inch slices

6 large dried Chinese mushrooms, soaked for 20 minutes, drained, stemmed and shredded

½ lb boneless pork butt, shredded

1½ tablespoons dried shrimp, soaked for 15 minutes and drained

2 pints chicken stock

1 teaspoon salt

¼ lb cellophane noodles, soaked for 5 minutes and drained

1 tablespoon soy sauce

1½ tablespoons red wine vinegar

2 scallions, cut into 1 inch pieces

1½ teaspoons sesame oil

freshly ground black pepper

Heat the oil in a large pan. Add the cabbage, mushrooms, pork and dried shrimps. Stir-fry over high heat for 3 minutes. Pour in the stock and add the salt. Bring to the boil, then simmer for 5 minutes.
Add the noodles and soy sauce. Bring back to the boil and simmer for 20 minutes.
Sprinkle in the vinegar, spring onions (shallots/scallions) and sesame seed oil. Simmer for a further 2 to 3 minutes. Add pepper to taste. Serve hot.

Root ginger

Root ginger is used much more extensively in Chinese cooking than in Western cooking. It is almost always used in the cooking of fish, seafood, and strong-tasting meats, such as beef and venison. To extract ginger juice from the root, place the small peeled slices of root ginger in a garlic crusher and squeeze firmly.

Stir-Fried Shredded Beef with Ginger

METRIC/IMPERIAL

0.5 kg/1 lb rump steak, shredded

1 × 5 ml spoon/1 teaspoon salt

1 × 15 ml spoon/1 tablespoon cornflour

3.5 × 15 ml spoons/3½ tablespoons oil

12 slices root ginger, shredded

2.5 × 15 ml spoons/2½ tablespoons soy sauce

1 × 5 ml spoon/1 teaspoon sugar

2 × 15 ml spoons/2 tablespoons dry sherry or yellow wine

2 × 5 ml spoons/2 teaspoons cornflour, dissolved in 2.5 × 15 ml spoons/2½ tablespoons water

3 spring onions (shallots), cut into 3.5 cm/1½ inch pieces

freshly ground black pepper

AMERICAN

1 lb flank steak, shredded

1 teaspoon salt

1 tablespoon cornstarch

3½ tablespoons oil

12 slices ginger root, shredded

2½ tablespoons soy sauce

1 teaspoon sugar

2 tablespoons pale dry sherry or yellow wine

2 teaspoons cornstarch, dissolved in 2½ tablespoons water

3 scallions, cut into 1½ inch pieces

freshly ground black pepper

Sprinkle the steak with the salt, cornflour (cornstarch) and 1.5 × 5 ml spoons/1½ teaspoons of the oil. Heat the remaining oil in a pan. Add the steak and ginger and stir-fry over high heat for 2 minutes. Stir in the soy sauce, sugar, sherry or wine and the cornflour (cornstarch) mixture. Continue stir-frying for a further 1 minute. Sprinkle in the spring onions (shallots/scallions) and add pepper to taste. Stir and turn a few times. Transfer to a serving dish and serve hot.

Fresh coriander leaves (Chinese parsley)

Coriander is sometimes called Chinese parsley, although its taste and aroma are much stronger and more distinct than the parsley we are familiar with. Coriander leaves (Chinese parsley) are most often used to garnish fish and chicken dishes. The herb is sold in Chinese food stores and quality greengrocers; if unobtainable, substitute flat-leaved parsley.

Fish Soup with Coriander (Chinese Parsley)

For delicacy of flavour and aroma, the Chinese use lightly seasoned chicken stock rather than fish stock.

METRIC/IMPERIAL

225–350 g/8–12 oz fish fillets (sole, halibut, cod, bream, bass, carp, etc.), cut into 3.5 × 2.5 cm/ 1½ × 1 inch slices

1 × 5 ml spoon/1 teaspoon salt

1 × 15 ml spoon/1 tablespoon cornflour

900 ml/1½ pints chicken stock

2 slices root ginger, shredded

1 egg white, lightly beaten

3 × 15 ml spoons/3 tablespoons red wine vinegar

1 × 2.5 ml spoon/½ teaspoon pepper

1.5 × 15 ml spoons/1½ tablespoons chopped coriander leaves

AMERICAN

½–¾ lb fish filets (sole, halibut, cod, sea bass, striped bass, carp, etc.), cut into 1½ × 1 inch slices

1 teaspoon salt

1 tablespoon cornstarch

3¾ cups chicken stock

2 slices ginger root, shredded

1 egg white, lightly beaten

3 tablespoons red wine vinegar

½ teaspoon pepper

1½ tablespoons chopped Chinese parsley

Rub the fish slices with the salt and cornflour (cornstarch). Bring the stock to the boil in a pan. Add the ginger, then taste and add salt if necessary. Dip the fish slices in beaten egg white, then add to the stock, a few at a time. Return the stock to the boil, then lower the heat and simmer gently for 5 minutes, or until the fish is tender. Sprinkle the soup with the vinegar, pepper and coriander (Chinese parsley). Stir a few times then transfer to a serving tureen. Serve hot.

Chinese edible fungi: wood (tree) ears and cloud ears

The Chinese fungi grow on trees. They are eaten not so much for their flavour – there is not much flavour to them—but for their unusual texture. They are often used in dishes to provide a contrast in colour. Cloud ear is often found in sweet soups but is used to a lesser extent than wood (tree) ears, which are most frequently used in stir-fried meat or fish dishes. Both are available dried and must be soaked, preferably in warm water, for 20 minutes before use. They should be rinsed thoroughly before and after soaking.

Quick-Fried Lambs' Kidneys with Wood (Tree) Ears

METRIC/IMPERIAL

3–4 lambs' kidneys

1 × 5 ml spoon/1 teaspoon salt

1 × 15 ml spoon/1 tablespoon red wine vinegar

3.5 × 15 ml spoons/3½ tablespoons oil

2 × 15 ml spoons/2 tablespoons soy sauce

2 × 15 ml spoons/2 tablespoons stock

1 × 15 ml spoon/1 tablespoon hoisin sauce

1 × 2.5 ml spoon/½ teaspoon chilli sauce

4 sticks celery, cut into 2.5 cm/ 1 inch pieces

4 × 15 ml spoons/4 tablespoons dried wood ears, soaked for 20 minutes, drained and stemmed

1.5 × 15 ml spoons/1½ tablespoons lard

AMERICAN

3–4 lamb kidneys

1 teaspoon salt

1 tablespoon red wine vinegar

3½ tablespoons oil

2 tablespoons soy sauce

2 tablespoons stock

1 tablespoon hoisin sauce

½ teaspoon chili sauce

4 stalks celery, cut into 1 inch pieces

¼ cup dried tree ears, soaked for 20 minutes, drained and stemmed

1½ tablespoons lard

Skin, halve and core the kidneys. Make criss-cross cuts in a lattice pattern halfway through the thickness of each kidney half. Sprinkle with the salt, vinegar and 1.5 × 5 ml spoons/1½ teaspoons of the oil. Mix together the soy sauce, stock, hoisin sauce and chilli sauce.

Heat the remaining oil in a pan. Add the kidneys and stir-fry quickly over high heat for 30 seconds. Remove the kidneys from the pan, using a slotted spoon.

Add the celery to the pan with the wood (tree) ears and stir-fry over high heat for 2 minutes. Add the lard and the soy sauce mixture and bring to the boil, stirring. Return the kidneys to the pan and turn them in the sauce with the other ingredients for 45 seconds. Serve hot.

Sesame seed oil, sesame seeds and sesame seed paste

The sesame seed and its derivatives – oil and paste—are widely used in China for their nutty flavour and aromatic quality. They combine well with soy sauce to produce a flavour which can only be described as 'nutty savouriness', which many find highly appealing. A little sesame oil is often added to soups, noodles, or stir-fried dishes just before serving to heighten their aromatic appeal.

Stir-Fried Chicken in Hot Sesame Sauce

METRIC/IMPERIAL

0.5 kg/1 lb boned chicken breasts, cut into 2.5 cm/1 inch cubes

1.5 × 5 ml spoons/1½ teaspoons cornflour

3.5 × 15 ml spoons/3½ tablespoons oil

1 green pepper, cored, seeded, and cut into 2.5 cm/1 inch pieces

2.5 × 15 ml spoons/2½ tablespoons soy sauce

15 g/½ oz lard

2.5 × 15 ml spoons/2½ tablespoons sesame seed paste

1 × 15 ml spoon/1 tablespoon sesame seed oil

1 × 15 ml spoon/1 tablespoon stock or water

1 × 5 ml spoon/1 teaspoon chilli sauce

1 × 15 ml spoon/1 tablespoon dry sherry

AMERICAN

1 lb boneless chicken breasts, cut into 1 inch cubes

1½ teaspoons cornstarch

3½ tablespoons oil

1 green pepper, cored, seeded, and cut into 1 inch pieces

2½ tablespoons soy sauce

1 tablespoon lard

2½ tablespoons sesame paste

1 tablespoon sesame oil

1 tablespoon stock or water

1 teaspoon chili sauce

1 tablespoon pale dry sherry

Toss the chicken cubes in the cornflour (cornstarch) until evenly coated. Heat the oil in a pan. Add the chicken and stir-fry over high heat for 45 seconds. Remove the chicken from the pan, using a slotted spoon.

Add the green pepper to the pan and stir-fry over moderate heat for 1 minute. Stir in 1 × 15 ml spoon/1 tablespoon of the soy sauce, then push to one side of the pan. Add the lard to the pan. When it has melted, add the remaining soy sauce, the sesame seed paste, sesame seed oil, stock or water, chilli sauce and sherry; mix these ingredients well.

Return the chicken cubes to the sauce mixture in the pan and stir over high heat for 45 seconds. Mix in the green pepper and cook for a further 30 seconds until just tender.

Serve hot.

Chinese pickles: winter pickle (salted cabbage) or Tung Tsai, snow pickle (salted mustard greens) or Hseuh Tsai and Szechuan hot pickle (kohlrabi) or Tsa Tsai

These are the most commonly used pickles in China. The winter pickle (salted cabbage), which is brownish-green in colour, savoury and mildly salty, is sold in jars. Snow pickle (salted mustard greens) is greenish in colour and has a salty and mildly sour flavour. Szechuan hot pickle (kohlrabi) is crunchy, yellowish-green in colour, hot and salty. The latter two pickles are both sold in cans and all of these pickles are available from Chinese food stores. They are cooked with meat, and with those vegetables which have a less pronounced flavour. They should always be rinsed thoroughly before use.

Noodle Soup with Pork and Winter Pickle (Salted Cabbage)

METRIC/IMPERIAL

0.5 kg/1 lb fresh or dried egg noodles

900 ml/1½ pints stock

1 chicken stock cube (optional)

2 × 15 ml spoons/2 tablespoons oil

225–350 g/8–12 oz minced pork

2 × 5 ml spoons/2 teaspoons soy bean paste

1 × 15 ml spoon/1 tablespoon soy sauce

4 × 15 ml spoons/4 tablespoons chopped winter pickle

AMERICAN

1 lb fresh or dried egg noodles

3¾ cups stock

2 chicken stock cubes (optional)

2 tablespoons oil

½–¾ lb ground pork

2 teaspoons bean sauce

1 tablespoon soy sauce

¼ cup pickled salted cabbage

Cook the noodles in plenty of boiling water for 7 minutes if fresh, 15 minutes if dried. Drain and rinse under cold running water.

Bring the stock to the boil in a saucepan. Crumble in the stock cube(s), if used. Add the noodles, bring to the boil and simmer for 2 to 3 minutes. Pour the noodles and soup into a large serving tureen or individual soup bowls. Keep hot.

Heat the oil in a pan. Add the pork and stir-fry over high heat for 3 minutes. Add the soy bean paste (sauce) and soy sauce. Mix well and continue to stir-fry for 1 minute. Add the pickle (cabbage) and stir-fry for a further 1 minute.

Spoon the pork mixture on top of the noodles and soup. Serve hot.

Five spices and 5-spice powder

The five spices are star anise, anise pepper (Szechuan peppercorns), fennel, cloves and cinammon. Ground and mixed together they make the fragrant, cocoa-coloured 5-spice powder, which is often the predominant smell in a Chinese grocery shop. 5-spice powder is essentially pungent and should be used very sparingly. It is normally used to season red-cooked (soy braised), or roasted meat and poultry. The five spices can be bought whole, mixed in a packet, and it is really safer to use them in this form rather than as powder because you are less likely to use too much and the individual spices can be removed as required.

Lotus root, lotus seeds and lotus leaves

In China, fresh lotus root is sometimes eaten as a sweet – chilled and sliced, with an apricot sauce poured over. However, in the West it is only available dried or canned, and is only suitable to be used as a constituent of a mixed vegetable dish. Dried lotus root should be soaked in water overnight before use. Lotus seeds are sold dried and canned in Chinese food stores. The seeds are oval in shape and about 1 cm/$\frac{1}{2}$ inch long. They are used in braised vegetable dishes, soups and savoury stuffings; sugared lotus seeds are eaten as a festival sweet. Dried lotus leaves are sold in packages in Chinese food stores and are used for wrapping foods to be steamed. They must be soaked, preferably in warm water, for about 20 minutes to soften before use. The lotus leaves are not eaten but they impart their delicate flavour to the wrapped food during steaming.

Steamed Chicken Wrapped in Lotus Leaves

METRIC/IMPERIAL

6 × 15 ml spoons/6 tablespoons glutinous rice

4 × 15 ml spoons/4 tablespoons canned or dried lotus seeds

4 × 15 ml spoons/4 tablespoons barley

6 dried Chinese mushrooms, soaked for 20 minutes, drained, stemmed and quartered

1 × 15 ml spoon/1 tablespoon dried shrimps, soaked for 15 minutes and drained

1 × 15 ml spoon/1 tablespoon dried tangerine peel, crumbled

4–5 slices Cha Shao Quick-Roast Pork (see page 188)

1 Chinese sausage, cut into 8–10 slices

4 × 15 ml spoons/4 tablespoons soy sauce

2 × 15 ml spoons/2 tablespoons stock

2 × 15 ml spoons/2 tablespoons dry sherry

1 × 2–2.25 kg/4$\frac{1}{2}$–5 lb oven-ready chicken

2 slices root ginger, minced

2 × 5 ml spoons/2 teaspoons sesame seed oil

2 large lotus leaves, soaked for 20 minutes and drained

AMERICAN

6 tablespoons glutinous or sweet rice

$\frac{1}{4}$ cup canned or dried lotus seeds

$\frac{1}{4}$ cup barley

6 dried Chinese mushrooms, soaked for 20 minutes, drained, stemmed and quartered

1 tablespoon dried shrimp, soaked for 15 minutes and drained

1 tablespoon dried tangerine peel, crumbled

4–5 slices Cha Shao Quick-Roast Pork (see page 188)

1 Chinese sausage, cut into 8–10 slices

$\frac{1}{4}$ cup soy sauce

2 tablespoons stock

2 tablespoons pale dry sherry

1 × 4$\frac{1}{2}$–5 lb roasting chicken

2 slices ginger root, minced

2 teaspoons sesame oil

2 large lotus leaves, soaked for 20 minutes and drained

Place the rice, lotus seeds and barley in a pan half-filled with water. Bring to the boil and boil steadily for 5 minutes; drain and allow to cool slightly. Combine the mushrooms, dried shrimps, tangerine peel, roast pork. Chinese sausage, 2 × 15 ml spoons/ 2 tablespoons of soy sauce, the stock and sherry in a bowl. Add the rice mixture and mix thoroughly. Stuff the mixture into the cavity of the chicken and secure the neck opening with skewers or string.

Combine the remaining soy sauce with the ginger and sesame seed oil. Pour over the chicken, wrap in the lotus leaves and tie securely with string. Steam for 3 hours.

To serve, bring the chicken still wrapped in the lotus leaves to the table. Unwrap, carve and serve.

Seaweed and golden needles (Tiger Lily buds)

Purple seawood (laver), hair seaweed and broad seaweed are the types of seaweed the Chinese most frequently use in cooking. The seaweeds are mostly used in conjunction with other vegetables in soups. They must be soaked in water for at least 20 minutes, but preferably overnight, before use and should be rinsed thoroughly before and after soaking.

Golden needles (or Tiger Lily buds) have a musty mouldy flavour, which is very much a cultivated taste. They are often used to garnish steamed fish, and form part of the well-known Peking dish *Mou Shu Rou,* or Yellow Flower Pork, in which they are stir-fried with pork, leeks, eggs, and wood (tree) ears. Like the seaweeds, they must be soaked in water for at least 20 minutes before use.

Lohan Tsai

Literally this is 'Buddhist's vegetable ensemble for the Gods'.

METRIC/IMPERIAL

5 × 15 ml spoons/5 tablespoons oil

1 × 5 ml spoon/1 teaspoon salt

4 × 15 ml spoons/4 tablespoons soy sauce

1.2 litres/2 pints chicken stock or clear broth (see page 15)

100 g/4 oz transparent pea-starch noodles, soaked for 20 minutes and drained

1 × 15 ml spoon/1 tablespoon sesame seed oil

Dried vegetables

40 g/1½ oz golden needles, soaked for 30 minutes and drained

5 large dried Chinese mushrooms, soaked for 20 minutes, drained, stemmed and quartered

2 × 15 ml spoons/2 tablespoons dried wood ears, soaked for 20 minutes, drained and stemmed

4 slices dried lotus root, soaked for 20 minutes and drained

4 × 15 ml spoons/4 tablespoons hair seaweed, soaked for at least 30 minutes and drained

4 × 15 ml spoons/4 tablespoons purple seaweed, soaked for at least 30 minutes and drained

Fresh vegetables

225 g/8 oz Chinese cabbage, cut into 2.5 cm/1 inch slices

225 g/8 oz broccoli florets

100 g/4 oz mange-tout peas

100 g/4 oz cauliflower florets

100 g/4 oz bean sprouts

100 g/4 oz button mushrooms

1 green pepper, cored, seeded and thinly sliced

1 small courgettte, sliced

AMERICAN

5 tablespoons oil

1 teaspoon salt

¼ cup soy sauce

2½ pints chicken stock or clear broth (see page 15)

¼ lb cellophane noodles, soaked for 20 minutes and drained

1 tablespoon sesame oil

Dried vegetables

1 cup Tiger Lily buds, soaked for 30 minutes and drained

5 large dried Chinese mushrooms, soaked for 20 minutes, drained, stemmed and quartered

2 tablespoons dried tree ears, soaked for 20 minutes, drained and stemmed

4 slices dried lotus root, soaked for 20 minutes and drained

4 tablespoons hair seaweed, soaked for at least 30 minutes and drained

4 tablespoons dried laver (purple), soaked for at least 30 minutes and drained

Fresh vegetables

½ lb Chinese cabbage (bok choy), cut into 1 inch slices

½ lb broccoli florets

¼ lb snow peas

¼ lb cauliflower florets

¼ lb bean sprouts

¼ lb button mushrooms

1 green pepper, cored, seeded and thinly sliced

1 small zucchini, sliced

Heat 2 × 15 ml spoons/2 tablespoons of the oil in a large pan. Add all of the dried vegetables and stir-fry over moderate heat for 4 to 5 minutes. Heat the remaining oil in another large pan. Add all of the fresh vegetables and stir-fry over moderate heat for 5 to 6 minutes. Add the fresh vegetables to the dried vegetables and mix together. Sprinkle in the salt, soy sauce and stock or broth and add the noodles. Bring to the boil, cover then simmer for 20 minutes. Sprinkle with the oil and serve hot.

1. Baby corn; 2. Mustard plant; 3. Dried lotus leaves;
4. Chinese spinach; 5. Bamboo shoot; 6. Chinese cabbage;
7. Gingko nuts; 8. Bok choy; 9. Chinese white radish;
10. Chinese sausages; 11. Water chestnuts; 12. Glutinous
rice; 13. Plain rice; 14. Bird's nest; 15. Oyster sauce;
16. Chilli bean sauce; 17. Maltose; 18. Dried mandarin
peels; 19. Dried shrimps; 20. Transparent noodles;
21. Crackling pork skin; 22. Dried black dates; 23. Dried
red dates; 24. Dried Chinese mushrooms.

How to Serve a Chinese Meal and Menu Suggestions

Kitty Sham

There are basically two ways to serve a Chinese meal, either as a formal dinner or a family-style dinner. In a formal dinner, there is always a fixed number of guests at the table – usually 10 or 12; the number of dishes is fixed and courses are served in an orderly fashion. In a family-style dinner, the number of dishes is determined by the number of guests attending and all courses are placed in the centre of the table, in a very casual manner.

Formal dinner

In ancient days, a formal dinner comprised no less than 100 dishes. The number has gradually diminished with time and nowadays there are generally 12 or 14 dishes, but always an even number. For the appetizer course, one cold dish and three hot dishes are usually served, followed by soup. The main course, consisting of about six dishes is served next, then fried rice and noodles or noodle soup. Normally two desserts complete the meal.

In preparing a formal dinner menu, certain points should be taken into consideration. 1. Main-course dishes should be chosen to complement each other in texture, flavour and colour; basic ingredients in each one should not be repeated. 2. Each cooking method (deep-frying, boiling, roasting, simmering, red-stewing, quick-stir-frying, etc.) should only be used once. 3. Each dish should be attractively garnished in a different way. Providing these basic rules are followed, one will have a richly varied formal dinner.

Family-style dinner

There are no strict rules regarding the preparation of family-style dinners but as a general guide, one main dish is normally allowed per guest and one soup is also served. Thus, a family dinner for two usually consists of two main dishes and one soup; a dinner for six is composed of five or six main dishes and one soup.

Sometimes a vegetable dish, such as Dry-cooked green beans *(page 144)* is eaten, either instead of, or in addition to the soup. Steamed rice, rather than fried rice, is served at a family dinner. Also unlike a formal dinner, all of the dishes are presented at the table simultaneously. Fresh fruit is more commonly served to complete the meal than a dessert at a small family dinner. However, when there is a gathering of old friends or guests staying up late, a dessert such as Peas pudding *(page 136)* is served for supper.

Dim Sum

Dim sum is a favourite Chinese snack and is particularly popular among Cantonese people; served with Chinese tea, and always in the morning or early afternoon. To go to a restaurant for *dim sum* is also known as 'going out to morning tea'. When Chinese people have *dim sum*, they usually start with salty snacks like Barbecued meat buns *(page 210)*, Spring rolls *(page 216)* and other steamed dumplings. These are followed by sweet snacks like Waterchestnut cake *(page 90)* and Walnut sweet *(page 64)*. Although *dim sum* is suitable for serving as afternoon tea, or cocktail party snacks in the West, it should never be served as an appetizer in a formal dinner. Preparing *dim sum* is time-consuming and requires skill so it is rarely prepared at home and only served in the most orthodox Chinese restaurants in Chinatown – in the morning and afternoon.

Southern Chinese Formal Wedding Party Dinner for Ten People

APPETIZERS

Selection of cold hors d'ouevre (illustrated on pages 6 and 7): White Cooked Chicken PAGE 12, Cantonese Roast Duck PAGE 200, Barbecued Pork PAGE 201, Roast Beef, Steamed Prawns (Shrimp), Abalone, Asparagus, Sweet and Sour Cucumber PAGE 128, Tea Eggs PAGE 49

Chicken Wings Stuffed with Ham PAGE 74

Deep-Fried Crab Claws in Prawns (Shrimp) PAGE 202

Stir-Fried Squid with Broccoli PAGE 109

SOUP

Shark's Fin Soup PAGE 67

MAIN COURSE

Oyster Sauce Abalone with Lettuce PAGE 208

Fried Whole Chicken PAGE 182

Triple Mushrooms Braised with Oyster Sauce PAGE 205

Deep-Fried Scallops PAGE 157

Steamed Fish with Ginger and Spring Onions (Scallions) PAGE 92

RICE AND NOODLES

Fried Rice with Ham PAGE 205
Prawn (Shrimp) Noodles PAGE 135

DESSERTS

Lotus Sweets PAGE 90

Deep-Fried Sweet Potato Balls PAGE 180

Family-Style Menu for Ten People

Stir-Fried Prawns (Shrimp) PAGE 65

Lemon Chicken PAGE 193

Stewed Duck with Onion PAGE 211

Fish in Vinegar Sauce PAGE 106

Deep-Fried Pork Spareribs with Tomato Sauce PAGE 183

Beef Steak with Mange-Tout (Snow Peas) PAGE 151

Fried Lamb Slices with Onions PAGE 125

Sweet and Sour Kidneys PAGE 94

Deep-Fried Bean Curd with Mushrooms PAGE 202

Chinese Cabbage in Cream Sauce PAGE 131

Sweet Corn and Fish Soup PAGE 212

Date Crisps PAGE 188

Special Northern Chinese Menu for Six People

Mohammedan Fire Kettle or Mongolian Hot Pot PAGE 83

Dan Dan Noodles or Noodles with Sesame Paste Sauce PAGE 176

Walnut Sweet PAGE 64

Family-Style Menus for Six People

NORTHERN CHINESE MENU

Steamed Prawns (Shrimp) PAGE 88

Smoked Chicken PAGE 77

Deep-Fried Beef Steak PAGE 82

Baked Fish with Sesame Seed Oil
PAGE 93

Stewed Pork PAGE 85

Sour Hot Soup PAGE 66

Caramel Apples PAGE 79

WESTERN CHINESE MENU

Prawns (Shrimp) with Tomato
Ketchup (Sauce) PAGE 169

Deep-Fried Spiced Fish PAGE 140

Poached Kidneys with Hot Sauce
PAGE 166

Red-Cooked Pork with Chestnuts
PAGE 177

Sautéed Beef with Mushrooms PAGE
149

Liver Soup PAGE 150

Aubergine (Eggplant) with Garlic
Sauce PAGE 144

EASTERN CHINESE MENU

Red-Cooked Fish PAGE 105

Braised Prawns (Shrimp) PAGE 102

Salted Chicken PAGE 113

Pork Slices with Bamboo Shoots
and Wood (Tree) Ears PAGE 120

Stir-Fried Liver PAGE 114

Bean Curd and Spinach Soup PAGE
132

Peas Pudding PAGE 136

SOUTHERN CHINESE MENU

Fried Crab with Black Beans PAGE
210

Chicken with Cashew Nuts PAGE 204

Fried Beef with Oyster Sauce PAGE
190

Fried Fish with Celery PAGE 190

Cantonese Sweet and Sour Pork
PAGE 214

Winter Melon Soup PAGE 206

Sweet Peanut Cream PAGE 180

Family-Style Menu for Two People

Braised Chinese Sausage with
Winter Melon PAGE 198

Dry-Fried Shredded Beef PAGE 151

Pork and Cucumber Soup PAGE 140

Scallop Fu-Yung PAGE 143

Chicken with Mushrooms PAGE 108

Stir-Fried Chinese Cabbage PAGE
194

Lion's Head PAGE 124

Golden Braised Fish PAGE 134

Beef and Tomato Soup PAGE 154

Sautéed Prawns (Shrimp) with
Pepper Sauce PAGE 140

Braised Beef with Turnips PAGE 164

Stir-Fried Lettuce with Oyster
Sauce PAGE 187

Family-Style Menus for Four People

NORTHERN CHINESE MENU
Stewed Chicken with Chestnuts PAGE 78

Deep-Fried Meatballs PAGE 86

Egg Foo-Yung with Prawns (Shrimp) PAGE 70

Fried Fish Fillets with Sweet and Sour Sauce PAGE 89

Bird's Nest Soup PAGE 67

EASTERN CHINESE MENU
Braised Duckling with Bamboo Shoots and Mushrooms PAGE 112

Fish Slices in White Sauce PAGE 105

Red-Cooked Beef with Broccoli PAGE 114

Shredded Pork with Eggs PAGE 119

Pork Spareribs Soup PAGE 113

WESTERN CHINESE MENU
Sautéed Frogs' Legs PAGE 161

Paper-Wrapped Fish PAGE 171

Chicken with Hot Oil Sauce PAGE 169

Stir-Fried Pork with Transparent Pea-Starch (Cellophane) Noodles PAGE 175

Sizzling Rice Soup PAGE 153

SOUTHERN CHINESE MENU
(illustrated on pages 2 & 3)

Chicken in Soy Sauce PAGE 199

Stewed Oxtail with Tangerine Peel PAGE 207

Fried Prawns (Shrimp) with Broad (Lima) Beans PAGE 184

Fried Pork with Baby Corn PAGE 213

Egg Flower Soup PAGE 212

COMPOSITE MENU
Tomatoes Stuffed with Meat PAGE 195

Shredded Chicken with Spiced Sesame Sauce PAGE 163

Deep-Fried Crab PAGE 88

Fish with Bean Curd in Hot and Sour Sauce PAGE 107

Pork and Mustard Green Soup PAGE 187

COMPOSITE MENU
Poached Fresh Fish PAGE 215

Steamed Beef with Semolina (Rice Powder) PAGE 154

Braised Duck PAGE 92

Spareribs in Sweet and Sour Sauce PAGE 121

Spinach and Bean Curd Soup PAGE 183

Special Northern Chinese Menu for Six People

Peking Roast Duck PAGE 96

Moo Shoo Pork PAGE 72

Diced Chicken with Brown Bean Sauce PAGE 78

Sliced Beef with Bamboo Shoots PAGE 80

Abalone or Scallops with Asparagus PAGE 91

Mandarin Pancakes PAGE 97

Dan Dan Noodles or Noodles with Sesame Paste Sauce PAGE 176

Chinese Festivals
Deh-ta Hsiung

Chinese festivals are based on the lunar calendar, which always puzzles people in the West who cannot understand why the Chinese New Year falls on a different day every year.

The words month and moon are identical in Chinese because a month equals one moon. The number of days in a month corresponds to the number of days which it takes the moon to make one complete revolution around the earth; therefore, some months have 29 days and others 30 days. Consequently, you cannot see the moon at all on the first day of the month, but a full moon appears on the fifteenth.

Apart from this, the rest of the Chinese calendar bears a remarkable similarlity to the Western one. For example, there are four seasons in the year, and each year normally has 12 months. I say normally because since a Chinese year consists of about 354 days, compared with 365 in the West, an extra month has to be added every two or three years in order to make it up with the two equinoxes and the two solstices. When there are 13 months in the year, it is called a leap year.

Every Chinese year is divided into 24 'terms', and each of these terms denotes a marked change of temperature or weather; therefore, they are a great help to farmers. Some of the terms are celebrated as festivals. The Chinese word for festival is *chieh*, which literally means a joint or division, because the festival usually punctuates the change of a season. For example, the New Year's Day (first day of the first moon) always falls at the inception of the second new moon after December 22nd, the winter solstice. It marks the coming of spring in China (and the

northern hemisphere) which is why the New Year celebration is called 'Spring Festival' in China.

Chinese New Year is a big event both for adults and children. For most people it is a kind of birthday as well, because in China birthdays are not normally celebrated except for a few milestones such as the first year and the tenth year. Only after the age of 70 is every birthday regarded as something worth making a fuss about. But on New Year's Day, everybody has an extra year added automatically to his or her age.

Young children, apart from receiving presents like new clothes and new toys, also get money in a red envelope. This is left under their pillows by their parents on New Year's Eve and is always eagerly opened at dawn by little hands, excited by the thought that not only are they a year older, but also by all the festivities in store for them.

The New Year festivities actually begin a week before the end of the old year, when the ritual of 'sending the Kitchen God to Heaven for the Annual Report' takes place. The God is welcomed back on New Year's Eve, when a big feast usually takes place.

Traditionally, New Year's Day is a rather low-key affair compared with other days of festivity. As early as four or five in the morning, the adults, who have been sitting up all night to see the New Year in, will perform the ceremony of 'Opening the Door to Welcome the Auspicious New Year'. What happens is this: the night before, the front doors of the house are sealed from outside with a piece of red paper with the word 'Blessing' written on it. When the door is opened from inside the next morning, the seal is broken to let in the New Year. Don't ask me how you can seal yourself inside; it remains a complete mystery to me because I was never allowed to stay up to watch the goings-on.

After the front doors (all Chinese houses have double front

doors) have been ceremoniously opened by the head of the household, candles and incense are lit, and fire-crackers are let off. Everything suddenly comes alive. Children put on their new clothes, and adults dress in their best. Everyone congratulates each other and exchanges the compliments of the season. People call on each other to offer New Year's greetings and are invariably offered hot tea and a box of 'treasures'. The 'treasures' usually consist of dried dates and other fruits and nuts, and in the case of a close relative or special guest, a bowl of hot noodles in soup topped with a poached egg or two. In some cases New Year Pudding is served, in steaming hot soup – if savoury, or fried – if sweet.

New Year Pudding is made with glutinous rice powder as its main ingredient, and takes quite a few days to prepare. In China one usually buys ready-made pudding from a shop, to save time and effort. Most households will also serve a dessert called Eight-Treasure Rice Pudding, colourfully decorated with eight different dried fruits and nuts, which are supposed to represent the eight charmed objects that will ward off evil spirits. The following recipe is a slightly modified version as some of the eight dried fruits and nuts are hard to come by outside China.

Eight-Treasure Rice Pudding

METRIC/IMPERIAL

225 g/8 oz glutinous rice

40 g/1½ oz lard

2 × 15 ml spoons/2 tablespoons sugar

15 dried red dates, stoned

30 raisins

10 walnut halves

10 glacé cherries

10 pieces candied angelica, chopped

1 × 225 g/8 oz can sweetened chestnut purée or red bean paste

Syrup

3 × 15 ml spoons/3 tablespoons sugar

300 ml/½ pint cold water

1 × 15 ml spoon/1 tablespoon cornflour blended with 2 × 15 ml spoons/2 tablespoons water

AMERICAN

1¼ cups glutinous or sweet pudding rice

3 tablespoons lard

2 tablespoons sugar

15 dried red dates (jujubes), pitted

30 raisins

10 walnut halves

10 candied cherries

10 pieces candied angelica, chopped

1 × ½ lb can sweetened chestnut purée or 1 cup red bean paste

Syrup

3 tablespoons sugar

1¼ cups cold water

1 tablespoon cornstarch blended with 2 tablespoons water

Place the rice in a saucepan, cover with water and bring to the boil. Reduce heat, cover tightly and cook for 10 to 15 minutes, or until the water is absorbed. Add 25g/ 1 oz (2 tablespoons) of the lard and the sugar to the cooked rice. Mix well.

Brush a 900 ml/1½ pint (3¾ cup capacity) mould or pudding basin (steaming mold) with the remaining lard. Cover the bottom and sides with a thin layer of the rice mixture. Gently press a layer of the fruits and nuts, attractively arranged in rows, into the rice so they will show through when the pudding is turned out.

Cover the fruits and nuts with another layer of rice, much thicker this time. Fill the centre with the chestnut purée or bean paste and cover with the remaining rice. Press gently to flatten the top. Cover with a pleated circle of greaseproof (waxed) paper and secure with string.

Steam the pudding for 1 hour. A few minutes before it is ready, make the syrup. Dissolve the sugar in the water in a small pan, bring to the boil. Stir in the cornflour (cornstarch) mixture and simmer gently, stirring, until thickened.

Invert the pudding onto a warmed serving plate. Pour over the syrup and serve immediately. As this is a very sweet, substantial pudding, it will easily serve 6 to 8.

The New Year festivities go on for quite a few days, during which a great deal of food and drink is consumed. On New Year's Day only vegetarian dishes are served, as a mark of respect for Heaven and Earth, but no restrictions exist for the following days. Chicken is eaten all year round, but duck is considered rather special and has therefore become a festival dish. Ham or a whole leg of pork makes another feast dish. To complete the 'three meats' of any feast, carp is served because it is regarded as a fish of good luck.

On the fifteenth day of the first moon there is the Lantern Festival which formally marks the end of the New Year celebration. In the evening there are processions of lanterns of all kinds, and the highlight is a magnificent dragon dance.

The traditional food served at the Lantern Festival is little round dumplings made out of glutinous rice powder.

Rice Dumplings in Syrup

METRIC/IMPERIAL

50 g/2 oz sago

225 g/8 oz glutinous rice powder

Filling

175g/6 oz canned sweetened chestnut purée

1 × 15 ml spoon/1 tablespoon sesame seeds

Syrup

100 g/4 oz brown sugar

1.2 litres/2 pints water

AMERICAN

⅓ cup sago

½ lb glutinous rice powder

Filling

½ cup canned sweetened chestnut purée

1 tablespoon sesame seeds

Syrup

⅔ cup brown sugar

2½ pints water

Soak the sago in cold water for at least 6 hours. Leave to drain in a sieve (strainer) for 30 minutes, then knead and pound until fine. Knead in the glutinous rice powder, mixing to a smooth dough. Roll into a long sausage shape, about 2.5 cm/1 inch in diameter, and cut into 1 cm/½ inch pieces. Flatten each piece of dough and place 1 × 2.5 ml spoon/½ teaspoon chestnut purée and a few sesame seeds in the centre. Carefully draw the edges of dough over the filling and shape into a small ball by rolling between the palms of the hands.

For the syrup: dissolve the sugar in the water in a large saucepan. Bring to the boil and drop in the dumplings. Bring back to the boil and, when all the dumplings float to the surface, reduce the heat and simmer gently for a further 10 minutes. Serve hot.

Chinese Sponge Cake (right)
Formal setting for a Chinese wedding party (below)

Chinese Sponge Cake

METRIC/IMPERIAL

4 eggs

100 g/4 oz caster sugar

120 ml/4 fl oz milk

225 g/8 oz self-raising flour

1 × 2.5 ml spoon/½ teaspoon bicarbonate of soda

pinch of salt

25 g/1 oz lard

3 × 15 ml spoons/3 tablespoons oil

AMERICAN

4 eggs

½ cup sugar

½ cup milk

2 cups self-rising flour

½ teaspoon baking soda

pinch of salt

2 tablespoons lard or shortening

3 tablespoons oil

Beat the eggs in a bowl. Add the sugar and continue beating until the mixture is thick and pale in colour. Stir in the milk. Sift the flour, soda and salt together and fold into the egg mixture.

Melt the lard and allow to cool, then mix with the oil. Gently stir into the egg mixture. Pour into a greased 20 cm/8 inch round cake tin and steam for 20 minutes. Remove the cake from the tin while still hot. Cut into 6 to 8 wedges and serve hot or cold.

Exactly 160 days after the winter solstice, usually on the third day of the third month, we have the *Ching Ming* festival, which means 'pure and clean'. We are now in the middle of spring and in most parts of

Tea Eggs

METRIC/IMPERIAL

6 eggs

2 × 5 ml spoons/2 teaspoons salt

3 × 15 ml spoons/3 tablespoons soy sauce

1 whole star anise (optional)

2 × 5 ml spoons/2 teaspoons black China tea

AMERICAN

6 eggs

2 teaspoons salt

3 tablespoons soy sauce

1 whole star anise (optional)

2 teaspoons black China tea

Hard-boil the eggs for 10 minutes. Drain and tap the shells gently with a spoon until they are cracked finely all over. Put the eggs back into the saucepan and cover with fresh water. Add the salt, soy sauce, star anise, if used, and tea. Bring to the boil, then simmer for 1 hour. Allow the eggs to cool in the liquid.

Just before serving, remove the egg shells carefully to reveal a beautiful marbled pattern.

China the atmosphere is clean and the weather fine. This is the time people pay a visit to their ancestral tombs in the countryside, put them in order and present food and other offerings to the departed. Hence it is sometimes referred to as the 'Festival of Tomb Sweeping'.

As a sign of respect to the dead, no fires are lit in the houses. Instead of hot meals, cold foods are prepared the day before and are taken to be eaten as a picnic by the graveside, in the company of the ancestors.

One particular favourite for children during this festival is a type of sponge cake (illustrated above).

The next major festival is on the fifth day of the fifth month, often corresponding with the first part of June, the Summer Festival. This is also known as the 'Dragon Boat Festival', in honour of an ancient poet-statesman, Chu Yuan, who drowned himself in a river as a protest against a corrupt government in 295 B.C. The story goes that on learning of Chu Yuan's death, people who admired his uprightness and integrity set off in a boat in search of his body. They also threw rice into the river to draw away the fishes in case they devoured the body. To this day, dragon boat races are still held, and people eat *tsungtse*, a kind of dumpling made of glutinous rice wrapped in large bamboo leaves – glutinous rice again! It is very much a festival food.

Now the summer is really upon us, and the weather grows hotter. Children go round wearing sachets of incense to ward off evil spirits, and are made to eat boiled garlic in order to clean the system. Salted duck eggs are also part of the Summer Festival celebrations for reasons nobody seems to know. Here is a rather unusual way of cooking eggs.

Towards the end of September, around the autumnal equinox, is the festival of Middle Autumn. It always occurs on the fifteenth day of the eighth moon when there is a full moon and is therefore called the 'Moon Festival'. At this time Moon Cakes are exchanged as gifts. These cakes are filled with rich red soy bean paste, and sometimes also filled with lotus seeds and salted duck's eggs. Moon Cakes are never made at home, for they are very difficult to prepare and require a long list of unusual ingredients as well as special cooking equipment.

For the true gourmet, at autumn festival time nothing can compare with eating crab, which is then at the height of its season, accompanied by rice wine, in a garden of chrysanthemums under a beautiful full moon. Poets and artists were often inspired by such happenings, and many great works of art were created in the past under such favourable circumstances.

The Festival of Winter Solstice is no longer celebrated in China, so the next major event is the New Year festival and we are back to where we started. The circle is complete. *Kung Ho Hsin Hsi* (Happy New Year)!

Drinks to Accompany Chinese Food

Deh-ta Hsiung

Tea is undoubtedly by far the most popular beverage in China. Traditionally, it is regarded as one of the seven essential daily items for any household at the start of the day, the other six being fuel, rice, oil, salt, soy sauce and vinegar.

Although tea-drinking is universal amongst the Chinese, tea is never drunk with food at meal times except in certain southern parts of China. The reason for this is that the greatest enemy of tea is oil, and nearly all foods are cooked with oil. If you go to a 'tea house' for refreshments or snacks (*dim sum* in Cantonese), you will find most people sipping tea before or after eating, but seldom accompanying the food.

Tea is served all day long in China. A visitor is automatically offered tea on entering a house, indeed, it is regarded as discourteous if a caller is sent away without receiving the offer. There was a time when poor people who could not afford tea would offer a guest plain boiled water, nicknamed 'white tea'.

It is generally agreed that tea is the ideal beverage after a Chinese meal. For this reason I will leave tea to the end of this chapter, and first answer the question: what do Chinese drink with their food?

During an everyday lunch or supper at home, soup is normally served throughout the meal. This is why Chinese soups are mostly clear broths to which small pieces of vegetable and/or meat are added just before serving. Very often, when a broth is not available, a Chinese housewife will simply stir-fry a small amount of, for example, greens, then add some water and bring it rapidly to the boil. *Voilà* – an instant soup.

When it comes to a more formal occasion or when entertaining, wines and spirits are essential parts of the fare. Indeed, a feast cannot be considered a feast without wine. It is universally accepted that good food should be accompanied by good wine, the only exception to this rule being on religious or health grounds.

As I said earlier, in China tea is seldom drunk with food, but wine is never drunk without food! Hardly anybody drinks before or after a meal (they drink tea both for an apéritif as well as a digestif). In a Chinese inn one always orders food to accompany the wine. Also, drinking is a social affair in China, and it is very rare for a person to be seen drinking alone.

The Chinese character for wine is *chiew*, which is applied to any type of alcoholic beverage, spirits included. *Chiew* is formed from the character for water and an ancient form of the word meaning eighth month (corresponding to September in the Western Calendar); the earliest type of wine was made from millet which was harvested at this time.

As you might well imagine, in a country where rice is the staple food, rice wine is the most popular alcoholic beverage. Rice wine is commonly known as 'yellow wine' because of its golden colour. It is very similar to dry sherry, both in colour and flavour. Indeed, it is so like sherry that in a blind tasting, it is sometimes extremely difficult, even for an expert, to distinguish one from the other.

Without a doubt, the best yellow wine comes from Shaoshing in the Chekiang province. It is made from a blend of glutinous rice, millet and ordinary rice, but its unique flavour is attributed to the special type of yeast used, and the mineral water taken from the lake nearby. The best known Shaoshing wine is called Hua Tiao (Carved Flower). It is amber in colour, because it has been well-matured in underground cellars, sometimes for as long as 40 years or more. Such wines are very rare, as they are usually at least 10 years old when offered for sale.

It was once the custom for people in the Shaoshing district to store a few urns of yellow wine at the birth of a daughter in order to drink them at her wedding feast – a charming tradition but alas, no longer observed.

Another famous yellow wine comes from Fukien. It is called Chen Gang, which means 'sunken urn', because the wine-urns are stored deeply during the maturing process. Like Shaoshing wine, it has a fragrant bouquet but tastes a little sweeter. It is often used as a tonic, particularly by women during pregnancy and after confinement.

There is also glutinous rice wine which is paler than other rice wines and is very often home-made. My grandmother used to make it for the New Year Festival and I was first introduced to it at an early age. I liked it so much that I got quite drunk for the first time in my life at the age of four!

After yellow wine, the next most popular Chinese 'wine' is Mao Tai (Thatched Terrace), which is not really a wine but a spirit. It is made from sorghum grain and its alcoholic strength is 55 per cent (110 proof), which is stronger than pure Russian vodka. Mao Tai is made in a town of the same name in the Kweichow province of South-West China. The special feature of this spirit is the water used, which is taken from a river flowing in a gorge between high mountains and on past the town. The climate there is moist and warm and a thin layer of mist permanently hovers over the fast-running river. In 1704, a salt merchant from Shansi in North China was so enchanted by the beauty of the scenery around Mao Tai that he decided to settle in, what was then only a small village. Following the technique used for Koaliang, the famous spirit distilled in his native province, he started making wine from sorghum grain and it soon attracted attention all over the country. *Mao Tai* was first introduced abroad at the 1919 Panama International Exposition, and its reputation is now world-wide.

Another famous spirit is called Fen Chiew and comes from a village called Apricot Blossoms in the Shansi province. It is made from sorghum and millet, and again owes its unique quality to the water of a river, a tributary of the famous Yellow River. Fen Chiew has a long history; it was first made over 1,400 years ago, and won a gold medal at the Panama Exposition in 1919.

Fen Chiew is used as the basis for a liqueur called Chu Yeh Ching (Bamboo-Leaf Green). It has no less than twelve different flavourings, including dried orange peel and bamboo leaves, hence the name. It tastes a little sweeter than both Mao Tai and Fen Chiew, and is quite refreshing; therefore it is more suitable as an after-dinner digestif.

Sweeter still is a liqueur called Mei Kuei Lu (Rose Dew). Distilled from sorghum and other grains, it is blended with rose petals and other aromatic herbs.

One other well-known spirit is Wu Chia Pi (Five-Layer Skin). Again it is made from sorghum but essence of caramel is added, which gives it a slight burnt taste not unlike Madeira. It is often used for medicinal purposes as well as for social occasions.

52

There are a number of wines and spirits which are used solely for medicinal purposes, most notable of which are Snake wine, Tiger Bones wine, and the most famous of them all, Ginseng wine. However, I do not think there is anything to beat 'Deer's Testicle Wine', which is supposed to aid rejuvenation!

Apart from yellow wine, none of the spirits mentioned is really a table wine in the Western sense, although a great number of Chinese would happily drink any of these spirits with food. However, wine made from grapes is now a rapidly expanding industry in China. It was during the Han dynasty (208 B.C. – 220 A.D.) that the vine, *vitis vinifera,* was first introduced into China from Iran via the silk route, although the art of wine-making was not acquired until the 7th Century from Turkestan. Grape wine-making has only really started to flourish during the last two decades or so.

At the start of this century, when Shantung was under German influence, a type of white wine was made there. Today Chefoo and Tsingtao are two of China's leading wine producing centres, making mainly white wine, which is sweeter than German hock. Elsewhere, grape wines are produced in Peking and Manchuria, and it is in Tunghwa in Manchuria that China's largest and most modern winery is situated. Both red and white wines are made there. The red resembles a tawny port and the white is not unlike a medium sherry. Dry wines mainly come from Peking, again both red and white, but neither of them has a distinct character, and therefore cannot seriously be considered as a table wine.

For any formal dinner or feast, the Chinese serve rice only at the end of the meal, when drinking will cease. This is because it is considered sacreligious to drink wine with rice, since most alcoholic beverages are made from grains of some sort.

In China, the sophistication of drinking different wines with different foods does not exist. Normally, only one type of wine is served throughout the meal, and the choice seems to rest entirely on taste and budget. In the case of the connoisseur, the best yellow wine is considered ideal for any food, be it fish, meat or poultry; others may prefer a strong spirit, of which Koaliang is the most popular, with Mao Tai as the best money can buy. There is also a geographical division. As rice is abundant south of the Yangtze River, rice wine is more popular in the south. Sorghum is essentially a northern crop so Kaoliang spirit is more popular in the North, also probably because the climate there is colder.

The Chinese, as a rule, only drink socially. At a dinner table, be it a formal occasion or an informal gathering, one only lifts up one's wine cup in drinking a toast, A Chinese dining table is either round or square, and there are usually eight to ten people at each table. The guest of honour's seat is always the head of the table, facing the doorway, while the host sits opposite with his back to the door. The next most important guests sit on either side of the guest of honour with somebody junior, either in rank or age or both, sitting next to the host and hostess, who usually sit side by side. When everybody is seated, the host will lift up his wine cup and offer a toast to the guest of honour, saying: '*Kan Pei!'* (Bottoms up!). This is the signal for the start of eating and drinking. After the first helping of food, the guest of honour returns a toast to the host and hostess. Then the host toasts the next guest, who in turn returns the toast, and so on. Now, even if you have no head for figures, it is not difficult to see that by the time everyone has toasted everybody else and in turn been toasted back, an alarming amount of wine or spirit will have been consumed by all.

To further increase the chance of inebriation, when a toast is exchanged, it goes without saying that everybody will raise their cups and take a sip. However, the two people actually toasting each other are expected to empty their cups in one gulp, then turn their cup upside-down to show it is empty, hence the toast 'bottoms up'.

As if not enough alcohol is drunk this way, the Chinese invented a finger game to be played at table to encourage more drinking. The game is called 'Guess the Fist' and is played between two people. Both fling out a fist simultaneously, with or without a number of fingers stretched, and at the same time call out a number from 0 to 10. If the first person who calls happens to match the total number of outstretched fingers, then he is the winner. But it is the loser who has to down the drink! The players get quite excited about this game, and often shout at the tops of their voices. Most Chinese restaurants have tables behind partitions, and although you cannot see what is going on, when you hear the guessing game, you know that a party is in full swing.

The order in which dishes or courses are served at a Chinese dinner seems to puzzle most people in the West when faced with the problems of choosing a wine or wines to accompany the food. The Western conventional order of soup, fish, meat, dessert is not observed. Instead, both fish and meat are served together, sometimes soup and sweet dishes are served between courses, then fish and chicken appear again, followed by soup as the very last course. As explained at the beginning of this chapter, tea is not an acceptable choice, nor is a white or rosé wine because in a well-balanced dinner there will always be a number of meat dishes cooked in rich sauces that call for a full-bodied red wine.

When you closely examine a well-planned Chinese dinner, you will find there is indeed a logical order in which dishes or courses make their appearance on the table. They follow a pattern which is not determined by the natural taste of the foods served, but by the method in which they are prepared and cooked. A well-planned dinner always includes fish, pork and poultry. These three ingredients are supplemented by others to form 6 to 10 different dishes. Care is taken to ensure that the combination of dishes is well-balanced, not only in taste but also in texture and colour.

A dinner, say, for 10 to 12 people, will start with four cold dishes as appetizers, served simultaneously. These will be followed by four or more hot dishes served one after another. These are light dishes, usually stir-fried or deep-fried, never too heavy nor too rich, and each dish should contrast its predecessor as well as the dish to follow. Sometimes 'neutral' dishes such as vegetables or soup will be served at this point before the 'big' dishes to come.

Choosing wine for a dinner like this presents no problems at all, as there are so many of you that you will need at least four, if not five bottles of wine. To start with, choose a medium sherry as an apéritif to accompany the cold appetizers. Alternatively select a Champagne or any light white wine, such as Muscadet, Chablis, Graves; or a less dry white, such as hock, Moselle or any white wine made from the Riesling grape.

For the next course, when stir-fried dishes are served, you need a stronger wine with more fruitiness and flavour such as a white Alsace, a Burgundy or Pouilly Blanc Fumé from France, an Orvieto Secco or Frascati from Italy, or a Pinot Chardonnay from California. For those who prefer red wine, choose a Beaujolais, Mâcon, Chinon, Bourgueil or a lightish claret from Bordeaux; or any other light red wine from Italy (Valpolicella, Bardolino or Barolo), Spain (Rioja), Australia (Cabernet or Shiraz) or California (Cabernet Sauvignon or Pinot Noir).

The final 'big' dishes call for a more robust and full-bodied red wine. For the claret lovers, there is plenty of suitable good red wine such as an aromatic Pomerol or St Emilion. Médoc or red Graves may be a shade too delicate for the really rich dishes, but the firmer and tastier Burgundy suits well. Any of the

commune type wines such as Gevrey-Chambertin, Chambolle-Musigny, Nuits-St-Georges, Aloxe Corton, Beaune, Pommard, Volnay or Sautenay are highly suitable, as is a powerful and fragrant Châteauneuf-du-Pape or a Hermitage from the Rhône valley. Italian Chianti Classico, or the Marques de Riscal from Spain will also do well. The list is really too large to go on here. Suffice it to say that almost any good quality red wine, be it French, Italian, Californian or Australian, immediately becomes the right wine as long as both you and your friends enjoy it.

For smaller gatherings, when there are not enough people to warrant opening more than two wine bottles, have a white and a red (always drink white before red). When only one single bottle is required, I would recommend a red, preferably Burgundy, which seems to have a greater affinity for Chinese food than other wines.

Both brandy and whisky are very popular in China, but usually after a good meal, nothing is more welcoming than hot Chinese tea. It is most invigorating and refreshing.

Oddly enough, tea was only discovered as a beverage as late as the 6th Century A.D., whereas wine was first made in China more than 2,000 years prior to that. Tea has been acclaimed as one of the greatest contributions to the pleasure of mankind. Indeed, life without tea would be unthinkable to many people. Tea grows in practically all parts of China, but because of the climate all the best teas are produced in the south. There are hundreds of varieties, but they all fall into two basic categories: green (unfermented) and red or black (fermented) tea. Green tea is dried in the sun, while red tea is first dried by sun or air, then fired over charcoal.

In China, Lung Ching (Dragon Well), a fragrant green tea from Hanchow in Chekiang, is generally regarded as the best green tea. For red tea, the crown must be awarded to Wuyi (Cliff) tea, which comes from the high mountains between the borders of Kiangsi and Fukien. It is said that because the cliffs are so steep, monkeys were trained to climb them to pluck the tea leaves. One of the best-known varieties is called 'Iron Goddess of Mercy'. It has an exquisite fragrance with a very full flavour, and is almost black in colour, hence the name iron.

Other well-known teas include green 'Water Nymph' and red 'Black Dragon' from Kwangtung, green 'Cloud Mist' from Kiangsi, and from Yunnan, a powerful reddish-black tea called 'Pu Erh', which is often used as a medicine. And there is of course Jasmin tea, probably the most popular Chinese tea abroad.

A Chinese tea connoisseur attaches great importance to the technique of tea-making, to the extent that he will be fastidious in his selection of kettle, teapot and water. People may travel miles to get water from a spring, or go to endless trouble to store rain-water. My grandfather used to boil up snow in the winter for tea and there are still people who keep snow for months for tea-making in the dry season.

Kettles should ideally be made of earthenware. Water must be freshly boiled; re-boiled water loses its oxygen content and this can impair the taste of tea. Teapots and cups must be of finest porcelain or earthenware, and they must never be washed together with greasy dishes.

Since most of us have to get our water from a tap and use a metal kettle, the least we can do is to observe a few basic rules in our tea-making. They are quite simple: 1. Use only freshly boiled water. 2. Avoid using silver or other metal teapots. 3. Always rinse the teapot thoroughly and warm with boiling water before putting in the tea. 4. Allow the tea to stand to infuse for about 3 minutes before pouring out. 5. Drink it while still hot – even in summer. 6. Never add milk or sugar to Chinese tea because it will spoil the fragrant aroma.

Northern China
Peking, Shantung and Honan

Nancy Chih Ma

The Great Wall of China enfolds more than a region, it encompasses a culinary history. In successive dynasties, governors visiting Peking from the provinces brought their own chefs to the Imperial capital. These chefs, in turn, brought with them a variety of culinary traditions from all of the different regions of China.

The preparation and service of food played such an important part in court rituals that many Emperors made it their first task to appoint a court chef. Naturally, each court chef in turn sought to excel the cooking of his predecessor. As a result of this concentration of culinary expertise, and encouragement from the Emperors to develop new dishes, a type of haute cuisine was created in Peking.

The importance that the Chinese attach to food and its preparation is shown by the following classification of doctors, which dates back to about 2,000 B.C. Doctors of the first class were the 'doctors of food', doctors of the second class were the physicians, the third class were surgeons and the fourth class were veterinarians. The 'doctor of food' in ancient days was the family cook or even the court cook, who, by way of an expert balance of spices, herbs and other ingredients, saw to it that everyone in the household was in good health.

Peking has been the capital of China for nearly 1,000 years, and it has been over-run more than once by Tartar invaders who brought with them Moslem traditions of Central Asia. Other cuisines, even those of Europe, have made an impression on Northern China. The cooking of this region is thus as ancient and varied as the history of the city itself.

Unlike Southern Chinese cuisine, Peking cooking is light rather than rich, and always extremely elegant. Strong flavours, such as those of leeks, onions and garlic, are enjoyed as well as more delicately seasoned foods. Mandarin pancakes, wrapped around spring onions (shallots/scallions) and garlic, and noodles are popular, but the greatest of all Northern China delicacies is undoubtedly Peking roast duck (*page 97*).

Outside the capital city, the region stretches to the borders of Inner Mongolia where the land is dry and arid. There are also thousands of miles of grassland in Northern China, and, unlike the rest of the country, the staple food here is wheat flour rather than rice. Wheat flour is used to make noodles, steamed breads and buns, dumplings and pancakes. Sesame seeds, and the oil and paste extracted from them, are widely used all over China, but they were originally introduced to the North by the Tartars, and are a staple food in the Northern diet.

In the provinces outside Peking, methods are simple – roasting, barbecuing and boiling. Strong-tasting dips served with the meat add a touch of refinement. Mutton and lamb are very popular, due no doubt to the lingering influence of the Mongol invasion and dynasty (1279–1368); elsewhere in China mutton and lamb are rarely eaten. The Mongolian hot pot (*page 83*), or Mohammedan fire kettle as it is sometimes known, is a good example of the style of cooking favoured.

Honan, on the Yellow River (Hwang Ho), is famous for its pungent sweet-and-sour specialities. Carp, caught in the Yellow River, is deliciously prepared in this way.

In Shantung, the people eat large quantities of raw spring onions (shallots/scallions) which they believe to have health-giving properties. Chefos, in Shantung province, is famous for its grapes, peaches and a crunchy type of pear called 'water pear'. The best-known vegetable of the region is the Tientsin white cabbage, called Chinese cabbage or bok choy elsewhere. In flavour and texture, it is a cross between cabbage, lettuce and celery. To the east is the Gulf of Chilli, which gives a plentiful supply of prawns (shrimp) and other shellfish. A popular way of cooking prawns (shrimp) is to stir-fry them in their shells.

According to Chinese belief, one needs the teaching of three generations to dress well and four generations in order to eat well. The cooks of northern China reflect this belief, and their delicate preparations are evidence of their sophisticated cooking traditions.

Shredded Lamb Stir-Fried with Noodles and Spring Onions (Scallions)

METRIC/IMPERIAL

1 egg, beaten

1 × 15 ml spoon/1 tablespoon cornflour

1.5 × 15 ml spoons/1½ tablespoons water

225 g/8 oz lean lamb, shredded

1 chicken stock cube

300 ml/½ pint stock

3 × 15 ml spoons/3 tablespoons oil

2 × 15 ml spoons/2 tablespoons soy sauce

4–5 spring onions (shallots), cut into 5 cm/2 inch pieces

100 g/4 oz transparent pea-starch noodles, soaked in hot water for 5 minutes and drained

1 × 15 ml spoon/1 tablespoon sesame seed oil

2 × 15 ml spoons/2 tablespoons dry sherry

Shredded Lamb Stir-Fried with Noodles and Spring Onions (Scallions)

AMERICAN

1 egg, beaten

1 tablespoon cornstarch

1½ tablespoons water

½ lb lean lamb, shredded

2 chicken stock cubes

1¼ cups stock

3 tablespoons oil

2 tablespoons soy sauce

4-5 scallions, cut into 2 inch pieces

¼ lb cellophane noodles, soaked in hot water for 5 minutes and drained

1 tablespoon sesame oil

2 tablespoons pale dry sherry

Beat the egg with the cornflour (cornstarch) and water. Add the lamb and turn to coat. Dissolve the stock cube(s) in the stock.

Heat the oil in a pan over high heat. Add the lamb and stir-fry for 1 minute. Sprinkle in the soy sauce and spring onions (shallots/scallions) and stir-fry for 1 minute. Add the stock and noodles and bring to the boil, stirring. Simmer gently for 5 minutes. Sprinkle with the sesame seed oil and sherry. Simmer for a further 1 minute. Serve hot.

Prawns (Shrimp) with Fresh Asparagus

METRIC/IMPERIAL

0.5 kg/1 lb raw prawns, shelled and deveined

1 × 5 ml spoon/1 teaspoon salt

1 × 5 ml spoon/1 teaspoon dry sherry

1 × 15 ml spoon/1 tablespoon cornflour

100 g/4 oz fresh asparagus, cut into 2.5 cm/1 inch pieces

6 × 15 ml spoons/6 tablespoons oil

1 × 2.5 ml spoon/½ teaspoon sugar

4 × 15 ml spoons/4 tablespoons water

AMERICAN

1½ lb raw shrimp, shelled and deveined

1 teaspoon salt

1 teaspoon pale dry sherry

1 tablespoon cornstarch

¼ lb fresh asparagus, cut into 1 inch pieces

6 tablespoons oil

½ teaspoon sugar

4 tablespoons water

Mix the prawns (shrimp) with half the salt, the sherry and 2 × 5 ml spoons/2 teaspoons of the cornflour (cornstarch). Cook the asparagus in boiling salted water until tender but still crisp. Drain well.

Heat the oil in a pan and add the prawns (shrimp). Stir-fry until they turn pink. Add the asparagus, sugar and remaining salt and mix well. Dissolve the remaining cornflour (cornstarch) in the water and add to the pan. Cook, stirring, until thickened. Serve hot.

Spinach Salad

METRIC/IMPERIAL

0.75 kg/1½ lb spinach

salt

2 × 15 ml spoons/2 tablespoons sesame seed oil

1 × 5 ml spoon/1 teaspoon sugar

2 × 15 ml spoons/2 tablespoons red wine vinegar

3 × 15 ml spoons/3 tablespoons soy sauce

1 × 5 ml spoon/1 teaspoon made mustard

AMERICAN

1½ lb spinach

salt

2 tablespoons sesame oil

1 teaspoon sugar

2 tablespoons red wine vinegar

3 tablespoons soy sauce

1 teaspoon prepared mustard

Trim the spinach and wash thoroughly in cold water.

Cook the spinach in a little boiling salted water until just tender. Drain well, then refresh under cold running water. Drain again, squeezing out all the water from the spinach. Cut each leaf into 3 or 4 pieces and place in a bowl. Allow to cool. Combine the sesame seed oil, sugar, vinegar, soy sauce and mustard in a bowl. Pour over the spinach and toss well before serving chilled.

Stir-Fried Liver with Spring Onions (Scallions)

METRIC/IMPERIAL

350 g/12 oz calves' or lambs' liver, cut into 5 mm/¼ inch thick slices

7 × 15 ml spoons/7 tablespoons oil

6 spring onions (shallots), cut into 5 cm/ 2 inch pieces

2 slices root ginger

50 g/2 oz dried wood ears, soaked for 20 minutes, drained and stemmed

2 × 15 ml spoons/2 tablespoons soy sauce

1 × 5 ml spoon/1 teaspoon sugar

1 × 15 ml spoon/1 tablespoon red wine vinegar

1 × 15 ml spoon/1 tablespoon dry sherry

1 × 15 ml spoon/1 tablespoon cornflour, dissolved in 250 ml/8 fl oz water

Marinade

1 × 2.5 ml spoon/½ teaspoon salt

1 × 2.5 ml spoon/½ teaspoon pepper

2 × 5 ml spoons/2 teaspoons dry sherry

2 × 5 ml spoons/2 teaspoons cornflour

2 × 5 ml spoons/2 teaspoons oil

Garnish

8 spring onion (shallot) flowers (see note)

AMERICAN

¾ lb veal or lambs' liver, cut into ¼ inch thick slices

7 tablespoons oil

6 scallions, cut into 2 inch pieces

2 slices ginger root

2 cups dried tree ears, soaked for 20 minutes, drained and stemmed

2 tablespoons soy sauce

1 teaspoon sugar

1 tablespoon red wine vinegar

1 tablespoon pale dry sherry

1 tablespoon cornstarch, dissolved in 1 cup water

Spinach Salad (top left)
Prawns (Shrimp) with Asparagus (below)
Stir-Fried Liver with Spring Onions (Scallions) (right)

Marinade

½ teaspoon salt

½ teaspoon pepper

2 teaspoons pale dry sherry

2 teaspoons cornstarch

2 teaspoons oil

Garnish

8 scallion flowers (see note)

Soak the liver in cold water for 30 minutes. Drain on absorbent kitchen paper. Mix the ingredients for the marinade in a bowl. Add the liver slices and marinate for 10 minutes. Heat 5 × 15 ml spoons/5 tablespoons of the oil in a pan over a high heat. Add the liver and stir-fry very rapidly until it changes colour. Transfer to a plate.

Heat the remaining oil in the pan and stir-fry the spring onions (shallots/scallions), ginger and mushrooms for 1 minute. Add the soy sauce, sugar, vinegar and sherry and bring to the boil. Return the liver to the pan. Add the cornflour (cornstarch) and simmer, stirring, until thickened. Garnish and serve hot.

Note: To prepare the garnish, make about four 2.5 cm/1 inch deep cuts across both ends of each spring onion (shallot/scallion) stalk. Leave in a bowl of iced water to open.

Shredded Duck Salad

METRIC/IMPERIAL

2 × 15 ml spoons/2 tablespoons red wine vinegar

2 × 15 ml spoons/2 tablespoons sugar

2 × 15 ml spoons/2 tablespoons sesame seed oil

2 × 15 ml spoons/2 tablespoons soy sauce

1 × 5 ml spoon/1 teaspoon made mustard

1 × 2.5 ml spoon/½ teaspoon salt

100 g/4 oz carrots, shredded

100 g/4 oz cucumber, peeled and shredded

75 g/3 oz cabbage or Chinese cabbage, cored and shredded

0.5 kg/1 lb roast duck or chicken meat, shredded

AMERICAN

2 tablespoons red wine vinegar

2 tablespoons sugar

2 tablespoons sesame oil

2 tablespoons soy sauce

1 teaspoon prepared mustard

½ teaspoon salt

1 cup shredded carrot

1 cup peeled and shredded cucumber

1 cup shredded cabbage or Chinese cabbage (bok choy)

1 lb roast duck or chicken meat, shredded

Combine the vinegar, sugar, sesame seed oil, soy sauce, mustard and salt in a bowl; mix thoroughly. Arrange the vegetables on a serving plate. Put the shredded duck or chicken on top. Pour over the dressing just before serving.

Shredded Duck Salad (top)
Stir-Fried Prawns (Shrimp) (below)
Walnut Sweet (right)

Walnut Sweet

METRIC/IMPERIAL

225 g/8 oz shelled walnuts

175 g/6 oz red dates

oil for deep frying

1.75 litres/3 pints water

250 g/8 oz crystal sugar or 275 g/10 oz granulated sugar

5 × 15 ml spoons/5 tablespoons cornflour, dissolved in 5 × 15 ml spoons/5 tablespoons water

AMERICAN

2 cups shelled walnuts

1 cup red dates (jujubes)

oil for deep frying

7 cups water

1 cup rock sugar or 1¼ cups granulated sugar

5 tablespoons cornstarch, dissolved in 5 tablespoons water

Soak the walnuts in boiling water for 5 minutes, then remove the skins. Dry on absorbent kitchen paper. Soak the red dates in boiling water for 5 minutes, then drain and remove the stones (seeds). Heat the oil to 180°C/350°F. Deep-fry the walnuts until golden brown. (Walnuts burn easily, so remove them from the oil as soon as the colour changes.) Drain on absorbent kitchen paper. Put the walnuts and dates in a blender and grind until very fine or rub through a sieve.

Bring the water to the boil in a saucepan. Stir in the sugar and the walnut mixture. When the sugar has dissolved, add the cornflour (cornstarch) mixture and simmer, stirring continuously, until thickened. Serve hot.

Note: 65 g/2½ oz (½ cup) rice powder or cornmeal may be used in place of the cornflour (cornstarch).

Stir-Fried Prawns (Shrimp)

METRIC/IMPERIAL

0.5 kg/1 lb large prawns, shelled and deveined

1 × 15 ml spoon/1 tablespoon dry sherry

1 egg white

salt

pepper

4 × 5 ml spoons/4 teaspoons cornflour

7 × 15 ml spoons/7 tablespoons oil

1 × 2.5 ml spoon/½ teaspoon finely chopped garlic

1 × 5 ml spoon/1 teaspoon soy sauce

100 g/4 oz cucumber, peeled and sliced

8 dried Chinese mushrooms, soaked for 20 minutes, drained, stemmed and sliced

1 × 5 ml spoon/1 teaspoon sugar

1 × 5 ml spoon/1 teaspoon red wine vinegar

1 × 15 ml spoon/1 tablespoon water (optional)

AMERICAN

1 lb large shrimp, shelled and deveined

1 tablespoon pale dry sherry

1 egg white

salt

pepper

4 teaspoons cornstarch

7 tablespoons oil

½ teaspoon finely chopped garlic

1 teaspoon soy sauce

1 cup peeled and sliced cucumber

8 dried Chinese mushrooms, soaked for 20 minutes, drained, stemmed and sliced

1 teaspoon sugar

1 teaspoon red wine vinegar

1 tablespoon water (optional)

Split the prawns (shrimp) in half lengthwise, then cut each half crosswise into 3 pieces. Mix together the sherry, egg white, a pinch of salt, pinch of pepper and 1 × 15 ml spoon/1 tablespoon of the cornflour (cornstarch) in a bowl. Add the prawns (shrimp) and turn to coat with the mixture. Heat 5 × 15 ml spoons/5 tablespoons of the oil in a pan. Add the prawns (shrimp) and stir-fry until they are no longer opaque. Transfer to a plate. Add the remaining oil to the pan and heat. Add the garlic, soy sauce, cucumber and mushrooms and stir-fry for 1 minute. Return the prawns (shrimp) to the pan with the sugar, vinegar and salt and pepper to taste. Stir a few times. If necessary, thicken with the remaining cornflour (cornstarch) dissolved in the water. Serve hot.

Sweet and Sour Cabbage

METRIC/IMPERIAL

3 × 15 ml spoons/3 tablespoons oil

15 g/½ oz butter

1 Chinese or Savoy cabbage, cored and shredded

1 × 5 ml spoon/1 teaspoon salt

Sauce

1.5 × 15 ml spoons/1½ tablespoons cornflour

5 × 15 ml spoons/5 tablespoons water

1.5 × 15 ml spoons/1½ tablespoons soy sauce

2.5 × 15 ml spoons/2½ tablespoons sugar

3.5 × 15 ml spoons/3½ tablespoons vinegar

3.5 × 15 ml spoons/3½ tablespoons orange juice

2.5 × 15 ml spoons/2½ tablespoons tomato purée

1.5 × 15 ml spoons/1½ tablespoons sherry

AMERICAN

3 tablespoons oil

1 tablespoon butter

1 Chinese (bok choy) or Savoy cabbage, cored and shredded

1 teaspoon salt

Sauce

1½ tablespoons cornstarch

5 tablespoons water

1½ tablespoons soy sauce

2½ tablespoons sugar

3½ tablespoons vinegar

3½ tablespoons orange juice

2½ tablespoons tomato paste

1½ tablespoons sherry

Heat the oil and butter in a pan. Add the cabbage and sprinkle with the salt. Stir-fry for 2 minutes. Reduce the heat to low and simmer gently for 5 to 6 minutes.

Mix the sauce ingredients in another pan. Bring to the boil and simmer for 4 to 5 minutes, stirring continuously, until the sauce thickens and becomes translucent.

Transfer the cabbage to a serving dish and pour over the sauce. Serve hot.

Sour Hot Soup

METRIC/IMPERIAL

1.2 lites/2 pints clear broth (see page 15)

100 g/4 oz lean pork, shredded

50 g/2 oz canned bamboo shoot, drained and shredded

3 dried Chinese mushrooms, soaked for 20 minutes, drained, stemmed and shredded

1 cake bean curd, shredded

1 × 15 ml spoon/1 tablespoon dry sherry

2 × 15 ml spoons/2 tablespoons red wine vinegar

1 × 2.5 ml spoon/½ teaspoon salt

large pinch of pepper

2 × 5 ml spoons/2 teaspoons soy sauce

2 × 15 ml spoons/2 tablespoons cornflour, dissolved in 4 × 15 ml spoons/4 tablespoons water

1 egg, beaten

few drops of sesame seed oil

1 spring onion (shallot), shredded

AMERICAN

5 cups clear broth (see page 15)

¼ lb lean shredded pork

¼ cup shredded canned bamboo shoot

3 dried Chinese mushrooms, soaked for 20 minutes, drained, stemmed and shredded

1 cake bean curd, shredded

1 tablespoon pale dry sherry

2 tablespoons red wine vinegar

½ teaspoon salt

large pinch of pepper

2 teaspoons soy sauce

2 tablespoons cornstarch, dissolved in ¼ cup water

1 egg, beaten

few drops of sesame oil

1 scallion, shredded

Bring the broth to the boil. Add the pork, bamboo shoot and mushrooms. Cover and simmer for 10 minutes. Add the bean curd, sherry, vinegar, salt, pepper and soy sauce. When the soup returns to the boil, add the cornflour (cornstarch) mixture. Simmer, stirring, until thickened.

Slowly pour in the beaten egg, through a strainer. Pour into soup bowls, then sprinkle over the sesame seed oil and spring onion (shallot/scallion). Serve hot.

Opposite page: Bird's Nest Soup (left)
Shark's Fin Soup (centre)
Sour Hot Soup (right)

Sweet and Sour Cabbage (below)

Bird's Nest Soup

Bird's nest is one of the most expensive Chinese ingredients, and is delicious.

METRIC/IMPERIAL

100 g/4 oz dried bird's nest, soaked overnight and drained

1.5 litres/2½ pints clear broth (see page 15)

100 g/4 oz cooked chicken meat, chopped

1 × 15 ml spoon/1 tablespoon dry sherry

10 pigeon or quail eggs, boiled and peeled

1 × 15 ml spoon/1 tablespoon cornflour, dissolved in 1 × 15 ml spoon/1 tablespoon water

1 × 2.5 ml spoon/½ teaspoon salt

pinch of pepper

2 egg whites

2 × 15 ml spoons/2 tablespoons shredded cooked ham

2 × 15 ml spoons/2 tablespoons chopped parsley

AMERICAN

¼ lb bird's nest, soaked overnight and drained

3 pints clear broth (see page 15)

¼ lb chopped cooked chicken meat

1 tablespoon pale dry sherry

10 pigeon or quail eggs, boiled and peeled

1 tablespoon cornstarch, dissolved in 1 tablespoon water

½ teaspoon salt

pinch of pepper

2 egg whites

2 tablespoons shredded cooked ham

2 tablespoons chopped parsley

Remove any loose feathers from the bird's nest with tweezers. Place in a saucepan, cover with water and boil for 15 minutes; drain and rinse. Cover with fresh cold water and soak for a few hours, then re-boil for 5 minutes.

Drain and soak in fresh water overnight. Drain the bird's nest, which will have separated into chips like transparent noodles. Place in a saucepan with half the broth and bring to the boil. Cover and simmer for 30 minutes. Drain, discarding the stock.

Put the remaining broth in the pan and bring to the boil. Add the chicken, bird's nest chips, sherry and pigeon or quail eggs. When the soup comes to the boil, add the cornflour (cornstarch) mixture and simmer, stirring, until thickened. Stir in the salt and pepper. Beat the egg whites until stiff, then fold into the soup. Pour into soup bowls and sprinkle with the ham and parsley. Serve hot.

Note: Canned pigeon or quail eggs may be used, if fresh ones are unobtainable.

Shark's Fin Soup

METRIC/IMPERIAL

225 g/8 oz shark's fin, soaked (see note)

1.75 litres/3 pints clear broth (see page 15)

2 spring onions (shallots)

3 slices root ginger

2 × 15 ml spoons/2 tablespoons oil

225 g/8 oz chicken meat or pork, shredded

65 g/2½ oz canned bamboo shoot, drained and shredded

50 g/2 oz mushrooms, shredded

100 g/4 oz cooked ham, shredded

1 × 15 ml spoon/1 tablespoon dry sherry

2 × 15 ml spoons/2 tablespoons soy sauce

1 × 15 ml spoon/1 tablespoon red wine vinegar

1 × 2.5 ml spoon/½ teaspoon sugar

1 × 2.5 ml spoon/½ teaspoon salt

3 × 15 ml spoons/3 tablespoons cornflour, dissolved in 3 × 15 ml spoons/3 tablespoons water

AMERICAN

½ lb shark's fin, soaked (see note)

7½ cups clear broth (see page 15)

2 scallions

3 slices ginger root

2 tablespoons oil

1 cup shredded chicken meat or pork

½ cup shredded canned bamboo shoot

½ cup shredded mushrooms

½ cup shredded cooked ham

1 tablespoon pale dry sherry

2 tablespoons soy sauce

1 tablespoon red wine vinegar

½ teaspoon sugar

½ teaspoon salt

3 tablespoons cornstarch, dissolved in 3 tablespoons water

Rinse the soaked shark's fin under cold running water for 10 minutes; drain. Place the shark's fin in a saucepan and add 750 ml/1¼ pints (3 cups) of the broth, the spring onions (shallots/scallions) and ginger. Bring to the boil, cover and boil for 15 minutes. Drain the shark's fin, discarding the broth.

Heat the oil in a clean saucepan. Add the meat and stir-fry until it changes colour. Stir in the remaining stock and bring to the boil. Add the bamboo shoot, mushrooms, ham, sherry, soy sauce, vinegar, sugar and salt and simmer for 15 to 20 minutes.

Add the cornflour (cornstarch) mixture and simmer, stirring, until thickened. Serve hot.

Note: Shark's fin is an expensive delicacy; thread-like, transparent and rich in vitamins and calcium, it takes one week to prepare. Trim the fin, wash then place in a saucepan. Cover with water, boil for 2 hours then drain. Cover with cold water and leave to soak overnight. Repeat this for 5 days.

Shark's fin can be obtained with the rough outer skin removed; this form requires less preparation. Canned shark's fin is also available.

Prawn (Shrimp) Cutlets

METRIC/IMPERIAL

8 Dublin Bay or Pacific (king) prawns

1 × 15 ml spoon/1 tablespoon dry sherry

1 egg, beaten

2 × 15 ml spoons/2 tablespoons cornflour

oil for deep frying

sprig of coriander (optional)

AMERICAN

8 jumbo shrimp

1 tablespoon pale dry sherry

1 egg, beaten

2 tablespoons cornstarch

oil for deep frying

sprig of Chinese parsley (optional)

Hold the prawns (shrimp) firmly by the tail and remove the shell, leaving the tail shell piece intact. Cut the prawns (shrimp) in half lengthwise almost through to the tail and remove the dark intestinal vein. Flatten the prawns (shrimp) to resemble cutlets. Sprinkle with the sherry.

Dip the cutlets in beaten egg, then in the cornflour (cornstarch); repeat. Heat the oil to 180°C/350°F. Deep-fry the prawns (shrimp) for 2 to 3 minutes. Drain on absorbent kitchen paper. Arrange on a serving plate and garnish with fresh coriander (Chinese parsley), if used. Serve plain or with sweet soy bean paste (sauce).

Steamed Chinese Cabbage

METRIC/IMPERIAL

0.75 kg/1½ lb Chinese cabbage

225 g/8 oz cooked ham

2 × 15 ml spoons/2 tablespoons oil

4 × 15 ml spoons/4 tablespoons chopped spring onions (shallots)

1 × 5 ml spoon/1 teaspoon salt

2 × 5 ml spoons/2 teaspoons cornflour, dissolved in 2 × 5 ml spoons/2 teaspoons water

AMERICAN

1½ lb Chinese cabbage (bok choy)

½ lb cooked ham

2 tablespoons oil

¼ cup chopped scallions

1 teaspoon salt

2 teaspoons cornstarch, dissolved in 2 teaspoons water

Discard the tough outer leaves of the cabbage. Separate the stalks, wash and cut into 10 × 15 cm/4 × 6 inch pieces. Cut the ham into pieces the same size as the cabbage. Heat the oil in a pan. Add the cabbage and stir-fry lightly. Remove from heat. Lightly oil a heatproof bowl, then sprinkle in the spring onions (shallots/scallions). Arrange the cabbage and ham in alternate layers in the bowl. Add the salt, cover and steam over high heat for 30 minutes.

Drain the juice from the bowl into a saucepan. Add the cornflour (cornstarch) mixture and simmer, stirring, until the sauce has thickened. Arrange the ham, cabbage and spring onions (shallots/scallions) on a serving plate. Pour the sauce over and serve hot.

Prawn (Shrimp) Cutlets (left)
Steamed Chinese Cabbage (centre)
Sour Chinese Cabbage (top right)

Sour Chinese Cabbage

This dish can be served as a soup or as a main-course dish.

METRIC/IMPERIAL

400 g/14 oz pork fillet

1 crab or 100 g/4 oz white crab meat, flaked

25 g/1 oz transparent pea-starch noodles, soaked for 5 minutes and drained

2.25 litres/4 pints clear broth (see page 15)

15 dried shrimps, soaked for 15 minutes and drained

4 dried scallops (optional), soaked for 15 minutes, drained and chopped

4 slices root ginger

3-4 spring onions (shallots), chopped

400 g/14 oz sour Chinese cabbage, shredded, or sauerkraut (see note)

225 g/8 oz beef, sliced

2 × 15 ml spoons/2 tablespoons dry sherry

2 × 5 ml spoons/2 teaspoons salt

large pinch of pepper

AMERICAN

14 oz pork tenderloin

$\frac{1}{4}$ lb white crab meat, flaked

1 oz cellophane noodles, soaked for 5 minutes and drained

5 pints clear broth (see page 15)

15 dried shrimp, soaked for 15 minutes and drained

4 dried scallops (optional), soaked for 15 minutes, drained and chopped

4 slices ginger root

$\frac{1}{4}$ cup chopped scallions

14 oz sour Chinese cabbage (bok choy), shredded, or sauerkraut (see note)

$\frac{1}{2}$ lb beef, sliced

2 tablespoons pale dry sherry

2 teaspoons salt

large pinch of pepper

Cook the pork in boiling water for 30 minutes. Drain, cool and slice very thinly.

If using a whole crab, open the shell and remove the soft spongy parts. Flake the white meat. Crack the claws and cut the meat into 6 pieces. Cut the noodles into 10 cm/4 inch pieces.

Put the broth in a large saucepan with the shrimps, scallops (if used), ginger and spring onions (shallots/scallions). Bring to the boil. Stir in the cabbage or sauerkraut, pork, crab meat and claw pieces. Cover and simmer for 20 minutes, then add the beef, noodles, sherry, salt and pepper. Simmer until the beef is no longer red in colour. Serve hot, accompanied by soy sauce and fermented bean curd.

Note: To make sour Chinese cabbage, cut a Chinese cabbage (bok choy) in half and leave to dry out overnight. The next day, separate the cabbage leaves and steep them, one at a time, in boiling water for a few seconds. Allow to cool, then layer the leaves in a big jar. Place a lid, which is smaller than the jar, on top of the cabbage. Put a small weight or stone on the lid to press down the cabbage. Leave for about 1 month for the cabbage to become sour. This is a popular winter preserved vegetable in North China.

Spiced Leg of Lamb

Lamb was introduced to Northern China by the Mongols, who invaded China and set up a dynasty which ruled from 1279 to 1368. This is one of a number of dishes adapted by the Chinese to suit their tastes.

METRIC/IMPERIAL

1 × 1.75–2.5 kg/4–5 lb leg of lamb

Sauce

6 garlic cloves, crushed

6 slices root ginger, shredded

2 onions, thinly sliced

1.2 litres/2 pints stock

5 × 15 ml spoons/5 tablespoons soy sauce

3 × 15 ml spoons/3 tablespoons soy bean paste or hoisin sauce

2 × 5 ml spoons/2 teaspoons dried chilli pepper or chilli sauce

1 × 2.5 ml spoon/½ teaspoon 5-spice powder

2 × 15 ml spoons/2 tablespoons sugar

300 ml/½ pint red wine

1 chicken stock cube

AMERICAN

1 × 4-5 lb leg of lamb

Sauce

6 garlic cloves, minced

6 slices ginger root, shredded

2 onions, thinly sliced

5 cups stock

5 tablespoons soy sauce

3 tablespoons bean sauce or hoisin sauce

2 teaspoons dried chili pepper or chili sauce

½ teaspoon 5-spice powder

2 tablespoons sugar

1¼ cups red wine

2 chicken stock cubes

Place the sauce ingredients in a saucepan and mix together. Bring to the boil and simmer gently for 45 minutes.

Put the leg of lamb into another large saucepan or flameproof casserole. Pour over the sauce. Bring to the boil, then simmer gently for 1½ hours, turning every 30 minutes. Remove from the heat and allow to cool in the sauce, then leave to marinate for a further 3 hours (or overnight).

About 1 hour before serving, place the lamb in a roasting pan and put into a preheated moderate oven (180°C/350°F, Gas Mark 4). Cook for 1 hour.

Slice the lamb into large bite-sized pieces and serve hot or cold with dips such as hoisin sauce, soy sauce and sherry mixed together, or soy sauce and vinegar mixed together.

Spiced Leg of Lamb

Egg Foo Yung with Prawns (Shrimp)

METRIC/IMPERIAL

6 eggs

1 × 2.5 ml spoon/½ teaspoon salt

5 × 15 ml spoons/5 tablespoons oil

225 g/8 oz prawns, shelled and deveined

AMERICAN

6 eggs

½ teaspoon salt

5 tablespoons oil

½ lb shrimp, shelled and deveined

Beat the eggs with the salt. Heat 2 × 15 ml spoons/2 tablespoons of the oil in a small pan. Add the prawns (shrimp) and stir-fry for 1 minute or until just cooked. Remove from the heat and add the prawns (shrimp) to the egg mixture.

Heat the remaining oil in the pan. When very hot, add the egg mixture. Cook, turning once, until golden brown on both sides. Serve hot.

Crab Rolls

METRIC/IMPERIAL

oil for deep frying

Wrapping

4 × 15 ml spoons/4 tablespoons plain flour

1 × 2.5 ml spoon/½ teaspoon salt

4 × 15 ml spoons/4 tablespoons water

4 eggs, beaten

Filling

2 × 15 ml spoons/2 tablespoons oil

1 egg, beaten

1 spring onion (shallot), shredded

300 g/11 oz crab meat, flaked

1 × 15 ml spoon/1 tablespoon dry sherry

pinch of salt

pinch of pepper

1 × 15 ml spoon/1 tablespoon cornflour, dissolved in 3 × 15 ml spoons/3 tablespoons water

Flour paste

1 × 15 ml spoon/1 tablespoon plain flour, dissolved in 1 × 15 ml spoon/1 tablespoon water

AMERICAN

oil for deep frying

Wrapping

¼ cup all-purpose flour

½ teaspoon salt

¼ cup water

4 eggs, beaten

Filling

2 tablespoons oil

1 egg, beaten

1 scallion, shredded

¾ lb crab meat, flaked

1 tablespoon pale dry sherry

pinch of salt

pinch of pepper

1 tablespoon cornstarch, dissolved in 3 tablespoons water

Flour paste

1 tablespoon all-purpose flour, dissolved in 1 tablespoon water

To make the wrapping, sift the flour and salt into a bowl. Gradually beat in the water and eggs to form a smooth batter. Place a small frying pan (skillet) over moderate heat and oil lightly. Pour 4 × 15 ml spoons/4 tablespoons of the batter into the pan and rotate until the bottom of the pan is covered with a thin sheet of batter. Cook until the edges curl, then turn and cook the other side. Continue making pancakes in this way until all of the batter is used.

To make the filling, heat the oil in a pan. Add the egg, spring onion (shallot/scallion) and crab meat. Stir-fry for a few seconds, then stir in the sherry, salt and pepper. Add the cornflour (cornstarch) mixture and cook, stirring, until thickened. Remove from the heat and allow to cool.

Place 2 × 15 ml spoons/2 tablespoons of the filling on the bottom half of each wrapping pancake and fold the top half over. Fold the right side towards the left and the left side towards the right. Roll up into a tight roll, and seal with the flour paste.

Heat the oil to 180 C/350 F. Deep-fry the rolls, a few at a time, until golden brown. Drain on absorbent kitchen paper and cut into pieces diagonally. Serve hot.

Variation: Minced (ground) pork or chopped prawns (shrimp) can be substituted for crab meat.

Crab Rolls (left)
Egg Foo Yung with Prawns (Shrimp) (right)

Moo Shoo Pork

METRIC/IMPERIAL

225 g/8 oz lean pork, shredded

1 × 15 ml spoon/1 tablespoon soy sauce

9 × 15 ml spoons/9 tablespoons oil

6 eggs, beaten

2 × 15 ml spoons/2 tablespoons dried wood ears, soaked for 20 minutes, drained and stemmed

2 spring onions (shallots), shredded

1 × 2.5 ml spoon/½ teaspoon sugar

Moo Shoo Pork (left)
Egg Foo Yung with Chicken (centre)
Steamed Egg Custard (right)

½ lb lean pork, shredded

1 tablespoon soy sauce

9 tablespoons oil

6 eggs, beaten

2 tablespoons dried tree ears, soaked for 20 minutes, drained and stemmed

2 scallions, shredded

½ teaspoon sugar

Mix the pork with the soy sauce. Heat 6 × 15 ml spoons/6 tablespoons of the oil in a pan. When very hot, add the eggs and stir-fry until set. Cut into thin strips, using a spatula, and transfer to a plate.

Add the remaining oil to the pan and heat. Add the pork, mushrooms and spring onions (shallots/scallions), and stir-fry until the pork is cooked. Add the egg pieces and the sugar; mix well. Serve immediately.

Note: This dish is traditionally served with Mandarin Pancakes (*see page 96*). Garnish with shredded spring onions (shallots/scallions) and thin strips of cucumber.

Steamed Egg Custard

METRIC/IMPERIAL

1 × 15 ml spoon/1 tablespoon oil

150 g/5 oz minced beef or pork

3 × 15 ml spoons/3 tablespoons chopped spring onions (shallots)

2 × 5 ml spoons/2 teaspoons soy sauce

4 eggs, beaten

350 ml/12 fl oz clear broth (see page 15) or water

large pinch of salt

AMERICAN

1 tablespoon oil

½ cup ground beef or pork, tightly packed

3 tablespoons chopped scallions

2 teaspoons soy sauce

4 eggs, beaten

1½ cups clear broth (see page 15) or water

large pinch of salt

Heat the oil in a pan, add the meat, spring onions (shallots/scallions) and soy sauce and stir-fry for 2 minutes. Mix the eggs with the broth or water and salt. Place the meat mixture in a heatproof serving bowl and pour the egg mixture over the top. Cover and steam for 15 minutes or until the custard is firm. Serve hot.

Egg Foo Yung with Chicken

METRIC/IMPERIAL

175 g/6 oz chicken meat (breast only)

6 × 15 ml spoons/6 tablespoons water

1 × 15 ml spoon/1 tablespoon dry sherry

1 × 2.5 ml spoon/½ teaspoon salt

4 egg whites

4 × 15 ml spoons/4 tablespoons oil

2 × 15 ml spoons/2 tablespoons chopped cooked ham

2 × 15 ml spoons/2 tablespoons chopped parsley

AMERICAN

1 boned medium chicken breast

6 tablespoons water

1 tablespoon pale dry sherry

½ teaspoon salt

4 egg whites

¼ cup oil

2 tablespoons chopped cooked ham

2 tablespoons chopped parsley

Chop the chicken meat, adding the water gradually during the chopping. (This will soften the meat and prevent it from sticking to the knife.) Add the sherry and salt. Beat the egg whites until stiff and fold into the chicken mixture.

Heat the oil in a pan. Add the chicken mixture and tilt the pan so that the mixture spreads out and covers the bottom. Cook gently until the mixture becomes white and puffy, then stir several times to break it up into small pieces, like chicken pieces; do not allow to brown. Transfer to a serving dish, sprinkle with ham and parsley and serve hot.

Steamed Eggs with Salt Eggs, Pickled Eggs and Quail Eggs

The different types of eggs in this dish provide an intriguing mixture of flavours.

METRIC/IMPERIAL

2 eggs, beaten

1 × 5 ml spoon/1 teaspoon salt

300 ml/½ pint clear broth (see page 15) or chicken stock

2 salt eggs, shelled and cut into 6-8 wedges

2 pickled eggs, shelled and cut into 6-8 wedges

4-5 canned quail eggs, drained (optional)

1.5 × 15 ml spoons/1½ tablespoons shredded smoked ham

1.5 × 15 ml spoons/1½ tablespoons shredded spring onions (shallots)

AMERICAN

2 eggs, beaten

1 teaspoon salt

1¼ cups clear broth (see page 15) or chicken stock

2 salt eggs, shelled and cut into 6-8 wedges

2 pickled eggs, shelled and cut into 6-8 wedges

4-5 canned quail eggs, drained (optional)

1½ tablespoons shredded smoked ham

1½ tablespoons shredded scallions

Beat the eggs with the salt and broth or stock in a bowl. Arrange the salt egg and pickled egg wedges alternately around the edge of a deep heatproof dish. Pour the stock mixture into the centre. If using the quail eggs, place them in the broth mixture. Steam for 10 to 12 minutes.

Sprinkle the ham on top of the quail eggs. Sprinkle the spring onions (shallots/scallions) over the beaten egg mixture. Steam for a further 3 to 4 minutes. Serve hot.

Chicken Wings Stuffed with Ham

METRIC/IMPERIAL

12 chicken wings

3 × 15 ml spoons/3 tablespoons soy sauce

oil for deep frying

350 ml/12 fl oz clear broth (see page 15) or water

1 × 15 ml spoon/1 tablespoon dry sherry

1-2 slices cooked ham, shredded

3 spring onions (shallots), chopped

5 dried Chinese mushrooms, soaked for 20 minutes, drained, stemmed and halved

1 × 15 ml spoon/1 tablespoon sugar

1 × 15 ml spoon/1 tablespoon cornflour, dissolved in 1 × 15 ml spoon/1 tablespoon water

AMERICAN

12 chicken wings

3 tablespoons soy sauce

oil for deep frying

1½ cups clear broth (see page 15) or water

1 tablespoon pale dry sherry

1-2 slices cooked ham, shredded

3 scallions, chopped

5 dried Chinese mushrooms, soaked for 20 minutes, drained, stemmed and halved

1 tablespoon sugar

1 tablespoon cornstarch, dissolved in 1 tablespoon water

Cut off the pointed ends of the chicken wings. Sprinkle with 1 × 15 ml spoon/1 tablespoon soy sauce and leave for 30 minutes. Heat oil to 180°C/350°F. Deep-fry the chicken wings until golden brown. Drain.

Bring the broth or water to the boil. Add the chicken wings, remaining soy sauce and the sherry; simmer for 30 minutes.

Remove the chicken wings from the pan and allow to cool, then carefully remove the bones, leaving the chicken wings whole. Insert ham into the cavity of each chicken wing. Return the stock mixture to the boil and add the spring onions (shallots/scallions), mushrooms, chicken wings and the sugar. Simmer for 5 minutes. Add the cornflour (cornstarch) mixture and simmer, stirring until thickened. Serve hot.

From top anti-clockwise: quail eggs, salt eggs, thousand year eggs (all sold in Chinese food stores), tea eggs (page 49) and painted egg shells

Peking Deep-Fried Chicken Pieces

METRIC/IMPERIAL

3 × 15 ml spoons/3 tablespoons soy sauce

1 × 15 ml spoon/1 tablespoon dry sherry

1 × 5 ml spoon/1 teaspoon peppercorns

4 × 15 ml spoons/4 tablespoons chopped spring onions (shallots)

0.75 kg/1½ lb boned chicken, cut into 2.5 cm/1 inch pieces

1 egg, beaten

5 × 15 ml spoons/5 tablespoons cornflour

2 × 15 ml spoons/2 tablespoons plain flour

oil for deep frying

AMERICAN

3 tablespoons soy sauce

1 tablespoon pale dry sherry

1 teaspoon peppercorns

¼ cup chopped scallions

1½ lb boneless chicken, cut into 1 inch pieces

1 egg, beaten

5 tablespoons cornstarch

2 tablespoons all-purpose flour

oil for deep frying

*Peking Deep-Fried Chicken Pieces with Szechuan
Peppery Hot Sauce (above)
Chicken Wings Stuffed with Ham (below)*

Mix together the soy sauce, sherry, pepper and spring onions (shallots/scallions). Add the chicken and leave for 15 minutes.

Beat together the egg, cornflour (cornstarch) and flour to make a smooth batter. Dip the chicken pieces into the batter to coat well.

Heat the oil to 180°C/350°F. Deep-fry the chicken pieces a few at a time until crisp and golden brown. Drain well on absorbent kitchen paper. Serve hot with Szechuan Peppery Hot Sauce (*see page 152*).

Stir-Fried Chicken with Bean Sprouts

METRIC/IMPERIAL

1 × 5 ml spoon/1 teaspoon dry sherry

1 × 5 ml spoon/1 teaspoon salt

2 × 5 ml spoons/2 teaspoons cornflour

1 egg white

350 g/12 oz chicken breasts, skinned, boned and cut into strips

6 × 15 ml spoons/6 tablespoons vegetable oil

200 g/7 oz bean sprouts

1 × 2.5 ml spoon/½ teaspoon sugar

2–3 spring onions (shallots), finely shredded

AMERICAN

1 teaspoon pale dry sherry

1 teaspoon salt

2 teaspoons cornstarch

1 egg white

¾ lb boneless chicken breasts, skinned and cut into strips

6 tablespoons vegetable oil

½ lb bean sprouts

½ teaspoon sugar

2–3 scallions, finely shredded

Mix together the sherry, 1 × 2.5 ml spoon/ ½ teaspoon of the salt, the cornflour (cornstarch) and egg white in a bowl. Add the chicken and toss to coat thoroughly.

Heat 4 × 15 ml spoons/4 tablespoons of the oil in a pan. Add the chicken and stir-fry until it is cooked through. Transfer to a plate.

Add the remaining oil to the pan and reheat. Add the bean sprouts and stir-fry for 30 seconds. Return the chicken to the pan with the remaining salt and the sugar and stir-fry for a few seconds.

Transfer to a serving plate and garnish with the shredded spring onions (shallots/scallions).

Empress Chicken

METRIC/IMPERIAL

8 chicken wings

7 × 15 ml spoons/7 tablespoons soy sauce

oil for deep frying

225 g/8 oz canned bamboo shoot, drained and sliced

4 dried Chinese mushrooms, soaked for 20 minutes, drained, stemmed and halved

2 spring onions (shallots), chopped

450 ml/¾ pint clear broth (see page 15)

1 × 5 ml spoon/1 teaspoon sugar

2 × 5 ml spoons/2 teaspoons dry sherry

3 × 15 ml spoons/3 tablespoons green peas

1 × 2.5 ml spoon/½ teaspoon salt

pinch of pepper

2 × 5 ml spoons/2 teaspoons cornflour, dissolved in 2 × 15 ml spoons/2 tablespoons water

AMERICAN

8 chicken wings

7 tablespoons soy sauce

oil for deep frying

1 cup sliced canned bamboo shoot

4 dried Chinese mushrooms, soaked for 20 minutes, drained, stemmed and halved

2 scallions, chopped

2 cups clear broth (see page 15)

1 teaspoon sugar

2 teaspoons pale dry sherry

3 tablespoons green peas

½ teaspoon salt

pinch of pepper

2 teaspoons cornstarch, dissolved in 2 tablespoons water

Cut off the pointed ends of the chicken wings. Sprinkle the wings with 2 × 15 ml spoons/2 tablespoons of the soy sauce and leave to marinate for 15 minutes.

Heat the oil to 180°C/350°F. Deep-fry the chicken wings until golden. Drain on absorbent kitchen paper and transfer to a clean pan. Add the bamboo shoot, mushrooms, spring onions (shallots/scallions), broth, remaining soy sauce, the sugar and sherry. Bring to the boil and simmer for 30 minutes. Add the peas, salt and pepper and simmer for a further 10 minutes. Add the cornflour (cornstarch) mixture and simmer, stirring, until thickened. Serve hot.

Smoked Chicken

METRIC/IMPERIAL

2 × 15 ml spoons/2 tablespoons whole Szechuan or black peppercorns

2 × 15 ml spoons/2 tablespoons salt

1 × 1 kg/2 lb chicken

100 g/4 oz sugar

40 g/1½ oz tea leaves

1 × 15 ml spoon/1 tablespoon sesame seed oil

sprig of coriander to garnish

AMERICAN

2 tablespoons whole Szechuan or black peppercorns

2 tablespoons salt

1 × 2 lb chicken

½ cup sugar

½ cup tea leaves

1 tablespoon sesame oil

sprig of Chinese parsley to garnish

Toast the peppercorns in a pan, then crush them coarsely and mix with the salt. Rub the chicken with the peppercorn mixture, inside and out. Leave to stand for a few hours.

Stir-Fried Chicken with Bean Sprouts (left)
Empress Chicken (centre)
Smoked Chicken (right)

Place a large sheet of foil in a roasting tin so the foil hangs well over the sides of the tin. Sprinkle the sugar and tea leaves over the foil, put a rack in the tin and place the chicken on it. Bring the foil up over the chicken and fold together to seal. Cook in a preheated moderately hot oven (190°C/375°F, Gas Mark 5) for 30 minutes. Unwrap the chicken and brush with the sesame seed oil. Return to the oven and roast, uncovered, for a further 5 to 10 minutes or until golden brown. Cut the chicken into serving pieces. Serve hot, garnished with coriander (Chinese parsley).

Note: If you prefer, the chicken can be boiled or steamed for 30 minutes or until tender and then roasted for 15 minutes. Chicken breasts or legs can be used instead of a whole chicken.

Steamed Sweet and Sour Fish

METRIC/IMPERIAL

1×0.75 kg/$1\frac{1}{2}$ lb whole fish (trout, bream, carp, mullet, salmon, etc.), cleaned

2×5 ml spoons/2 teaspoons salt

1.5×15 ml spoons/$1\frac{1}{2}$ tablespoons oil

40 g/$1\frac{1}{2}$ oz lard

2 small chilli peppers, seeded and shredded

6 spring onions (shallots), cut into 5 cm/2 inch pieces

6 slices root ginger, shredded

1 red pepper, cored, seeded and shredded

3 pieces canned bamboo shoot, shredded

3×15 ml spoons/3 tablespoons soy sauce

3×15 ml spoons/3 tablespoons wine vinegar

1.5×15 ml spoons/$1\frac{1}{2}$ tablespoons sugar

1.5×15 ml spoons/$1\frac{1}{2}$ tablespoons tomato pureé

3×15 ml spoons/3 tablespoons orange juice

1×15 ml spoon/1 tablespoon cornflour, dissolved in 5×15 ml spoons/5 tablespoons chicken stock

Steamed Sweet and Sour Fish

AMERICAN

$1 \times 1\frac{1}{2}$ lb whole fish (trout, bream, mullet, salmon, etc.), cleaned

2 teaspoons salt

$1\frac{1}{2}$ tablespoons oil

3 tablespoons lard

2 small chili peppers, seeded and shredded

6 scallions, cut into 2 inch pieces

6 slices ginger root, shredded

1 red pepper, cored, seeded and shredded

3 pieces canned bamboo shoot, shredded

3 tablespoons soy sauce

3 tablespoons wine vinegar

$1\frac{1}{2}$ tablespoons sugar

$1\frac{1}{2}$ tablespoons tomato paste

3 tablespoons orange juice

1 tablespoon cornstarch, dissolved in 5 tablespoons chicken stock

Rub the fish inside and out with the salt and oil and leave for 30 minutes. Place the fish on an oval heatproof serving dish and put the dish in a steamer. Steam vigorously for 15 minutes.

Melt the lard in a pan over moderate heat. Add the chilli peppers and stir-fry for 1 minute. Add all the remaining ingredients, except the cornflour (cornstarch) paste, and stir-fry for a further 15 seconds.

Add the cornflour (cornstarch) mixture and stir until the sauce thickens. Garnish the fish with the solid ingredients from the pan and carefully pour the sauce over the fish. Serve hot.

Stewed Chicken with Chestnuts

METRIC/IMPERIAL

6×15 ml spoons/6 tablespoons soy sauce

1×15 ml spoon/1 tablespoon dry sherry

1×1 kg/2 lb chicken, boned and cut into 3.5 cm/$1\frac{1}{2}$ inch pieces

2×15 ml spoons/2 tablespoons oil

2 slices root ginger, chopped

4 spring onions (shallots), chopped

0.5 kg/1 lb chestnuts, peeled and skinned

450 ml/$\frac{3}{4}$ pint water

1×15 ml spoon/1 tablespoon sugar

AMERICAN

6 tablespoons soy sauce

1 tablespoon pale dry sherry

1×2 lb chicken, boned and cut into $1\frac{1}{2}$ inch pieces

2 tablespoons oil

2 slices ginger root, chopped

4 scallions, chopped

1 lb chestnuts, peeled and skinned

2 cups water

1 tablespoon sugar

Mix together the soy sauce and sherry in a dish and add the chicken. Leave to marinate for 15 minutes.

Heat the oil in a large pan. Add the chicken mixture, ginger and half of the spring onions (shallots/scallions); stir-fry until the chicken is golden. Add the chestnuts, water and sugar. Bring to the boil, cover and simmer for 40 minutes or until tender. Serve hot, garnished with the remaining spring onions (shallots/scallions).

Note: If fresh chestnuts are unobtainable, canned or dried ones may be used instead. Canned chestnuts should be drained and added to the chicken mixture 10 minutes before the end of the cooking time. If dried chestnuts are used, they should be soaked in warm water overnight before using; cook as fresh chestnuts.

Diced Chicken with Brown Bean Sauce

METRIC/IMPERIAL

350 g/12 oz chicken meat, skinned and cut into 2.5 cm/1 inch cubes

pinch of salt

2×5 ml spoons/2 teaspoons dry sherry

2×5 ml spoons/2 teaspoons cornflour

2×15 ml spoons/2 tablespoons soy bean paste or hoisin sauce

2×15 ml spoons/2 tablespoons water

7 × 15 ml spoons/7 tablespoons oil

1 garlic clove, crushed

3 dried Chinese mushrooms, soaked for 20 minutes, drained, stemmed and cut into 2.5 cm/1 inch cubes

50 g/2 oz canned bamboo shoot, drained and diced

1 green pepper, cored, seeded and diced

AMERICAN

¾ lb boneless chicken, skinned and cut into 1 inch cubes

pinch of salt

2 teaspoons pale dry sherry

2 teaspoons cornstarch

2 tablespoons bean sauce or hoisin sauce

2 tablespoons water

7 tablespoons oil

1 garlic clove, minced

3 dried Chinese mushrooms, soaked for 20 minutes, drained, stemmed and cut into 1 inch cubes

¼ cup diced canned bamboo shoot

½ cup diced green pepper

Sprinkle the chicken with the salt, sherry and cornflour (cornstarch) and leave to marinate for 15 minutes. Mix the bean paste (sauce) or hoisin sauce with the water.

Heat 5 × 15 ml spoons/5 tablespoons of the oil in a pan. Add the chicken cubes and stir-fry until golden brown. Transfer to a plate. Add the remaining oil to the pan and heat. Add the garlic and stir-fry for 1 minute. Add the mushrooms, bamboo shoot and green pepper; stir-fry for a few seconds. Add the chicken with the bean paste (sauce) mixture and stir well. Serve hot.

Caramel Apples

METRIC/IMPERIAL

6 apples, peeled, cored and quartered

40 g/1½ oz plain flour

1 × 15 ml spoon/1 tablespoon cornflour

2 egg whites

oil for deep-frying

225 g/8 oz sugar

4 × 15 ml spoons/4 tablespoons water

1 × 15 ml spoon/1 tablespoon sesame seeds

AMERICAN

6 apples, peeled, cored and quartered

6 tablespoons all-purpose flour

1 tablespoon cornstarch

Stewed Chicken with Chestnuts (above)
Diced Chicken with Brown Bean Sauce
(below)
Caramel Apples (left)

2 egg whites

oil for deep-frying

1 cup sugar

4 tablespoons water

1 tablespoon sesame seeds

Dust the apple quarters lightly with a little of the flour. Sift the remaining flour and cornflour (cornstarch) into a bowl. Add the egg whites and mix to a smooth paste.

Heat the oil to 180°C/350°F. Coat the apple quarters, one at a time, with the paste, then drop them carefully into the oil. Fry until golden brown. Drain on absorbent kitchen paper.

Put the sugar and water in a small saucepan and stir to dissolve the sugar. Bring to the boil and boil until the syrup is a light golden brown. Stir in the apple quarters and sesame seeds.

Transfer to lightly oiled serving dishes. A bowl of cold water may be placed on the table, so that diners can pick up their apple pieces with chopsticks and lower them into the water before eating, to harden the caramel.

Peking Fried Duckling

METRIC/IMPERIAL

2 × 15 ml spoons/2 tablespoons coarsely
ground Szechuan or black peppercorns

1 × 1.5 kg/3 lb duckling

2 × 15 ml spoons/2 tablespoons salt

2 spring onions (shallots), minced

2 × 15 ml spoons/2 tablespoons chopped root
ginger

50 g/2 oz plain flour, sifted

5 × 15 ml spoons/5 tablespoons water

1 × 15 ml spoon/1 tablespoon soy sauce

1 egg white

oil for deep frying

sprigs of coriander to garnish

AMERICAN

2 tablespoons coarsely ground Szechuan or
black peppercorns

1 × 3 lb duckling

2 tablespoons salt

2 scallions, ground

2 tablespoons chopped ginger root

½ cup all-purpose flour, sifted

5 tablespoons water

1 tablespoon soy sauce

1 egg white

oil for deep frying

sprigs of Chinese parsley to garnish

Toast the peppercorns in a pan over low heat
for 2 minutes. Remove pan from the heat.
Rub the duckling inside and out with the
salt, pepper, spring onions (shallots/
scallions) and ginger. Place the duck in a
large heatproof dish, cover and leave for 5 to
6 hours.

Steam the duckling for 1¾ to 2 hours or until
tender. Remove the duckling from the bowl.
Mix together the flour, water, soy sauce and
egg white in a bowl and beat until smooth.
Rub over the duckling.

Heat the oil in a large deep-fryer to
180°C/350°F. Deep-fry the duckling until
golden brown. Drain. Serve the duckling cut
into pieces, or allow diners to separate the
meat with chopsticks. Serve the dish garnished with coriander (Chinese parsley) and
accompanied by tomato ketchup (sauce), if
liked.

Sliced Beef with Bamboo Shoots

METRIC/IMPERIAL

2 × 5 ml spoons/2 teaspoons dry sherry

5 × 5 ml spoons/5 teaspoons soy sauce

1 egg white

Deep-Fried Pork Slices (top left)
Peking Fried Duckling (centre)
Sliced Beef with Bamboo Shoots
(below)

1 × 15 ml spoon/1 tablespoon cornflour

225 g/8 oz beef (rump or topside), thinly
sliced and cut into bite-sized pieces

4 × 15 ml spoons/4 tablespoons oil

100 g/4 oz canned bamboo shoots, drained
and thinly sliced

4 large dried Chinese mushrooms, soaked for
20 minutes, drained, stemmed and quartered

1 × 2.5 ml spoon/½ teaspoon salt

pinch of pepper

1 spring onion (shallot), shredded (optional)

AMERICAN

2 teaspoons pale dry sherry

5 teaspoons soy sauce

1 egg white

1 tablespoon cornstarch

½ lb flank steak, thinly sliced and cut into
bite-sized pieces

¼ cup oil

½ cup thinly sliced canned bamboo shoots

4 large dried Chinese mushrooms, soaked for
20 minutes, drained, stemmed and quartered

½ teaspoon salt

pinch of pepper

1 scallion, shredded (optional)

Combine the sherry, 2 × 5 ml spoons/2 teaspoons of the soy sauce, the egg white and
cornflour (cornstarch) in a bowl. Add the
beef and toss to coat thoroughly.

Heat the oil in a pan. Add the beef and stir-
fry until just brown. Add the bamboo shoots
and mushrooms and stir-fry for a few seconds. Stir in the remaining soy sauce, the salt
and pepper. Transfer to a serving dish and
garnish with the shredded spring onion
(shallot/scallion), if used.

Deep-Fried Pork Slices

METRIC/IMPERIAL

350 g/12 oz pork fillet

3 × 15 ml spoons/3 tablespoons chopped spring onions (shallots)

large pinch of salt

2 × 5 ml spoons/2 teaspoons dry sherry

1 × 2.5 ml spoon/½ teaspoon cornflour

pinch of black pepper

0.5 kg/1 lb pork suet

oil for deep frying

Batter

1 egg

65 g/2½ oz plain flour, sifted

2 × 15 ml spoons/2 tablespoons cornflour

6 × 15 ml spoons/6 tablespoons water

Garnish

few cucumber slices

sprig of parsley

AMERICAN

¾ lb pork tenderloin

3 tablespoons chopped scallions

large pinch of salt

2 teaspoons pale dry sherry

½ teaspoon cornstarch

pinch of black pepper

1 lb pork suet

oil for deep frying

Batter

1 egg

½ cup plus 2 tablespoons all-purpose flour, sifted

2 tablespoons cornstarch

6 tablespoons water

Garnish

few cucumber slices

sprig of parsley

Cut the pork into slices, 7.5 cm/3 inches long and 5 mm/¼ inch thick. Combine the spring onions (shallots/scallions), salt, sherry, cornflour (cornstarch) and black pepper in a bowl. Add the pork slices and toss to coat thoroughly.

Boil the suet for 15 minutes. Drain and cut into slices the same length as the pork slices but only 3 mm/⅛ inch thick.

Sprinkle the suet slices with a little cornflour (cornstarch). Place a pork slice on top of each, dust with cornflour (cornstarch) and place another slice of suet on top.

Place the batter ingredients in a bowl and beat until smooth. Heat the oil to 180°C/350°F. Dip the meat sandwiches in the batter then deep-fry until golden brown. The suet should turn crisp and the pork become tender. Drain on absorbent kitchen paper.

Transfer to a serving plate and garnish with cucumber slices and parsley. Serve with tomato ketchup (sauce), if liked.

Simmered Pork Leg (Ham)

METRIC/IMPERIAL

1×2 kg/4 lb leg of pork
250 ml/8 fl oz soy sauce
1×15 ml spoon/1 tablespoon sugar
4×15 ml spoons/4 tablespoons dry sherry
1×5 ml spoon/1 teaspoon salt
750 ml/$1\frac{1}{4}$ pints water
$\frac{1}{2}$ red pepper (optional)
1-2 spring onions, shredded (optional)

AMERICAN

1×4 lb portion of fresh ham
1 cup soy sauce
1 tablespoon sugar
$\frac{1}{4}$ cup pale dry sherry
1 teaspoon salt
$1\frac{1}{2}$ pints water
$\frac{1}{2}$ red pepper (optional)
1-2 scallions, shredded (optional)

Place the pork (ham) in a saucepan and add sufficient water to cover. Bring to the boil and simmer for 10 minutes. Drain.

Return pork (ham) to the pan and add the soy sauce, sugar, sherry, salt and water. Bring to the boil, cover and simmer for $2\frac{3}{4}$ to 3 hours. Drain and carve into slices.

Arrange the slices on a serving plate. Garnish with the red pepper, attractively cut and topped with shredded spring onion (scallion), if used.

Deep-Fried Beef Steak

METRIC/IMPERIAL

0.5 kg/1 lb lean rump steak, thinly sliced
1×5 ml spoon/1 teaspoon grated root ginger
4×15 ml spoons/4 tablespoons soy sauce
2 egg whites
2×15 ml spoons/2 tablespoons cornflour
oil for deep frying
4-6 spring onions (shallots), shredded

AMERICAN

1 lb flank steak, thinly sliced
1 teaspoon minced ginger root
$\frac{1}{4}$ cup soy sauce
2 egg whites
2 tablespoons cornstarch
oil for deep frying
4-6 scallions, shredded

Simmered Pork Leg (Ham) (above)
Deep-Fried Beef Steak (below)

Beat the steak slices until very thin. Mix the ginger and soy sauce in a bowl, add the meat and leave to marinate for 30 minutes, turning occasionally.

Lightly beat the egg whites then beat in the cornflour (cornstarch) to make a smooth batter.

Heat the oil to 180°C/350°F. Dip the beef slices into the batter, then deep-fry a few slices at a time until golden brown. Drain on absorbent kitchen paper. Transfer to a plate and garnish with the shredded spring onions (shallots/scallions).

Serve hot with a selection of dips, such as soy sauce with grated garlic, hoisin sauce and tomato ketchup (sauce).

Mohammedan Fire Kettle or Mongolian Hotpot

Fire Kettle or Mongolian Hotpot is North China's winter dish, served either as soup or a main course.

METRIC/IMPERIAL

1 kg/2 lb boned loin of lamb

Soup

1 kg/2 lb Chinese cabbage

225 g/8 oz spinach

50 g/2 oz transparent pea-starch noodles, soaked in warm water for 5 minutes and drained

1 cake bean curd, thinly sliced

50 g/2 oz plain or egg noodles, cooked (optional)

2.25 litres/4 pints clear broth (see page 15) or water

Sauce

6 × 15 ml spoons/6 tablespoons chopped spring onions (shallots)

2 × 15 ml spoons/2 tablespoons chopped coriander

6 × 15 ml spoons/6 tablespoons soy sauce

6 × 15 ml spoons/6 tablespoons sesame seed paste

2 × 15 ml spoons/2 tablespoons dry sherry

2 × 15 ml spoons/2 tablespoons sugar

2 × 15 ml spoons/2 tablespoons hot chilli or Tabasco sauce

2 × 15 ml spoons/2 tablespoons sesame seed oil

1 × 15 ml spoon/1 tablespoon salt or fermented bean curd

AMERICAN

2 lb boned loin of lamb

Soup

2 lb Chinese cabbage (bok choy)

½ lb spinach

2 oz cellophane noodles, soaked in warm water for 5 minutes and drained

1 cake bean curd, thinly sliced

2 cups cooked plain or egg noodles (optional)

5 pints clear broth (see page 15) or water

Mohammedan Fire Kettle or Mongolian Hot Pot

Sauce

6 tablespoons chopped scallions

2 tablespoons chopped Chinese parsley

6 tablespoons soy sauce

6 tablespoons sesame paste

2 tablespoons pale dry sherry

2 tablespoons sugar

2 tablespoons hot chilli or Tabasco sauce

2 tablespoons sesame oil

1 tablespoon salt or fermented bean curd

Cut the lamb into paper-thin slices, 3.5 × 7.5 cm/1½ × 3 inches and arrange on a platter. Place the cabbage, spinach, transparent (cellophane) noodles, bean curd and cooked noodles in dishes. Put the sauce ingredients in individual bowls (to allow each person to prepare his own sauce).

When the diners are seated, bring the broth or water to the boil in a fondue pot, chafing dish, electric wok or other pot suitable for cooking at the table. Each person should dip meat slices into the pot—using long forks or chopsticks, cook until just tender, then immediately dip into the sauce and eat.

When all the meat has been eaten, add the vegetables, bean curd and transparent (cellophane) noodles to the pot and simmer until just tender. The soup in the pot becomes richer as the cooking progresses. Add the cooked noodles and heat through. Serve this noodle soup to end the meal.

Jellied Mutton

METRIC/IMPERIAL

0.5 kg/1 lb mutton or lamb

100 g/4 oz pork skin or 7 g/$\frac{1}{4}$ oz gelatine

1.5 litres/$2\frac{3}{4}$ pints water

225 g/8 oz turnips, sliced

5 spring onions (shallots)

3 slices root ginger

3 garlic cloves

2.5 cm/1 inch cinnamon stick

2 whole star anise

1 × 15 ml spoon/1 tablespoon Szechuan or black peppercorns

4 × 15 ml spoons/4 tablespoons soy sauce

2 × 15 ml spoons/2 tablespoons dry sherry

2 × 5 ml spoons/2 teaspoons sugar

slices of carrot and cucumber to garnish

Braised Pork with Carrots (above)
Jellied Mutton (below left)
Stewed Pork (below right)

AMERICAN

1 lb boneless lamb

¼ lb pork skin or 1 envelope unflavored gelatin

6¼ cups water

½ lb turnips, sliced

5 scallions

3 slices ginger root

3 garlic cloves

1 inch cinnamon stick

2 whole star anise

1 tablespoon Szechuan or black peppercorns

¼ cup soy sauce

2 tablespoons pale dry sherry

2 teaspoons sugar

slices of carrot and cucumber to garnish

Put the mutton or lamb and pork skin, if using, in a large pan and cover with water. Bring to the boil, then discard the water. Pour the measured water into the pan and bring to the boil. Add the meat and pork skin, if using, and the remaining ingredients. Simmer for 1 hour.

Remove the mutton or lamb from the pan. Continue boiling the liquid until reduced to about 250 ml/8 fl oz (1 cup); strain. If using gelatine, dissolve in 120 ml/4 fl oz (½ cup) warm water and add to the strained liquid. Shred the meat and place in a 1 litre/2 pint capacity mould. Pour over the strained liquid. Cool, then chill until firm. Invert onto a serving plate and garnish with attractively cut slices of carrot and cucumber.

Braised Pork with Carrots

METRIC/IMPERIAL

1 garlic clove, crushed

1 × 15 ml spoon/1 tablespoon dry sherry

120 ml/4 fl oz soy sauce

0.5 kg/1 lb pork fillet, cut into strips

2 × 15 ml spoons/2 tablespoons plain flour

2 × 15 ml spoons/2 tablespoons oil

2 onions, each cut into 6 sections

1 × 15 ml spoon/1 tablespoon sugar

4 carrots, cut into strips

chopped parsley to garnish

AMERICAN

1 garlic clove, minced

1 tablespoon pale dry sherry

½ cup soy sauce

1 lb pork tenderloin, cut into strips

2 tablespoons all-purpose flour

2 tablespoons oil

2 onions, each cut into 6 sections

1 tablespoon sugar

4 carrots, cut into strips

chopped parsley to garnish

Mix together the garlic, sherry and 3 × 15 ml spoons/3 tablespoons of the soy sauce. Add the pork strips and toss to coat well. Leave to marinate for at least 20 minutes, then stir in the flour.

Heat the oil in a pan. Add the onions and meat mixture and stir-fry until the meat is browned. Add the remaining soy sauce, the sugar and just enough water to cover the meat. Bring to the boil. Add the carrots and simmer for 40 minutes or until the meat is tender.

Serve hot, garnished with chopped parsley.

Stewed Pork

METRIC/IMPERIAL

2 × 15 ml spoons/2 tablespoons oil

1 kg/2 lb lean pork, cut into 5 cm/2 inch cubes

3 slices root ginger

4 spring onions (shallots), cut into 5 cm/ 2 inch pieces

3 whole star anise

5 × 15 ml spoons/5 tablespoons dry sherry

175 ml/6 fl oz soy sauce

2 × 15 ml spoons/2 tablespoons granulated or brown sugar

spring onion (shallot) rings to garnish

AMERICAN

2 tablespoons oil

2 lb pork shoulder, butt or lean sides, cut into 2 inch cubes

3 slices ginger root

4 scallions, cut into 2 inch pieces

3 whole star anise

5 tablespoons pale dry sherry

¾ cup soy sauce

2 tablespoons granulated or brown sugar

scallion rings to garnish

Heat the oil in a pan and add the pork, ginger and spring onions (shallots/scallions). Stir-fry until the pork is lightly browned.

Transfer the meat to a saucepan, using a slotted spoon. Reserve the ginger and spring onions (shallots/scallions). Add the anise, sherry, soy sauce, sugar and sufficient water to cover the meat. Bring to the boil, then cover and simmer for 1 hour or until the pork is tender, shaking the pan occasionally to prevent sticking.

Arrange the spring onions (shallots/scallions) around the edge of a warmed serving plate. Place the ginger in the centre and pile the pork on top. Serve hot garnished with a few spring onion (shallot/scallion) rings.

Stir-Fried Bean Curd with Pork and Cabbage

METRIC/IMPERIAL

1 cake bean curd, cut into 3.5 cm/1½ inch squares

3 × 15 ml spoons/3 tablespoons oil

225 g/8 oz lean pork, cut into thin bite-sized pieces

1 spring onion (shallot), chopped

2 slices root ginger, chopped

2 × 5 ml spoons/2 teaspoons salt

1 × 15 ml spoon/1 tablespoon dry sherry

1 litre/1¾ pints clear broth (see page 15)

0.5 kg/1 lb Chinese cabbage, shredded

AMERICAN

1 cake bean curd, cut into 1½ inch squares

3 tablespoons oil

½ pork butt or loin, cut into thin bite-sized pieces

1 scallion, chopped

2 slices ginger root, chopped

2 teaspoons salt

1 tablespoon pale dry sherry

2 pints clear broth (see page 15)

1 lb Chinese cabbage (bok choy), shredded

Freeze the bean curd squares overnight. Thaw in hot water, then drain.

Heat the oil in a saucepan. Add the pork, spring onion (shallot/scallion), ginger and bean curd and stir-fry until the meat is lightly browned. Add the salt, sherry and broth and bring to the boil. Cover and simmer for 10 minutes.

Add the cabbage and simmer until it is tender; about 10 minutes. Serve hot.

Note: Small holes may be left in the bean curd after thawing. These permit the delicious juices to penetrate the bean curd. Do not freeze the bean curd for more than 12 hours or it will toughen.

Deep-Fried Meatballs

METRIC/IMPERIAL

0.5 kg/1 lb minced pork

1 × 5 ml spoon/1 teaspoon grated root ginger

2 × 15 ml spoons/2 tablespoons cornflour

1 × 2.5 ml spoon/½ teaspoon salt

1 egg

1 × 15 ml spoon/1 tablespoon soy sauce

2 × 15 ml spoons/2 tablespoons plain flour

oil for deep frying

lemon slices and tomato rose (see note), to garnish

AMERICAN

1 lb ground pork

1 teaspoon minced ginger root

2 tablespoons cornstarch

½ teaspoon salt

1 egg

1 tablespoon soy sauce

2 tablespoons all-purpose flour

oil for deep frying

lemon slices and tomato rose (see note), to garnish

Mix together all the ingredients and form into small balls. Heat the oil to 180°C/350°F. Deep-fry the meatballs, a few at a time, turning frequently, until they float to the surface. Drain and cool slightly.

Reheat the oil to 180°C/350°F. Return the meatballs to the oil and fry for a further 1 minute to make them extra crispy. Drain on absorbent kitchen paper and transfer to a serving dish.

Garnish with lemon slices and the tomato rose.

Serve hot with hoisin sauce, tomato ketchup (sauce) and peppercorn-salt dip.

Note: To prepare a tomato rose, peel a firm tomato to make a continuous strip of peel. Coil the strip to form a rose and use a parsley sprig to form the flower centre.

Sautéed Lamb with Spring Onions (Scallions)

METRIC/IMPERIAL

2 × 15 ml spoons/2 tablespoons soy sauce

1 × 2.5 ml spoon/½ teaspoon salt

1 × 15 ml spoon/1 tablespoon dry sherry

120 ml/4 fl oz oil

225 g/8 oz lean lamb, very thinly sliced

1 × 15 ml spoon/1 tablespoon red wine vinegar

1 × 15 ml spoon/1 tablespoon sesame seed oil

1 × 2.5 ml spoon/½ teaspoon ground Szechuan or black peppercorns

2 garlic cloves, crushed

225 g /8 oz spring onions (shallots)

AMERICAN

2 tablespoons soy sauce

½ teaspoon salt

1 tablespoon pale dry sherry

½ cup oil

½ lb lean lamb, very thinly sliced

1 tablespoon red wine vinegar

1 tablespoon sesame oil

½ teaspoon ground Szechuan or black peppercorns

2 garlic cloves, minced

½ lb scallions (2 bunches)

Mix together 1 × 15 ml spoon/1 tablespoon of the soy sauce, the salt, sherry and 2 × 15 ml spoons/2 tablespoons of the oil. Add the lamb slices and leave to marinate for 5 minutes. Mix the remaining soy sauce with the vinegar, sesame seed oil and pepper in a small bowl.

Heat the remaining oil in a pan. Add the garlic and stir-fry for 10 seconds. Add the meat and stir-fry until browned. Shred a few of the spring onions (shallots/scallions) and set aside for garnish. Cut the remainder into 5 cm/2 inch pieces and add to the meat together with the vinegar mixture. Stir-fry for a few seconds. Serve hot, garnished with the reserved spring onions (shallots/scallions).

Note: Beef may be substituted for lamb, if preferred.

Deep-Fried Meatballs (left)
Stir-Fried Bean Curd with Pork and Cabbage (above right)
Sautéed Lamb with Spring Onions (Scallions) (below right)

Deep-Fried Crab

METRIC/IMPERIAL

2 live crabs, well scrubbed

75 g/3 oz plain flour

1 × 2.5 ml spoon/½ teaspoon salt

3 eggs, beaten

oil for deep frying

Sauce

1 × 15 ml spoon/1 tablespoon finely chopped root ginger

3 × 15 ml spoons/3 tablespoons soy sauce

2 × 5 ml spoons/2 teaspoons sugar

3 × 15 ml spoons/3 tablespoons wine vinegar

2 × 15 ml spoons/2 tablespoons dry sherry

Garnish

few tomato slices, halved

½ cucumber, cut into long thin strips

AMERICAN

2 live hard-shell crabs, well scrubbed

¾ cup all-purpose flour

½ teaspoon salt

3 eggs, beaten

oil for deep frying

Sauce

1 tablespoon finely chopped ginger root

3 tablespoons soy sauce

2 teaspoons sugar

3 tablespoons wine vinegar

2 tablespoons pale dry sherry

Garnish

few tomato slices, halved

½ cucumber, cut into long thin strips

Place the crabs in a large steamer and steam for 20 minutes. Cool, then open the shells. Remove the top shells and discard all the spongy parts—gills, stomach and intestines. Break the undershells crosswise in half. Cut each half into two sections, leaving a leg attached to each to use as a handle. Remove the meat from the top shell.

Sift the flour and salt into a bowl. Add the eggs and beat to form a smooth batter. Heat the oil to 180°C/350°F. Dip each crab section and bite-sized pieces of crabmeat into the batter. Deep-fry until golden brown; drain. Transfer to a serving dish and garnish with the tomato and cucumber slices. Combine the sauce ingredients in a dish and serve as an accompaniment.

Steamed Prawns (Shrimp)

METRIC/IMPERIAL

0.5 kg/1 lb large prawns

2 × 15 ml spoons/2 tablespoons oil

2 × 15 ml spoons/2 tablespoons chopped mushrooms

2 × 15 ml spoons/2 tablespoons chopped cooked ham

2 × 15 ml spoons/2 tablespoons chopped canned bamboo shoot

1 × 15 ml spoon/1 tablespoon dry sherry

1 × 2.5 ml spoon/½ teaspoon salt

large pinch of sugar

150 ml/¼ pint clear broth (see page 15)

2 × 5 ml spoons/2 teaspoons cornflour, dissolved in 2 × 15 ml spoons/2 tablespoons water

parsley sprigs, carrot slices and pepper strips, to garnish

AMERICAN

1 lb large shrimp

2 tablespoons oil

2 tablespoons chopped mushrooms

2 tablespoons chopped cooked ham

2 tablespoons chopped canned bamboo shoot

1 tablespoon pale dry sherry

½ teaspoon salt

large pinch of sugar

⅔ cup clear broth (see page 15)

2 teaspoons cornstarch, dissolved in 2 tablespoons water

parsley sprigs, carrot slices and pepper strips, to garnish

Remove the heads and shells from the prawns (shrimp) but keep on the tails. Make a shallow incision down the back of each prawn (shrimp) and remove the dark intestinal vein. Make a small cut in the back and pull the tail through it so the prawn (shrimp) is curled up. Steam the prawns (shrimp) for 5 minutes. Transfer to a serving dish and keep hot.

Heat the oil in a pan. Add the mushrooms, ham, bamboo shoot, sherry, salt, sugar and broth and bring to the boil. Add the cornflour (cornstarch) mixture and cook, stirring, until the sauce is thickened. Pour over the prawns (shrimp) and serve garnished with parsley, carrot slices and pepper strips.

Fried Fish Fillets with Sweet and Sour Sauce

METRIC/IMPERIAL

2 egg whites

1 × 2.5 ml spoon/½ teaspoon salt

2 × 5 ml spoons/2 teaspoons dry sherry

3 × 15 ml spoons/3 tablespoons cornflour

350 g/12 oz sole, plaice, whiting or bream fillets, cut into pieces

oil for deep frying

250 ml/8 fl oz clear broth (see page 15)

1 × 15 ml spoon/1 tablespoon sugar

1 × 15 ml spoon/1 tablespoon wine vinegar

1 × 2.5 ml spoon/½ teaspoon grated root ginger

sprig of parsley to garnish

Deep-Fried Crab (above left)
Steamed Prawns (Shrimp) (below left)
Fried Fish Fillets with Sweet and Sour Sauce (right)

AMERICAN

2 egg whites

½ teaspoon salt

2 teaspoons pale dry sherry

3 tablespoons cornstarch

¾ lb sole fillets, cut into serving pieces

oil for deep frying

1 cup clear broth (see page 15)

1 tablespoon sugar

1 tablespoon wine vinegar

½ teaspoon minced ginger root

sprig of parsley to garnish

Beat the egg whites lightly, then beat in the salt, sherry and 2 × 15 ml spoons/2 tablespoons of the cornflour (cornstarch) to make a smooth batter. Use to coat the fish pieces. Heat the oil to 160°C/325°F. Deep-fry the fish, a few at a time, until golden. Drain. Bring the broth to the boil in a pan. Add the sugar, vinegar and ginger. Dissolve the remaining cornflour (cornstarch) in a little water and add to the pan. Simmer, stirring until the sauce thickens. Add the fish and reheat. Serve hot, garnished with parsley.

Lotus Sweets

Water lily seeds have a delicate flavour and are oval like small olives. They are available in cans. They can be served fresh, candied, or as a pastry filling.

METRIC/IMPERIAL

0.5 kg/1 lb lotus seeds, soaked in boiling water for 10 minutes and drained

1 litre/1¾ pints water

250 g/8 oz sugar

2 eggs, beaten

AMERICAN

1 lb lotus seeds, soaked in boiling water for 10 minutes and drained

2 pints water

1 cup sugar

2 eggs, beaten

Rub the lotus seeds with your fingers to remove the skins. Use a toothpick to draw out the green bud from the centre of the lotus seeds.

Put the water in a pan and bring to the boil. Add the sugar and stir to dissolve. Add the lotus buds and simmer for 40 minutes.

Gradually stir in the eggs to form 'an egg flower'. When the egg has set, pour into a serving bowl and serve hot.

Waterchestnut Cake

METRIC/IMPERIAL

150 g/5 oz waterchestnut flour

350 ml/12 fl oz water

0.5 kg/1 lb peeled fresh or drained canned waterchestnuts

40 g/1½ oz lard

150 ml/¼ pint milk

275 g/10 oz sugar

AMERICAN

1¼ cups waterchestnut flour

1½ cups water

1 lb peeled fresh or drained canned waterchestnuts

1½ tablespoons lard

⅔ cup milk

1¼ cups sugar

Waterchestnut Cake (above)
Lotus Sweets (below)

Sift the waterchestnut flour into a bowl and gradually stir in half of the water. Beat to yield a smooth, soft dough.

Finely chop the waterchestnuts and place in a saucepan with the lard, milk, sugar and remaining water. Bring to the boil, stirring. Add one third of the flour mixture and stir constantly until the mixture comes to the boil again. Take off the heat and allow to cool for 2 minutes. Gradually add the remaining flour mixture, beating thoroughly. Brush a deep 20 cm/8 inch square cake tin with oil. Pour in the batter. Cover the tin with a sheet of foil or greaseproof (waxed) paper and secure with string. Place the tin in a large saucepan, half-filled with water. Cover the saucepan and steam for 25 to 30 minutes. Allow the cake to cool before turning out of the tin.

Serve cold, cut into slices. Alternatively, to serve hot, fry the cake slices in a little oil until golden brown on both sides. Drain on absorbent kitchen paper and serve immediately.

Abalone or Scallops with Asparagus

METRIC/IMPERIAL

425 g/15 oz can abalone, drained, or
0.5 kg/1 lb frozen scallops, thawed

425 g/15 oz can asparagus spears, drained

225 g/8 oz boned chicken breast, thinly sliced

1 × 5 ml spoon/1 teaspoon salt

3 × 5 ml spoons/3 teaspoons cornflour

4 × 15 ml spoons/4 tablespoons rendered chicken fat or oil (see note)

1 × 15 ml spoon/1 tablespoon dry sherry

1 × 2.5 ml spoon/½ teaspoon sugar

300 ml/½ pint clear broth (see page 15)

3 × 15 ml spoons/3 tablespoons water

AMERICAN

15 oz can abalone, drained, or 1 lb frozen scallops, thawed

15 oz can asparagus spears, drained

½ lb boneless chicken breast, thinly sliced

1 teaspoon salt

3 teaspoons cornstarch

¼ cup rendered chicken fat or oil (see note)

1 tablespoon pale dry sherry

½ teaspoon sugar

1¼ cups clear broth (see page 15)

3 tablespoons water

Slice the abalone thinly; if using scallops, cut into chunks. Set aside one third of the asparagus spears for garnish; cut the rest into 5 cm/2 inch pieces. Sprinkle the chicken with half the salt and 1 × 2.5 ml spoon/½ teaspoon of the cornflour (cornstarch). Heat the fat or oil in a pan. Add the chicken and stir-fry for a few seconds. Add the abalone or scallops, stir-fry for a few seconds, then add the asparagus pieces, sherry, sugar and remaining salt. Stir in the broth and bring to the boil.

Dissolve the remaining cornflour (cornstarch) in the water and add to the pan. Simmer, stirring, until thickened. Transfer to a serving dish and garnish with the reserved asparagus.

Note: Rendered chicken fat imparts an excellent flavour to this dish. Prepare by trimming fat from chicken, chop and melt before using.

Abalone or Scallops with Asparagus

Braised Duck

METRIC/IMPERIAL

1 × 1.75 kg/4 lb duck, cut into serving pieces

5 × 15 ml spoons/5 tablespoons soy sauce

4 × 15 ml spoons/4 tablespoons oil

3 spring onions (shallots)

4 slices root ginger

3 whole star anise

1 × 5 ml spoon/1 teaspoon black peppercorns

2 × 15 ml spoons/2 teaspoons dry sherry

4 dried Chinese mushrooms, soaked for 20 minutes, drained and stemmed

100 g/4 oz canned bamboo shoots, drained and sliced

2 × 15 ml spoons/2 tablespoons cornflour, dissolved in 2 × 15 ml spoons/2 tablespoons water

2-3 spring onions (shallots) to garnish

AMERICAN

1 × 4 lb duck, cut into serving pieces

5 tablespoons soy sauce

4 tablespoons oil

3 scallions

4 slices ginger root

3 whole star anise

1 teaspoon black peppercorns

2 tablespoons pale dry sherry

4 dried Chinese mushrooms, soaked for 20 minutes, drained and stemmed

1 cup sliced canned bamboo shoots

2 tablespoons cornstarch, dissolved in 2 tablespoons water

2-3 scallions to garnish

Rub the duck pieces with a little of the soy sauce. Heat the oil in a pan and add the duck pieces. Fry, turning, until golden brown on all sides. Transfer to a saucepan and add the spring onions (shallots/scallions), ginger, star anise, peppercorns, dry sherry, the remaining soy sauce and sufficient water to cover. Bring to the boil, then reduce the heat and cover. Simmer for 1½ to 2 hours or until the duck is tender, adding the mushrooms and bamboo shoots 20 minutes before the end of the cooking time.

Add the cornflour (cornstarch) mixture to the pan. Stir until the liquid has thickened. Serve hot, garnished with spring onions (shallots/scallions).

Steamed Fish with Ginger and Spring Onions (Scallions)

METRIC/IMPERIAL

0.75 kg/1½ lb whole fish or 4 fish steaks (see note)

1 × 5 ml spoon/1 teaspoon salt

2 × 15 ml spoons/2 tablespoons red wine vinegar

1 × 15 ml spoon/1 tablespoon sugar

3 × 15 ml spoons/3 tablespoons soy sauce

10-12 spring onions (shallots)

1 × 5 ml spoon/1 teaspoon shredded root ginger

AMERICAN

1½ lb whole fish or 4 fish steaks (see note)

1 teaspoon salt

2 tablespoons red wine vinegar

1 tablespoon sugar

3 tablespoons soy sauce

10-12 scallions

1 teaspoon shredded ginger root

If using a whole fish, clean thoroughly and remove the scales. Dry well on absorbent kitchen paper. Sprinkle the fish or steaks with salt and place in a heatproof dish. Steam for 15 minutes or until cooked.

Meanwhile, mix together the vinegar, sugar and soy sauce in a small serving bowl. Shred a few of the spring onions (shallots/scallions) and arrange the rest on a serving plate.

Transfer the fish to the serving plate and garnish with the ginger. Sprinkle with the shredded spring onions (shallots/scallions) and serve hot, with the vinegar sauce.

Note: Use grey mullet, halibut, cod, bass, snapper or John Dory.

Baked Fish with Sesame Seed Oil

METRIC/IMPERIAL

0.75 kg/1½ lb whole fish or 4 fish steaks (see note)

2 × 5 ml spoons/2 teaspoons salt

pinch of pepper

2 × 15 ml spoons/2 tablespoons dry sherry

25 g/1 oz plain flour

2 × 15 ml spoons/2 tablespoons oil

1 spring onion (shallot), sliced

3 × 15 ml spoons/3 tablespoons sesame seed oil

AMERICAN

1½ lb whole fish or 4 fish steaks (see note)

2 teaspoons salt

pinch of pepper

2 tablespoons pale dry sherry

¼ cup all-purpose flour

2 tablespoons oil

1 scallion, sliced

3 tablespoons sesame oil

If using a whole fish, clean thoroughly and remove the scales. Make 3 or 4 parallel diagonal slashes in each side of the fish, about 2.5 cm/1 inch apart, cutting through to the bone. Sprinkle the fish or steaks with the salt, pepper, sherry and then the flour.

Heat the oil in a pan. Add the fish and cook gently until golden brown on both sides. Transfer to a warmed serving plate and garnish with the spring onion (shallot/scallion). Heat the sesame seed oil and pour over the fish. Serve immediately.

Note: Mackerel, bass, snapper or John Dory may be used.

Braised Duck (left)
Steamed Fish with Ginger and Spring Onions (Scallions) (above right)
Baked Fish with Sesame Seed Oil (below right)

Sweet and Sour Kidneys

METRIC/IMPERIAL

0.75 kg/1½ lb pigs' kidneys, thinly sliced

1 × 15 ml spoon/1 tablespoon dry sherry

2 × 15 ml spoons/2 tablespoons soy sauce

2 × 15 ml spoons/2 tablespoons red wine vinegar

1 × 15 ml spoon/1 tablespoon sugar

4 × 15 ml spoons/4 tablespoons oil

2 × 15 ml spoons/2 tablespoons chopped spring onions (shallots)

1 × 5 ml spoon/1 teaspoon grated root ginger

175 g/6 oz mange-tout or shelled green peas

1 × 5 ml spoon/1 teaspoon cornflour, dissolved in 1 × 15 ml spoon/1 tablespoon water

AMERICAN

1½ lb pork kidneys, thinly sliced

1 tablespoon pale dry sherry

2 tablespoons soy sauce

2 tablespoons red wine vinegar

1 tablespoon sugar

¼ cup oil

2 tablespoons chopped scallions

1 teaspoon minced ginger root

1 cup snow peas or podded green peas

1 teaspoon cornstarch, dissolved in 1 tablespoon water

Soak the kidney slices in water for 30 minutes, then drain and parboil in boiling water for 5 minutes. Drain and cool under cold running water. Drain well.

Mix together the sherry, soy sauce, vinegar and sugar in a small bowl. Heat the oil in a pan and add the spring onions (shallots/scallions) and ginger. Stir-fry for 1 minute, then add the kidney and mange-tout (snow peas) or peas. Stir-fry for a few seconds, then stir in the sherry mixture. Add the dissolved cornflour (cornstarch) and simmer, stirring continuously, until thickened. Serve hot.

Quick-Fried French (Green) Beans in Onion and Garlic Sauce

This is an excellent dish to accompany rice and meat.

METRIC/IMPERIAL

½ chicken stock cube

150 ml/¼ pint clear broth (see page 15) or stock

0.5 kg/1 lb French beans

3 × 15 ml spoons/3 tablespoons oil

25 g/1 oz butter

4-6 garlic cloves, crushed

2 spring onions (shallots), sliced

1 × 5 ml spoon/1 teaspoon salt

1 × 15 ml spoon/1 tablespoon soy sauce

1 × 5 ml spoon/1 teaspoon sugar

1 × 15 ml spoon/1 tablespoon dry sherry

AMERICAN

1 chicken stock cube

⅔ cup clear broth (see page 15) or stock

1 lb green beans

3 tablespoons oil

2 tablespoons butter

4-6 garlic cloves, minced

2 scallions, sliced

1 teaspoon salt

1 tablespoon soy sauce

1 teaspoon sugar

1 tablespoon pale dry sherry

Dissolve the stock cube in the broth or stock in a large saucepan over moderate heat. Add the beans and simmer until nearly all the liquid has evaporated, turning them constantly.

Heat the oil and butter in a pan. Add the garlic, spring onions (shallots/scallions) and the salt. Stir-fry for 30 seconds. Add the beans and toss in the fat until well coated. Sprinkle with the soy sauce, sugar and sherry. Stir-fry for 1 minute. Serve hot.

Quick-Fried French (Green) Beans in Onion and Garlic Sauce

Sweet and Sour Pork

METRIC/IMPERIAL

350 g/12 oz pork fillet

2 × 15 ml spoons/2 tablespoons dry sherry

salt

freshly ground black pepper

1 × 15 ml spoon/1 tablespoon cornflour

120 ml/4 fl oz water

1 × 15 ml spoon/1 tablespoon tomato ketchup
(sauce)

5 × 15 ml spoons/5 tablespoons sugar

1 × 15 ml spoon/1 tablespoon soy sauce

2 × 5 ml spoons/2 teaspoons red wine vinegar

oil for deep frying

3 × 15 ml spoons/3 tablespoons oil

1 green pepper, cored, seeded and thinly
sliced

½ onion, sliced into rings

Batter

2 egg yolks

2 × 15 ml spoons/2 tablespoons plain flour

2 × 15 ml spoons/2 tablespoons water

Garnish

3-4 lemon slices

few carrot slices and onion rings

AMERICAN

¾ lb boneless pork tenderloin

2 tablespoons pale dry sherry

salt

freshly ground black pepper

1 tablespoon cornstarch

½ cup water

1 tablespoon tomato ketchup

5 tablespoons sugar

1 tablespoon soy sauce

2 teaspoons red wine vinegar

oil for deep frying

3 tablespoons oil

1 green pepper, cored, seeded and thinly
sliced

½ onion, sliced into rings

Batter

2 egg yolks

2 tablespoons all-purpose flour

2 tablespoons water

Sweet and Sour Pork (above)
Sweet and Sour Kidneys (below)

Garnish

3-4 lemon slices

few carrot slices and onion rings

Cut the pork into strips. Sprinkle with half of the sherry and a pinch each of salt and pepper. Mix the cornflour (cornstarch) with a little of the water, then stir in the remainder, together with the tomato ketchup (sauce), sugar, soy sauce, remaining sherry, the vinegar and 1 × 5 ml spoon/1 teaspoon salt.

Beat together the egg yolks, flour and water to make a smooth batter. Heat oil to 180°C/350°F. Dip the pork into the batter, then deep-fry until golden brown. Drain and keep hot.

Heat 3 × 15 ml spoons/3 tablespoons oil in a pan. Add the green pepper and onion and stir-fry for 2 minutes. Add the soy sauce mixture and cook, stirring, until thickened. Add the deep-fried pork strips and mix well. Transfer to a serving dish and garnish with the lemon slices, topped with carrot slices and onion rings. Serve hot.

95

Peking Roast Duck

Peking Roast Duck is considered one of the greatest Chinese dishes. In China ducks are particularly raised and fattened for this dish and special ovens, with jujube (date) wood providing the fuel, are used for cooking. The skin of the duck is considered the prime delicacy and is cut from the duck in thin slices.

METRIC/IMPERIAL

1×2 kg/$4\frac{1}{2}$ lb duck

3×15 ml spoons/3 tablespoons honey or black treacle

2×15 ml spoons/2 tablespoons red wine vinegar

2×15 ml spoons/2 tablespoons dry sherry

250 ml/8 fl oz hot water

Accompaniments

8-12 spring onion (shallot) brushes (see note)

120 ml/4 fl oz soy bean paste or hoisin sauce

16 mandarin pancakes

1 cucumber, sliced

4 spring onions (shallots), shredded

AMERICAN

$1 \times 4\frac{1}{2}$ lb duck

3 tablespoons honey or molasses

2 tablespoons red wine vinegar

2 tablespoons pale dry sherry

1 cup hot water

Accompaniments

8-12 scallion brushes (see note)

$\frac{1}{2}$ cup bean sauce or hoisin sauce

16 mandarin pancakes

1 cucumber, sliced

4 scallions, shredded

Place the duck in a large saucepan and cover with boiling water. Boil for 5 minutes, then drain and cool under running water. Dry on absorbent kitchen paper.

Combine the honey or treacle (molasses), vinegar, sherry and hot water. Brush the duck skin with this mixture. Brace the wings away from the body with two skewers. Hang the duck by the neck in a well-ventilated place to dry overnight.

Roast in a preheated moderately hot oven (200°C/400°F, Gas Mark 6) for 30 minutes. Reduce the heat to 190°C/375°F, Gas Mark 5 and roast for a further 40 minutes or until the duck is tender.

To serve: Cut off the crispy skin from the breast, sides and back of the duck and cut into 5×7.5 cm/2×3 inch slices. Arrange these slices on a warmed serving dish. Cut the wings and drumsticks from the duck. Slice the meat from the breast and carcass and arrange on a separate serving dish, with the drumsticks and wings.

To eat: Each diner dips a spring onion (shallot/scallion) brush in the soy bean paste (bean sauce) or hoisin sauce and brushes the sauce onto a mandarin pancake. He then places two pieces of cucumber and a little shredded spring onion (shallot/scallion) in the centre of the pancake. This is topped with a slice of meat and a slice of duck skin. The pancake is then rolled up, using the fingers, and eaten while still warm.

Note: Peking Roast Duck is traditionally served with spring onion (shallot/scallion) brushes. To prepare these make several deep cuts across both ends of each spring onion (shallot/scallion). Place in a bowl of iced water and leave until open. Drain, then wrap a thin strip of pepper around the centre of each brush.

Mandarin Pancakes

The pancakes for Peking Duck can either be bought ready-made from Chinese food stores or supermarkets or made in the following way.

METRIC/IMPERIAL

225 g/8 oz plain flour

250 ml/8 fl oz boiling water

2 × 15 ml spoons/2 tablespoons sesame seed oil

Peking Roast Duck with Mandarin Pancakes and other accompaniments

AMERICAN

2 cups all-purpose flour

1 cup boiling water

2 tablespoons sesame oil

Sift the flour into a bowl. Add the boiling water, a little at a time, beating well with a wooden spoon after each addition. Knead the dough for 5 to 6 minutes, then cover and rest for 10 minutes.

Form the dough into a long roll, about 5 cm/2 inches in diameter. Cut the roll into 1 cm/½ inch slices. Roll the slices into thin 15 cm/6 inch diameter pancakes. Brush the tops of two pancakes with sesame seed oil and sandwich together, oiled sides facing inwards. Sandwich the remaining pancakes in the same way.

Heat a heavy, ungreased frying-pan (skillet). Place a double-pancake in the pan and cook for 3 minutes on each side. (Brown spots will appear and some parts will start to bubble when the pancake is cooked.) Remove from the pan and cool slightly. Pull the two pancakes apart and fold each one in half, oiled side inwards. Stack on a heatproof dish and keep hot while cooking the remaining pancakes. When all the pancakes are cooked, place in a steamer and steam for 10 minutes.

These pancakes will keep in the refrigerator for 2 to 3 days, but should be steamed again for 7 to 8 minutes if they are to be kept for any length of time before serving.

Spring Rolls

METRIC/IMPERIAL

oil for deep frying

Wrapping

100 g/4 oz plain flour

250 ml/8 fl oz water

pinch of salt

Filling

3 × 15 ml spoons/3 tablespoons oil

225 g/8 oz lean pork, shredded

100 g/4 oz celery, shredded

100 g/4 oz mushrooms, shredded

1 × 15 ml spoon/1 tablespoon soy sauce

1 × 2.5 ml spoon/½ teaspoon salt

1 × 15 ml spoon/1 tablespoon cornflour,
dissolved in 3 × 15 ml spoons/3 tablespoons
water

Flour paste

1 × 15 ml spoon/1 tablespoon plain flour
mixed with 1 × 15 ml spoon/1 tablespoon
water

AMERICAN

oil for deep frying

Wrapping

1 cup all-purpose flour

1 cup water

pinch of salt

Filling

3 tablespoons oil

½ lb lean pork, shredded

1 cup shredded celery

1 cup shredded mushrooms

1 tablespoon soy sauce

½ teaspoon salt

1 tablespoon cornstarch, dissolved in 3
tablespoons water

Flour paste

1 tablespoon all-purpose flour mixed with 1
tablespoon water

To make the wrapping, sift the flour into a
bowl and gradually beat in the water to form
a smooth batter. Stir in the salt. Let stand for
at least 30 minutes.

Lightly grease a heated 23 cm/9 inch frying
pan (skillet). Use a pastry brush to spread a
thin sheet of batter on the bottom of the pan.
Cook until set. If holes appear, brush with a
little more batter. Remove from the pan and
keep warm. Continue making wrapping pancakes in this way until all of the batter is
used.

For the filling, heat the oil in a pan. Add the
pork and stir-fry until it changes colour. Add
the vegetables, soy sauce and salt. Add the
cornflour (cornstarch) mixture and stir until
thickened. Remove from the heat and allow
to cool.

Place 2 × 15 ml spoons/2 tablespoons of the
filling on the bottom half of each wrapping

pancake and fold the top over. Fold the right
side towards the left and the left side towards
the right. Roll up into a tight roll and seal
with the flour paste.

Heat the oil to 180°C/350°F. Deep-fry the
rolls a few at a time until golden brown.
Drain on absorbent kitchen paper and serve
hot.

Note: The professional way to make the
wrapping is to make the dough as soft in
consistency as marshmallow. Hold the
dough in one hand and rub on a heavy pan's
surface to form paper-thin sheets. Ready-
made wrapping may be purchased.

Boiled Pork with Lotus Root

In July and August in Peking, wherever there
is a pond, you will see lovely pink and white
water lilies. The tuberous stem, which is
about 20 cm/8 inches long and 5 cm/2 inches
in diameter, is lotus root, one of the most
popular Chinese vegetables.

METRIC/IMPERIAL

0.5 kg/1 lb fresh, peeled, or canned lotus root

1 × 15 ml spoon/1 tablespoon vinegar

1 kg/2 lb pork fillet, cut into 4 pieces

1 × 5 ml spoon/1 teaspoon salt

3 slices root ginger

3 spring onions (shallots)

2 × 5 ml spoons/2 teaspoons crushed garlic

3 × 15 ml spoons/3 tablespoons soy sauce

few spring onions (shallots) to garnish

AMERICAN

1 lb fresh, peeled, or canned lotus root

1 tablespoon vinegar

2 lb pork tenderloin or fresh sides, cut into 4
pieces

1 teaspoon salt

3 slices ginger root

3 scallions

2 teaspoons minced garlic

3 tablespoons soy sauce

few scallions to garnish

If using fresh lotus root, place in a bowl.
Cover with cold water, to which the vinegar
has been added to prevent discoloration.
Leave to soak for 15 minutes.

Place the pork, salt, ginger and spring onions
(shallots/scallions) in a saucepan. Pour in
sufficient boiling water to cover. Simmer for
40 minutes to 1 hour or until the pork is
tender. Drain the pork and allow to cool.

Slice the pork and lotus root and arrange on
a serving plate. Garnish with spring onions
(shallots/scallions). Combine the garlic and
soy sauce in a dish and serve as a dip for the
pork.

Chilled Aubergine (Eggplant) Salad

METRIC/IMPERIAL

0.75 kg/1½ lb aubergines

100 g/4 oz dried shrimps, soaked for 15
minutes, then drained

2 × 15 ml spoons/2 tablespoons oil

4 × 15 ml spoons/4 tablespoons sesame seed
paste

4 × 15 ml spoons/4 tablespoons water

4 × 15 ml spoons/4 tablespoons chopped
spring onions (shallots)

1 garlic clove, crushed (optional)	3 tablespoons soy sauce
3 × 15 ml spoons/3 tablespoons soy sauce	2 tablespoons red wine vinegar
2 × 15 ml spoons/2 tablespoons red wine vinegar	1 teaspoon sugar
1 × 5 ml spoon/1 teaspoon sugar	

AMERICAN

1½ lb eggplant

1½ cups dried shrimp, soaked for 15 minutes, then drained

2 tablespoons oil

¼ cup sesame paste

¼ cup water

¼ cup chopped scallions

1 garlic clove, minced (optional)

Peel the skin from the aubergines (eggplant) then soak for 5 minutes to prevent discoloration; drain. Steam the aubergines (eggplants) for about 20 minutes or until just tender.

Cut each one lengthwise into quarters and arrange on a plate. Allow to cool, then chill. If using the shrimps, chop them finely. Heat the oil in a pan. Add the shrimps and stir-fry for 1 minute. Remove from the heat and cool.

Gradually mix the sesame seed paste with the water, then add the shrimps, spring onions (shallots/scallions), garlic, if used, soy sauce, vinegar and sugar. Mix well. Pour on top of the chilled aubergines (eggplant) and serve cold.

Note: Aubergines (eggplant) may be baked in the oven rather than steamed. Grated sesame seeds mixed with oil, or peanut butter, can be used instead of the sesame seed paste.

Boiled Pork with Lotus Root (left)
Spring Rolls (right)

Eastern China
Kiangche, Fukien and Shanghai
Deh-ta Hsiung

The great Yangtze River flows down from the Plateau of Tibet, winds its way through the gorges of Szechuan, rushes on to the basin of Hupei and Anpwei where a net of lakes, canals and tributary rivers slows down its progress until it reaches its journey's end, by roaring into the East China Sea a few miles north of Shanghai.

The Yangtze has travelled more than 3,000 miles by the time it reaches the lower plain. This is one of China's leading agricultural regions, for the river delta contains some of the most fertile land in China. Both wheat and rice are grown here, and other crops including barley, corn, sweet potatoes, peanuts and soy beans. Fishes abound in the multitude of lakes and rivers, and deep-sea fishing has long been established in the coastal provinces of Kiangsu and Chekiang.

Eastern Chinese food is traditionally divided into a number of regional styles. Starting in the north, we have the school known as *Huai Yang* with its centre in Yangchow in the Yangtze delta, just north of the river. Besides being famous for its noodles and dumplings, it boasts a host of other popular dishes. These include the famous Lion's Head (*page 125*).

Once we cross to the south of the river we are in the place known as the 'Land of fish and rice', one of the most densely populated parts of China, as well as the wealthiest and most industrialized. The school known as *Kiangche*, combining the cuisines of the coastal provinces Kiangsu and Chekiang, has a tremendous variety of gourmet dishes. To name but a few, there are the duck dishes of Nanking, and spareribs of Wusih; Kinhwa is known for its ham, Hangchow for its Dragon Well tea and, from Shaohsing, comes the best rice wine in China. The list can go on endlessly for over the centuries, Nanking has three times the capital of China, and Hangchow was the capital during one of the most cultural and economically prosperous periods in Chinese history. Therefore, it is hardly surprising that the cuisine has absorbed numerous gastronomic delights from all over the Empire. Nowadays the centre of the *Kiangche* school is Shanghai, which also has a cuisine style of its own.

In the days of primitive transportation the Grand Canal terminated at Hangchow, linking the city with Peking in the north. We have an old saying: 'In heaven, there is Paradise; on earth, we have Soochow and Hangchow', for not only is the scenery extremely beautiful in those places, they also produce the world famous silk and embroideries.

Shanghai, situated on the Yangtze estuary, is the largest city in China and one of the world's most populous of metropoli. During the 19th Century, Shanghai was the focus of foreign trade and very cosmopolitan; even today it remains China's greatest port and the centre of her trade and industry. Western influences are apparent in the cuisine of Shanghai; for example such ingredients as milk and butter are used. The characteristics of Shanghai cuisine can be summarized as rich in flavour, sweet in taste, exquisite in appearance and employing a great deal of lard to enrich the natural flavour of vegetables as well as meats.

South of Chekiang we come to Fukien province with its capital Foochow (*Chow* in Chinese means country or department). We leave the sophistication of Shanghai behind for here the accent is on locally produced delicacies, particularly seafood and agricultural products. Also, as the southern tip of Fukien borders on Kwangtung, its culinary art is strongly influenced by its great Cantonese neighbour.

West of Fukien is Kiangsi, 'Land of fish and rice', where you will see people either busily working on the land, or fishing in the shallow ponds or small rivers. Here the style of cooking is truly 'national' for besides its neighbour Fukien to the east, it also draws inspiration from Kwangtung in the south, Hunan with its hot and piquant food in the west, and the vast northern school of Anpwei and Chekiang.

Eastern Chinese food can be said to include the best of other schools of cuisine in China, as well as retaining an individual style of its own. Here you will find a selection of specialities from the region.

Braised Prawns (Shrimp)

METRIC/IMPERIAL

1 × 5 ml spoon/1 teaspoon salt

1 egg white

2 × 15 ml spoons/2 tablespoons cornflour

225 g/8 oz raw prawns, shelled and deveined

225 g/8 oz lard

2 × 15 ml spoons/2 tablespoons dry sherry

4 × 15 ml spoons/4 tablespoons stock

1 × 15 ml spoon/1 tablespoon water

1 × 5 ml spoon/1 teaspoon sesame seed oil

AMERICAN

1 teaspoon salt

1 egg white

2 tablespoons cornstarch

$\frac{1}{2}$ lb raw shrimp, shelled and deveined

1 cup lard or oil

2 tablespoons pale dry sherry

$\frac{1}{4}$ cup stock

1 tablespoon water

1 teaspoon sesame seed oil

Mix together the salt, egg white and 1 × 15 ml spoon/1 tablespoon of the cornflour (cornstarch). Add the prawns (shrimp) and leave to marinate in the refrigerator for 1 to 2 hours.

Heat the lard (or oil) in a pan. Add the prawns (shrimp). Stir to separate them, then lift them out with a perforated spoon. Pour off the excess lard (oil), leaving a small amount in the pan. Add the sherry, stock and prawns (shrimp) and bring to the boil.

Dissolve the remaining cornflour (cornstarch) in the water and add to the pan. Stir until thickened. Add the sesame seed oil and serve hot or cold on a bed of lettuce.

Prawns (Shrimp) in Shells

This is an ideal appetizer. You put a whole prawn in your mouth and lick off the sauce while extracting the meat from its shell.

METRIC/IMPERIAL

225 g/8 oz Pacific prawns (or Dublin Bay Prawns)

300 ml/$\frac{1}{2}$ pint oil

2 × 15 ml spoons/2 tablespoons soy sauce

2 × 15 ml spoons/2 tablespoons dry sherry

1 × 15 ml spoon/1 tablespoon sugar

2 spring onions (shallots), chopped

2 slices root ginger, chopped

chopped parsley to garnish

AMERICAN

$\frac{1}{2}$ lb jumbo shrimp

1$\frac{1}{4}$ cups oil

2 tablespoons soy sauce

2 tablespoons pale dry sherry

1 tablespoon sugar

2 scallions, chopped

2 slices ginger root, chopped

chopped parsley to garnish

Trim the legs off the prawns (shrimp) but keep the body shells on.

Heat the oil in a pan. Add the prawns (shrimp) and fry for a few seconds or until they just start to turn pink. Lift out with the perforated spoon.

Pour off the oil, then return the prawns (shrimp) to the pan. Add the soy sauce, sherry, sugar, spring onions (shallots/scallions) and ginger. Stir-fry vigorously for a few seconds. Serve hot, garnished with parsley.

Braised Prawns (Shrimp) (below)

Stir-Fried Crab with Spring Onions (Scallions)

METRIC/IMPERIAL

| 0.5 kg/1 lb crab |
| 6 spring onions (shallots), chopped |
| 6 slices root ginger, finely chopped |
| 2 × 15 ml spoons/2 tablespoons dry sherry |
| 4 × 15 ml spoons/4 tablespoons oil |
| 2 eggs, beaten |
| 3 × 15 ml spoons/3 tablespoons cornflour |
| 2 garlic cloves, crushed |
| 2 × 15 ml spoons/2 tablespoons soy sauce |
| 1 × 15 ml spoon/1 tablespoon sugar |
| 2 × 15 ml spoons/2 tablespoons red wine vinegar |
| 1 × 15 ml spoon/1 tablespoon water |

AMERICAN

| 3–4 hard-shelled crabs |
| 6 scallions, chopped |
| 6 slices ginger root, finely chopped |
| 2 tablespoons pale dry sherry |
| ¼ cup oil |
| 2 eggs, beaten |
| 3 tablespoons cornstarch |
| 2 garlic cloves, minced |
| 2 tablespoons soy sauce |
| 1 tablespoon sugar |
| 2 tablespoons red wine vinegar |
| 1 tablespoon water |

Twist the legs and claws from the crabs and break each crab into 3 or 4 pieces. Discard the feathery gills and the grey stomach sac. Place the crab pieces, legs and claws in a dish. Add 3 of the spring onions (shallots/scallions), half of the ginger and the sherry and leave to marinate for about 10 minutes. Take out the crab and set aside the marinade ingredients.

Heat the oil in a pan. Beat eggs with 2 × 15 ml spoons/2 tablespoons of the cornflour (cornstarch) until smooth. Coat the crab pieces with the egg mixture and add to the pan. Fry until golden brown, then lift out with a perforated spoon and drain on absorbent kitchen paper.

Fry the remaining spring onions (shallots/scallions) and ginger together with the garlic in the oil remaining in the pan. Add the soy sauce, sugar and vinegar. Replace the crab in the pan. Dissolve the remaining cornflour (cornstarch) in the water and stir into the pan. Cook, stirring, until thickened. Transfer to a serving dish and sprinkle with the reserved spring onions (shallots/scallions) and ginger. Serve hot.

Prawns (Shrimp) in Shells (above)
Stir-Fried Crab with Spring Onions (Scallions) (below)

103

'Smoked' Fish Slices

METRIC/IMPERIAL

3 × 15 ml spoons/3 tablespoons soy sauce

2 × 15 ml spoons/2 tablespoons dry sherry

pinch of salt

0.5 kg/1 lb cod fillets, cut into
5 × 2.5 cm/2 × 1 inch pieces

3 spring onions (shallots), chopped

2 slices root ginger, chopped

250 ml/8 fl oz water

50 g/2 oz sugar

1 × 2.5 ml/½ teaspoon 5-spice powder

oil for deep frying

AMERICAN

3 tablespoons soy sauce

2 tablespoons pale dry sherry

pinch of salt

1 lb cod fillets, cut into 2 × 1 inch pieces

3 scallions, chopped

2 slices ginger root, chopped

1 cup water

¼ cup sugar

½ teaspoon 5-spice powder

oil for deep frying

Mix together the soy sauce, sherry and salt in a bowl. Add the fish and leave to marinate for 30 minutes.

Remove the fish pieces from the marinade. Put the marinade in a saucepan with the spring onions (shallots/scallions), ginger, water, sugar and 5-spice powder. Bring to the boil and simmer gently for 10 minutes. Strain the sauce into a bowl and set aside.

Heat the oil to 180°C/350°F. Deep-fry the fish pieces, in batches, for about 4 minutes or until they are crisp and golden. Lift out using chopsticks or a slotted spoon and put them in the sauce. Leave for about 5 minutes before laying the fish pieces out side by side on a plate to cool. Serve cold.

Soy-Braised Cod or Halibut Steaks

METRIC/IMPERIAL

50 g/2 oz lard

3–4 spring onions (shallots), finely chopped

2–3 slices root ginger, finely chopped

0.5 kg/1 lb cod or halibut fillets, quartered

2 × 15 ml spoons/2 tablespoons sherry

2 × 15 ml spoons/2 tablespoons soy sauce

1 × 15 ml spoon/1 tablespoon sugar

120 ml/4 fl oz water

1 × 15 ml spoon/1 tablespoon cornflour, dissolved in 1.5 × 15 ml spoons/1½ tablespoons water

1 × 5 ml spoon/1 teaspoon sesame seed oil

shredded spring onion (shallot) to garnish

AMERICAN

¼ cup lard

3–4 scallions, finely chopped

2–3 slices ginger root, finely chopped

1 lb cod or halibut fillets, quartered

2 tablespoons pale dry sherry

2 tablespoons soy sauce

1 tablespoon sugar

½ cup water

1 tablespoon cornstarch, dissolved in 1½ tablespoons water

1 teaspoon sesame oil

shredded scallion to garnish

Melt the lard in a pan over high heat. Add the spring onions (shallots/scallions) and ginger and stir-fry for a few seconds. Add the fish pieces and stir very gently to separate. Add the sherry and bring to the boil, then stir in the soy sauce, sugar and water. Simmer for about 10 minutes.

Add the cornflour (cornstarch) mixture and simmer, stirring, until thickened. Add the sesame seed oil and serve hot, garnished with shredded spring onion (shallot/scallion).

Fish Slices in White Sauce

METRIC/IMPERIAL

1 egg white

1 × 5 ml spoon/1 teaspoon salt

1 × 15 ml spoon/1 tablespoon cornflour

0.5 kg/1 lb plaice or sole fillets, cut into small pieces

3 × 15 ml spoons/3 tablespoons oil

2 spring onions (shallots), finely chopped

1 garlic clove, finely chopped

2 × 15 ml spoons/2 tablespoons dry sherry

1 × 15 ml spoon/1 tablespoon water

AMERICAN

1 egg white

1 teaspoon salt

1 tablespoon cornstarch

1 lb flounder or sole fillets, cut into small pieces

3 tablespoons oil

2 scallions, chopped

1 garlic clove, finely chopped

2 tablespoons pale dry sherry

1 tablespoon water

Mix together the egg white, salt and 1 × 5 ml spoon/1 teaspoon of the cornflour (cornstarch). Add the fish and turn to coat. Heat the oil in a pan. Add the fish and fry gently until golden. Remove from the pan with a slotted spoon.

Add the spring onions (shallots/scallions) and garlic to the pan and stir-fry for 30 seconds. Return the fish slices to the pan with the sherry. Dissolve the remaining cornflour (cornstarch) in the water and stir into the pan. Stir well so the sauce covers the fish evenly and cook until the sauce thickens. Serve hot.

Soy-Braised Cod or Halibut Steaks (top left)
Red-Cooked Fish (below left)
Fish Slices in White Sauce (below)

Red-Cooked Fish

METRIC/IMPERIAL

1 kg/2 lb whole fish (carp, bream, mullet or mackerel), cleaned and scaled

4 × 15 ml spoons/4 tablespoons soy sauce

3 × 15 ml spoons/3 tablespoons oil

15 g/½ oz dried wood ears, soaked for 20 minutes, drained and stemmed

50 g/2 oz canned bamboo shoots, drained and sliced

3–4 spring onions (shallots), shredded

3 slices root ginger, shredded

2 × 5 ml spoons/2 teaspoons cornflour, dissolved in 1 × 15 ml spoon/1 tablespoon water

Sauce

2 × 15 ml spoons/2 tablespoons soy sauce

2 × 15 ml spoons/2 tablespoons dry sherry

2 × 5 ml spoons/2 teaspoons sugar

4 × 15 ml spoons/4 tablespoons stock

AMERICAN

2 lb whole fish (carp, porgy, mullet or mackerel), cleaned and scaled

¼ cup soy sauce

3 tablespoons oil

½ cup dried tree ears, soaked for 20 minutes, drained and stemmed

½ cup sliced canned bamboo shoots

3–4 scallions, shredded

3 slices ginger root, shredded

2 teaspoons cornstarch, dissolved in 1 tablespoon water

Sauce

2 tablespoons soy sauce

2 tablespoons pale dry sherry

2 teaspoons sugar

¼ cup stock

Marinate the fish in the soy sauce for 30 minutes. Mix together the sauce ingredients. Heat the oil in a pan. When it is very hot, add the fish pieces and fry until golden. Add the sauce, wood (tree) ears and bamboo shoots and continue cooking for about 10 minutes. Add the spring onions (shallots/scallions) and ginger and cook until the sauce is reduced by half. Add the cornflour (cornstarch) mixture and cook, stirring, until thickened. Transfer to a serving dish. Pour over the sauce and serve hot.

Quick-Fried Prawns (Shrimp) with Bacon, Mushrooms and Cucumber

METRIC/IMPERIAL

350 g–0.5 kg/12 oz–1 lb shelled prawns

2 garlic cloves, crushed

2 slices root ginger, finely chopped (optional)

4 × 15 ml spoons/4 tablespoons oil

1 × 5 ml spoon/1 teaspoon salt

freshly ground black pepper

1 onion, thinly sliced

2–3 streaky bacon rashers, cut into thin strips

225–350 g/8–12 oz mushrooms, chopped

½ medium cucumber, diced

1 × 5 ml spoon/1 teaspoon sugar

1.5 × 15 ml spoons/1½ tablespoons soy sauce

2 × 15 ml spoons/2 tablespoons dry sherry

0.5 kg/1 lb hot cooked rice

AMERICAN

¾–1 lb shelled shrimp

2 garlic cloves, minced

2 slices ginger root, finely chopped (optional)

¼ cup oil

1 teaspoon salt

freshly ground black pepper

1 onion, thinly sliced

2–3 fatty bacon slices, cut into thin strips

½–¾ lb mushrooms, chopped

½ medium cucumber, diced

1 teaspoon sugar

1½ tablespoons soy sauce

2 tablespoons pale dry sherry

6 cups hot cooked rice

Place the prawns (shrimp) in a bowl, and add the garlic, ginger (if used) and 1 × 15 ml spoon/1 tablespoon of the oil. Sprinkle with salt and pepper.

Heat the remaining oil in a pan over high heat. Add the onion and stir-fry for 1 minute. Add the bacon and mushrooms and stir-fry for 1 minute.

Add the prawns (shrimp) and cucumber and sprinkle in the sugar and soy sauce. Stir-fry for 2 minutes. Stir in the sherry and cook for a few seconds longer.

Arrange the cooked rice in a serving dish and spoon the prawn (shrimp) mixture on top. Serve hot.

Fish in Vinegar Sauce

METRIC/IMPERIAL

50 g/2 oz lard

2–3 spring onions (shallots), white part only, cut into 2.5 cm/1 inch pieces

0.5 kg/1 lb fish fillets (cod, halibut, snapper or John Dory), cut into pieces

2 × 15 ml spoons/2 tablespoons dry sherry

2 × 15 ml spoons/2 tablespoons soy sauce

150 ml/¼ pint stock or water

1 × 5 ml spoon/1 teaspoon finely chopped root ginger

3 × 15 ml spoons/3 tablespoons wine vinegar

2 × 15 ml spoons/2 tablespoons sugar

2 × 5 ml spoons/2 teaspoons cornflour, dissolved in 1 × 15 ml spoon/1 tablespoon water

1 × 5 ml spoon/1 teaspoon sesame seed oil

AMERICAN

¼ cup lard

2–3 scallions, white part only, cut into 1 inch pieces

1 lb fish fillets (cod or halibut), cut into pieces

2 tablespoons pale dry sherry

2 tablespoons soy sauce

⅔ cup stock or water

1 teaspoon finely chopped ginger root

3 tablespoons wine vinegar

2 tablespoons sugar

2 teaspoons cornstarch, dissolved in 1 tablespoon water

1 teaspoon sesame oil

Melt the lard in a pan. Add the spring onions (shallots/scallions) and fry until golden. Add the fish pieces and sherry and cook until almost all of the sherry has evaporated. Add the soy sauce, stock or water, ginger and half the vinegar and sugar. Bring to the boil, then simmer for 5 minutes.

Add the remaining vinegar and sugar, and the cornflour (cornstarch) mixture. Cook, stirring, until thickened. Add the sesame seed oil and serve hot.

Fish with Bean Curd in Hot and Sour Sauce

METRIC/IMPERIAL

0.5 kg/1 lb fish fillets (cod, halibut, snapper or John Dory), cut into 5 × 2.5 cm/2 × 1 inch pieces

3 × 15 ml spoons/3 tablespoons soy sauce

4 × 15 ml spoons/4 tablespoons oil

2–3 spring onions (shallots), finely chopped

2–3 slices root ginger, finely chopped

1 garlic clove, crushed

2 cakes bean curd, each cut into 12 cubes

1 × 5 ml spoon/1 teaspoon salt

2 × 15 ml spoons/2 tablespoons dry sherry

1 × 5 ml spoon/1 teaspoon sugar

1 × 15 ml spoon/1 tablespoon chilli sauce

2 × 15 ml spoons/2 tablespoons wine vinegar

120 ml/4 fl oz water

chopped parsley to garnish

AMERICAN

1 lb fish fillets (cod or halibut), cut into 2 × 1 inch pieces

3 tablespoons soy sauce

¼ cup oil

2–3 scallions, finely chopped

2–3 slices ginger root, finely chopped

1 garlic clove, minced

2 cakes bean curd, each cut into 12 cubes

1 teaspoon salt

2 tablespoons pale dry sherry

1 teaspoon sugar

1 tablespoon chili sauce

2 tablespoons wine vinegar

½ cup water

chopped parsley to garnish

Sprinkle the fish pieces with 1 × 15 ml spoon/ 1 tablespoon of the soy sauce and leave to marinate.

Heat 3 × 15 ml spoons/3 tablespoons of the oil in a pan. Add the fish pieces and fry until golden. Remove the fish from the pan and set aside.

Heat the remaining oil in the pan. Add the spring onions (shallots/scallions), ginger and garlic and fry for a few seconds. Add the bean curd cubes, fish pieces, salt, sherry, sugar, remaining soy sauce, the chilli sauce, vinegar and water. Bring to the boil, then simmer for 10 minutes.

Serve hot, garnished with chopped parsley.

Quick-Fried Prawns (Shrimp) with Bacon, Mushrooms and Cucumber

Fish in Vinegar Sauce (top right)
Fish with Bean Curd in Hot and Sour Sauce (below right)

Chicken with Mushrooms (top left)
Bean Sprouts with Shredded Chicken (top right)
Stir-Fried Squid with Broccoli (centre)

Chicken with Mushrooms

METRIC/IMPERIAL

350 g/12 oz boned chicken breasts, skinned and cut into 2.5 cm/1 inch slices

pinch of salt

1 egg white

1 × 15 ml spoon/1 tablespoon cornflour

75 g/3 oz lard

50 g/2 oz fermented bean curd

1 × 5 ml spoon/1 teaspoon sugar

1 × 15 ml spoon/1 tablespoon dry sherry

225 g/8 oz mushrooms, sliced

1 small green pepper, cored, seeded and sliced

50 g/2 oz canned bamboo shoots, sliced

AMERICAN

¾ lb boned chicken breasts, skinned and cut into 1 inch slices

pinch of salt

1 egg white

1 tablespoon cornstarch

6 tablespoons lard

¼ cup fermented bean curd

1 teaspoon sugar

1 tablespoon pale dry sherry

½ lb mushrooms, sliced

½ cup sliced green pepper

½ cup sliced canned bamboo shoots

Rub the chicken slices with salt, then coat with the egg white and cornflour (cornstarch). Melt the lard in a pan. Add the chicken and stir-fry until each piece is coated with lard. Lift the chicken out with a perforated spoon. Increase the heat and add the fermented bean curd. Fry for 2 minutes, then add the sugar and sherry. Mix well, then add the mushrooms, green pepper and bamboo shoots. Stir-fry for a few seconds, then add the chicken. Cook for a further 1 to 2 minutes and serve hot.

Stir-Fried Squid with Broccoli

METRIC/IMPERIAL

0.5 kg/1 lb squid

2 × 5 ml spoons/2 teaspoons salt

1 × 15 ml spoon/1 tablespoon dry sherry

1 × 15 ml spoon/1 tablespoon cornflour

75 g/3 oz lard

5 spring onions (shallots), cut into 2.5 cm/
1 inch pieces

225 g/8 oz broccoli, broken into florets

1 × 5 ml spoon/1 teaspoon sesame seed oil
(optional)

AMERICAN

1 lb squid

2 teaspoons salt

1 tablespoon pale dry sherry

1 tablespoon cornstarch

6 tablespoons lard

5 scallions, cut into 1 inch pieces

½ lb broccoli, broken into florets

1 teaspoon sesame oil (optional)

Clean the squid, discarding the head and transparent backbone. Cut into thin slices, then blanch in boiling water for 2 to 3 minutes. Drain the squid and place in a bowl with 1 × 5 ml spoon/1 teaspoon of the salt, the sherry and cornflour (cornstarch). Leave to marinate for 10 minutes.

Melt half the lard in a pan. Add the spring onions (shallots/scallions) and squid and stir-fry briskly for about 2 minutes. Transfer the squid mixture to a serving plate and keep hot.

Melt the remaining lard in a clean pan. Add the broccoli, the remaining salt and a little water if the mixture seems too dry. Stir-fry until just tender. Arrange the broccoli spears around the edge of the squid. Sprinkle the sesame seed oil (if used) over the squid and serve hot.

Bean Sprouts with Shredded Chicken

METRIC/IMPERIAL

3 × 15 ml spoons/3 tablespoons oil

100 g/4 oz boned chicken breast, shredded

salt

1 × 5 ml spoon/1 teaspoon sugar

1 × 15 ml spoon/1 tablespoon dry sherry

2 spring onions (shallots), shredded

225 g/8 oz bean sprouts

AMERICAN

3 tablespoons oil

½ cup shredded chicken breast meat

salt

1 teaspoon sugar

1 tablespoon pale dry sherry

2 scallions, shredded

½ lb bean sprouts

Heat 1 × 15 ml spoon/1 tablespoon of the oil in a pan. Add the chicken and a pinch of salt and stir-fry for 2 minutes. Add the sugar and sherry. When the liquid starts to bubble, remove the chicken mixture from the pan. Heat the remaining oil in a clean pan. When it is very hot, sprinkle in 1 × 5 ml spoon/ 1 teaspoon salt followed by the spring onions (shallots/scallions). Stir-fry for a few seconds, then add the bean sprouts. Continue stir-frying for 1 minute, then add the chicken mixture. Stir well. As soon as the juice starts to bubble, serve.

Red-Cooked Pork with Spring Onions (Scallions) and Eggs

This dish is also known as the 'Pork of Four Happiness'. A dark soy sauce should be used for red-cooked pork to impart a deep colour and a rich flavour.

METRIC/IMPERIAL

1.5 kg/3–4 lb lean pork

1 × 5 ml spoon/1 teaspoon salt

1.5 × 5 ml spoons/1½ teaspoons sugar

120 ml/4 fl oz water

200 ml/⅓ pint soy sauce

5 × 15 ml spoons/5 tablespoons dry sherry

4 hard-boiled eggs

3.5 × 15 ml spoons/3½ tablespoons oil

4–5 spring onions (shallots), cut into 2.5 cm/1 inch pieces

3 garlic cloves, crushed

AMERICAN

3–4 lb lean pork

1 teaspoon salt

1½ teaspoons sugar

½ cup water

1 cup soy sauce

5 tablespoons pale dry sherry

4 hard-cooked eggs

3½ tablespoons oil

4–5 scallions, cut into 1 inch pieces

3 garlic cloves, minced

Cut the pork into 4 cm/1½ inch pieces. Place the pork in a pan and pour over just enough boiling water to cover. Cook for 15 minutes, then drain off all the water. Combine the salt, sugar, water and 5 × 15 ml spoons/5 tablespoons of the soy sauce; pour this mixture over the pork. Stir, then bring to the boil. Cover and simmer very gently for 30 minutes. Stir in the sherry and simmer, covered, for a further 30 minutes.

Put the eggs and remaining soy sauce in a separate pan and bring to the boil. Simmer for 7 to 8 minutes or until the eggs are brown. Heat the oil in another pan. Add the spring onions (shallots/scallions) and garlic and stir-fry for 3 minutes. Add to the pork, together with the eggs, and serve hot.

Red-Cooked Pork with Spring Onions (Scallions) and Eggs

Fried Eight-Piece Chicken

METRIC/IMPERIAL

1 × 1.25 kg/2½ lb spring chicken

2–3 spring onions (shallots), finely chopped

2–3 slices root ginger, finely chopped

2 × 15 ml spoons/2 tablespoons dry sherry

1 × 15 ml spoon/1 tablespoon sugar

3 × 15 ml spoons/3 tablespoons soy sauce

3 × 15 ml spoons/3 tablespoons cornflour

100 g/4 oz lard

1 × 5 ml spoon/1 teaspoon sesame seed oil

chopped parsley to garnish

AMERICAN

1 × 2½ lb spring chicken

2–3 scallions, finely chopped

2–3 slices ginger root, finely chopped

2 tablespoons pale dry sherry

1 tablespoon sugar

3 tablespoons soy sauce

3 tablespoons cornstarch

½ cup lard

1 teaspoon sesame oil

chopped parsley to garnish

Cut the legs, wings and breasts from the chicken, then cut each breast in half.

Mix the spring onions (shallots/scallions) and ginger with 1 × 15 ml spoon/1 tablespoon of the sherry, 1 × 5 ml spoon/1 teaspoon of the sugar and 1 × 15 ml spoon/1 tablespoon of the soy sauce. Add the chicken and leave to marinate for 3 minutes.

Coat each piece of chicken with cornflour (cornstarch). Heat the lard in a pan. Add the chicken pieces and fry until golden. Pour off the excess lard and add the remaining sherry, sugar and soy sauce to the pan. Bring to the boil, stirring. Add the sesame seed oil just before serving, garnished with parsley.

Braised Chicken Breast with Chestnuts

METRIC/IMPERIAL

0.5 kg/1 lb boned chicken breasts, cut into 2.5 cm/1 inch cubes

1 × 2.5 ml spoon/½ teaspoon salt

1 × 5 ml spoon/1 teaspoon cornflour

50 g/2 oz lard

100 g/4 oz dried chestnuts, soaked for 1 hour and drained

4 spring onions (shallots), cut into 4 cm/ 1½ inch pieces

120 ml/4 fl oz chicken stock

Sauce

2 × 15 ml spoons/2 tablespoons dry sherry

3 × 15 ml spoons/3 tablespoons soy sauce

1 × 15 ml spoon/1 tablespoon sugar

1 × 15 ml spoon/1 tablespoon cornflour

Fried Eight-Piece Chicken (left)
Braised Chicken Breast with Chestnuts (right)

AMERICAN

1 lb boneless chicken breasts, cut into 1 inch cubes

½ teaspoon salt

1 teaspoon cornstarch

¼ cup lard

¼ lb dried chestnuts, soaked for 1 hour and drained

4 scallions, cut into 1½ inch pieces

½ cup chicken stock

Sauce

2 tablespoons pale dry sherry

3 tablespoons soy sauce

1 tablespoon sugar

1 tablespoon cornstarch

Mix the chicken cubes with the salt and cornflour (cornstarch) until well coated. Mix together the sauce ingredients.

Melt the lard in a pan. When it is really hot, add the chicken and chestnuts and stir-fry together for about 1½ minutes. Remove from the pan. Add the spring onions (shallots/scallions) to the pan and fry until they start to turn yellow. Return the chicken and chestnuts to the pan with the sauce and stock. Continue cooking, stirring, until the sauce thickens. Serve hot.

111

Jellied Duckling

METRIC/IMPERIAL

1 × 2 kg/4½ lb oven-ready duckling

0.5 kg/1¼ lb belly pork

225 g/8 oz pork skin

250 ml/8 fl oz soy sauce

1 × 15 ml spoon/1 tablespoon salt

150 ml/¼ pint dry sherry

3 × 15 ml spoons/3 tablespoons sugar

1 × 5 ml spoon/1 teaspoon 5-spice powder

3 spring onions (shallots)

4 slices root ginger

watercress leaves to garnish

AMERICAN

1 × 4½ lb oven-ready duckling

1¼ lb fresh pork sides

½ lb pork skin

1 cup soy sauce

1 tablespoon salt

⅔ cup pale dry sherry

3 tablespoons sugar

1 teaspoon 5-spice powder

3 scallions

4 slices ginger root

watercress leaves to garnish

Put the duckling in a large pan with the pork and the pork skin. Cover with water and bring to the boil. Boil for 2 to 3 minutes, then pour off the water. Rinse the duckling, pork and pork skin under cold running water and put them back in the pot. Cover with fresh water. Add all the other ingredients, cover and bring to the boil. Simmer over low heat for about 4 hours.

Remove the duckling from the pan. Strain the stock into a bowl, discarding the pork, pork skin and flavourings. Bone the duckling, keeping the skin on. Put the duckling in the strained stock. Refrigerate until the stock sets into a jelly.

Invert the duckling onto a serving plate and garnish with watercress leaves.

Pepper Chicken (top)
Salted Chicken (centre)
Jellied Duckling (below)

Braised Duckling with Bamboo Shoots and Mushrooms

METRIC/IMPERIAL

1 × 2 kg/4½ lb oven-ready duckling

4 dried Chinese mushrooms, soaked for 20 minutes, drained, stemmed and sliced

6 × 15 ml spoons/6 tablespoons soy sauce

3 × 15 ml spoons/3 tablespoons sugar

225 g/8 oz canned bamboo shoots, drained and sliced

15 g/½ oz lard

3 spring onions (shallots), finely chopped

AMERICAN

1 × 4½ lb oven-ready duckling

4 dried Chinese mushrooms, soaked for 20 minutes, drained, stemmed and sliced

6 tablespoons soy sauce

3 tablespoons sugar

2 cups sliced canned bamboo shoots

1 tablespoon lard

3 scallions, finely chopped

Put the duckling in a large pan and cover with cold water. Bring to the boil, then take the duckling out and rinse under cold running water. Return the duckling to the pot after skimming off all impurities from the surface of the cooking water. Bring back to the boil and add the mushrooms, soy sauce and sugar. Cover tightly and simmer gently for 2 hours.

Add the bamboo shoots and continue cooking for 1 hour.

Just before serving, melt the lard in a pan. Add the spring onions (shallots/scallions) and fry until aromatic. Pour over the duckling and serve hot.

Salted Chicken

METRIC/IMPERIAL

1 × 1.75 kg/4 lb oven-ready chicken

1 × 15 ml spoon/1 tablespoon salt

2 × 5 ml spoons/2 teaspoons freshly ground black pepper

2.5 litres/4½ pints chicken stock

300 ml/½ pint dry sherry

1 × 5 ml spoon/1 teaspoon monosodium glutamate

3 spring onions (shallots), finely chopped (optional)

3 slices root ginger (optional)

3–4 spring onions (shallots) to garnish

AMERICAN

1 × 4 lb oven-ready chicken

1 tablespoon salt

2 teaspoons freshly ground black pepper

5½ pints chicken stock

1¼ cups pale dry sherry

1 teaspoon msg

3 scallions, finely chopped (optional)

3 slices ginger root, (optional)

3–4 scallions to garnish

Prick the skin of the chicken with a fork, then rub the salt and pepper all over it. Put the chicken in a large heatproof bowl, cover with foil and place a heavy weight on top. Leave in the refrigerator for 12 hours.

Place the chicken stock, sherry and mono-sodium glutamate (msg) in a pan and bring to the boil. Remove from the heat and allow to cool, then pour over the chicken. Leave to marinate for 5 to 6 hours.

Either steam the chicken with the spring onions (shallots/scallions) and ginger for 1 hour or cook it in the boiling sauce for 30 minutes until tender. Serve hot or cold, sprinkled with the garnish.

Pepper Chicken

METRIC/IMPERIAL

1 × 1.5 kg/3 lb oven-ready chicken

1 × 15 ml spoon/1 tablespoon oil

1.5 × 5 ml spoons/1½ teaspoons Szechuan or black peppercorns

Sauce

2 × 15 ml spoons/2 tablespoons soy sauce

1 × 15 ml spoon/1 tablespoon wine vinegar

1 × 5 ml spoon/1 teaspoon salt

1 × 2.5 ml spoon/½ teaspoon monosodium glutamate

2 spring onions (shallots), finely chopped

1 × 5 ml spoon/1 teaspoon finely chopped root ginger

Garnish

2 spring onions (shallots), chopped

AMERICAN

1 × 3 lb oven-ready chicken

1 tablespoon oil

1½ teaspoons Szechuan or black peppercorns

Sauce

2 tablespoons soy sauce

1 tablespoon wine vinegar

1 teaspoon salt

½ teaspoon msg

2 scallions, finely chopped

1 teaspoon finely chopped ginger root

Garnish

2 scallions, chopped

Blanch the chicken in boiling water for 10 minutes. Drain and, using a heavy cleaver, chop the chicken into small pieces. Arrange the chicken pieces neatly, skin side down, in a large heatproof bowl.

Heat the oil in a pan. Add the peppercorns and fry until they become aromatic. Pour the peppercorns and oil onto the chicken pieces. Combine the sauce ingredients and pour over the chicken.

Cover the bowl with foil and steam vig-orously for 30 minutes. To serve, invert onto a round plate and garnish with chopped spring onions (shallots/scallions).

Red-Cooked Beef with Broccoli

METRIC/IMPERIAL

0.5 kg/1 lb shin of beef, cubed

0.75 kg/1½ lb brisket of beef, cubed

4–5 slices root ginger, chopped

1 × 5 ml spoon/1 teaspoon salt

1 × 2.5 ml spoon/½ teaspoon peppercorns

3 × 15 ml spoons/3 tablespoons soy sauce

600 ml/1 pint water

300 ml/½ pint white wine

1 chicken stock cube

0.5 kg/1 lb broccoli, broken into florets

AMERICAN

1 lb shin of beef, cubed

1½ lb brisket of beef, cubed

4–5 slices ginger root, chopped

1 teaspoon salt

½ teaspoon peppercorns

3 tablespoons soy sauce

2½ cups water

1¼ cups white wine

2 chicken stock cubes

1 lb broccoli, broken in florets

Blanch the beef cubes in boiling water for 2 minutes and drain. Put the beef in a large pan. Add the ginger, salt, peppercorns, soy sauce and water. Bring to the boil, then cover and simmer gently for 2 hours, stirring occasionally.

Add the wine and crumbled stock cube. Simmer for a further 1 hour. Add the broccoli and cook for a further 10 minutes. Drain most of the cooking liquor into a bowl. Transfer the meat to a serving bowl and arrange the broccoli around the edge of the bowl. Serve the reserved liquor as a clear broth to accompany the meal.

Stir-Fried Liver

METRIC/IMPERIAL

pinch of salt

2 × 5 ml spoons/2 teaspoons cornflour

225 g/8 oz pig's liver, thinly sliced into 5 × 2.5 cm/2 × 1 inch pieces

50 g/2 oz lard

2 spring onions (shallots), cut into 2.5 cm/ 1 inch pieces

25g/1 oz dried wood ears, soaked for 20 minutes, drained and stemmed

1 × 15 ml spoon/1 tablespoon soy sauce

1 × 15 ml spoon/1 tablespoon dry sherry

1 × 5 ml spoon/1 teaspoon sugar

2 × 5 ml spoons/2 teaspoons stock or water

1 × 5 ml spoon/1 teaspoon sesame seed oil

AMERICAN

pinch of salt

2 teaspoons cornstarch

½ lb pork liver, thinly sliced into 2 × 1 inch pieces

¼ cup lard

2 scallions, cut into 1 inch pieces

1 cup dried tree ears, soaked for 20 minutes, drained and stemmed

1 tablespoon soy sauce

1 tablespoon pale dry sherry

1 teaspoon sugar

2 teaspoons stock or water

1 teaspoon sesame oil

Red-Cooked Beef with Broccoli

Mix together the salt and 1 × 5 ml spoon/ 1 teaspoon of the cornflour (cornstarch). Add the liver and turn to coat thoroughly. Melt the lard in a pan.

When the lard is hot, add the liver and stir-fry for about 30 seconds, or until each piece is coated with lard. Lift out with a perforated spoon and set aside.

Add the spring onions (shallots/scallions) and mushrooms to the pan. Stir-fry for a few seconds until the spring onions (shallots/scallions) begin to soften, then return the liver to the pan and add the soy sauce, sherry and sugar. Stir-fry for a few seconds.

Dissolve the remaining cornflour (cornstarch) in the stock or water and stir into the pan. Cook, stirring, until thickened. Add the sesame seed oil. Transfer to a shallow serving dish and serve hot.

Crispy Skin Fish

METRIC/IMPERIAL

| 0.75 kg/1½ lb small fish (whiting, herring, small trout, etc) |
| 3–4 slices root ginger, chopped |
| 1 × 15 ml spoon/1 tablespoon salt |
| 1.5 × 15 ml spoons/1½ tablespoons plain flour |
| oil for deep-frying |
| parsley sprigs to garnish |

AMERICAN

| 1½ lb small fish (whiting, herring, small trout, etc) |
| 3–4 slices ginger root, chopped |
| 1 tablespoon salt |

Crispy Skin Fish

| 1½ tablespoons all-purpose flour |
| oil for deep-frying |
| parsley sprigs to garnish |

Slit the fish along the belly, clean and rinse thoroughly but leave the heads and tails intact.

Rub the fish inside and out with the ginger and salt. Leave for 3 hours. Rub with the flour and leave for a further 30 minutes.

Heat the oil to 180°C/350°F. Deep-fry the fish in batches for 3 to 4 minutes, or until they are crisp and golden brown. Drain on absorbent kitchen paper and keep hot while frying the remaining fish. When all the fish have been fried, return all of them to the oil and fry for 2½ to 3 minutes, or until very crisp. Serve hot, garnished with parsley.

Red, White and Green Kidney

METRIC/IMPERIAL

2 eggs, beaten

3 × 15 ml spoons/3 tablespoons cornflour

salt

225 g/8 oz cooked chicken breast meat, finely chopped

175 g/6 oz cooked ham, minced

2–3 spring onions (shallots), finely chopped

4 × 100 g/4 oz pigs' kidneys, cored and each cut into 8 slices

25 g/1 oz lard

225 g/8 oz Brussels sprouts

150 ml/¼ pint stock

AMERICAN

2 eggs, beaten

3 tablespoons cornstarch

salt

1 cup finely chopped cooked chicken breast meat

¾ cup ground cooked ham

2–3 scallions, finely chopped

4 × ¼ lb pork kidneys, cored and each cut into 8 slices

2 tablespoons lard

½ lb Brussels sprouts

⅔ cup stock

Beat the eggs with 2 × 15 ml spoons/2 tablespoons of the cornflour (cornstarch) and a little salt. Mix together the chicken, ham and spring onions (shallots/scallions).

Dip each slice of kidney into the egg mixture, then coat with a little of the chicken and ham mixture. Arrange in rows on a well-greased heatproof plate. Steam for 30 minutes.

Meanwhile, melt the lard in a pan. Add the Brussels sprouts and stir-fry with a little salt and about half of the stock until just tender. Arrange the sprouts around the kidney and keep hot.

Heat the remaining stock in a saucepan. Mix in the remaining cornflour (cornstarch) and a little salt and cook, stirring, until thickened. Pour over the kidney and serve hot.

Shredded Pork with Fermented Bean Curd

METRIC/IMPERIAL

25 g/1 oz lard

50 g/2 oz red fermented bean curd

0.5 kg/1 lb pork fillet, cut into small cubes

2 × 15 ml spoons/2 tablespoons dry sherry

1 × 15 ml spoon/1 tablespoon soy sauce

1 × 15 ml spoon/1 tablespoon brown sugar

300 ml/½ pint stock

AMERICAN

2 tablespoons lard

¼ cup red fermented bean curd

1 lb pork tenderloin, cut into small cubes

2 tablespoons pale dry sherry

1 tablespoon soy sauce

1 tablespoon brown sugar

1¼ cups stock

Melt the lard in a saucepan. Add the fermented bean curd and stir-fry for 30 seconds. Add the pork, sherry, soy sauce, sugar and stock. Bring to the boil, then simmer for at least 2 hours, stirring occasionally to break up the meat into small pieces.

Transfer to a large frying-pan (skillet) or wok. Cook over a very low heat, stirring constantly with a wooden spoon to separate the meat fibres. This process will take 1½ to 2 hours, by which time all the juice will have evaporated, and the meat fibres will be fluffy and woolly. Place the meat on a sheet of greaseproof paper or non-stick parchment to cool.

Serve as part of an hors d'oeuvre.

Red, White and Green Kidney (left)
Soy Duckling (below)

Kidney in Sweet and Sour Sauce

METRIC/IMPERIAL

4 × 100 g/4 oz pig's kidneys, cored and each cut into 8 pieces

40 g/1½ oz lard

2 spring onions (shallots), finely chopped

2 slices root ginger, finely chopped

Sauce

2 × 15 ml spoons/2 tablespoons soy sauce

2 × 15 ml spoons/2 tablespoons wine vinegar

1 × 15 ml spoon/1 tablespoon sugar

1 × 15 ml spoon/1 tablespoon cornflour

2 × 15 ml spoons/2 tablespoons water

AMERICAN

4 × ¼ lb pork kidneys, cored and each cut into 8 pieces

3 tablespoons lard

2 scallions, finely chopped

2 slices ginger root, finely chopped

Sauce

2 tablespoons soy sauce

2 tablespoons wine vinegar

1 tablespoon sugar

1 tablespoon cornstarch

2 tablespoons water

Blanch the kidneys in boiling water for about 5 minutes. Drain. Mix together the sauce ingredients.

Melt the lard in a pan. Add the spring onions (shallots/scallions) and half the ginger and stir-fry for 30 seconds. Add the sauce and stir until it thickens. Strain, discarding the spring onions (shallots/scallions) and ginger, then return the sauce to the pan. Add the kidneys and stir until heated through. Garnish with the remaining ginger and serve hot.

Soy Duckling

METRIC/IMPERIAL

1 × 2.25 kg/5 lb oven-ready duckling

2 × 5 ml spoons/2 teaspoons salt

4 spring onions (shallots)

4 slices root ginger

1 × 5 ml spoon/1 teaspoon 5-spice powder

2.25 litres/4 pints water

2 × 15 ml spoons/2 tablespoons dry sherry

6 × 15 ml spoons/6 tablespoons soy sauce

50 g/2 oz sugar

1 × 15 ml spoon/1 tablespoon sesame seed oil

chopped parsley to garnish

AMERICAN

1 × 5 lb oven-ready duckling

2 teaspoons salt

4 scallions

4 slices ginger root

1 teaspoon 5-spice powder

5 pints water

2 tablespoons pale dry sherry

6 tablespoons soy sauce

¼ cup sugar

1 tablespoon sesame oil

chopped parsley to garnish

Blanch the duckling in boiling water for 1 minute, then drain and dry thoroughly inside and out. Rub about 1 × 5 ml spoon/1 teaspoon of the salt into the cavity. Put the spring onions (shallots/scallions), ginger, 5-spice powder and water in a large pan. Bring to the boil and boil for 2 to 3 minutes, then add the duckling, sherry, soy sauce, sugar and the remaining salt. Cover and simmer for 2 to 3 hours until the duckling is tender. Lift the duckling out of the cooking liquid and rub it all over with the sesame seed oil. Keep hot. Boil the cooking liquid until reduced by about half. Baste the duckling with the liquor several times, then cut it into small pieces. Arrange on a serving plate and garnish with parsley. Serve hot.

Stir-Fried Beans with Pork Slices
(top)
Shredded Pork with Eggs (below)

1 × 15 ml spoon/1 tablespoon dry sherry

1 × 5 ml spoon/1 teaspoon sugar

225 g/8 oz runner (green) beans, broken into 4 cm/1½ inch pieces

1 × 5 ml spoon/1 teaspoon salt

stock or water

AMERICAN

¼ cup lard

½ lb pork tenderloin, thinly sliced into bite-size pieces

1 tablespoon soy sauce

1 tablespoon pale dry sherry

1 teaspoon sugar

½ lb string beans, broken into 1½ inch pieces

1 teaspoon salt

stock or water

Melt about half the lard in a pan. Add the pork and stir-fry until it turns pale in colour. Add the soy sauce, sherry and sugar. When the juice starts to bubble, remove the pan from the heat.

Melt the remaining lard in a clean pan. When very hot, add the beans and salt. Stir-fry for 3 to 4 minutes, adding a little stock or water if the mixture becomes dry. Add the pork mixture and stir well. As soon as the juice starts to bubble, transfer to a serving plate and serve hot.

Stir-Fried Green Pepper with Pork

METRIC/IMPERIAL

75 g/3 oz lard

100 g/4 oz pork fillet, shredded

1 × 15 ml spoon/1 tablespoon soy sauce

1 × 5 ml spoon/1 teaspoon sugar

1 × 15 ml spoon/1 tablespoon dry sherry

2 green peppers, cored, seeded and cut into thin strips

1 × 5 ml spoon/1 teaspoon salt

stock or water

AMERICAN

6 tablespoons lard

¼ lb pork tenderloin, shredded

1 tablespoon soy sauce

1 teaspoon sugar

1 tablespoon pale dry sherry

2 green peppers, cored, seeded and cut into thin strips

1 teaspoon salt

stock or water

Melt 25 g/1 oz (2 tablespoons) of the lard in a pan. Add the pork and stir-fry until it turns pale in colour. Add the soy sauce, sugar and sherry. When the juice starts to bubble, remove from the heat.

Melt the remaining lard in a clean pan. Add the green peppers, salt and, if the mixture seems too dry, a little stock or water. Stir-fry for 1 minute. Mix in the cooked pork mixture. When the sauce starts to bubble, transfer to a serving dish and serve hot.

Note: The green pepper should retain its crispness so take care not to overcook.

Stir-Fried Beans with Pork Slices

METRIC/IMPERIAL

50 g/2 oz lard

225 g/8 oz pork fillet, thinly sliced into bite-size pieces

1 × 15 ml spoon/1 tablespoon soy sauce

Shredded Pork with Eggs

METRIC/IMPERIAL

4 eggs

pinch of salt

50 g/2 oz lard

100 g/4 oz pork fillet, shredded

1 × 15 ml spoon/1 tablespoon dry sherry

1 × 15 ml spoon/1 tablespoon soy sauce

4 × 15 ml spoons/4 tablespoons stock

AMERICAN

4 eggs

pinch of salt

¼ cup lard

¼ lb pork tenderloin, shredded

1 tablespoon pale dry sherry

1 tablespoon soy sauce

¼ cup stock

Beat the eggs with the salt. Melt the lard in a pan. Add the pork and stir-fry until lightly browned. Lower the heat, pour the eggs over the pork and stir gently until set. Turn the 'omelet' over and break it into small pieces. Add the sherry, soy sauce and stock and continue cooking for about 2 to 3 minutes. Serve hot as an appetizer.

Pork and Bamboo Shoot Slices

METRIC/IMPERIAL

1 × 2.5 ml spoon/½ teaspoon salt

2 × 5 ml spoons/2 teaspoons cornflour

225 g/8 oz pork fillet, thinly sliced into bite-size pieces

75 g/3 oz lard

2 spring onions (shallots), cut into 2.5 cm/1 inch pieces

1 × 150 g/5 oz can bamboo shoots, drained and thinly sliced

1.5 × 15 ml spoons/1½ tablespoons soy sauce

1 × 15 ml spoon/1 tablespoon dry sherry

1 × 5 ml spoon/1 teaspoon sugar

2 × 5 ml spoons/2 teaspoons stock or water

1 × 5 ml spoon/1 teaspoon sesame seed oil

AMERICAN

½ teaspoon salt

2 teaspoons cornstarch

½ lb pork tenderloin, thinly sliced into bite-size pieces

6 tablespoons lard

2 scallions, cut into 1 inch pieces

1 × 5 oz can bamboo shoots, drained and thinly sliced

1½ tablespoons soy sauce

1 tablespoon pale dry sherry

1 teaspoon sugar

2 teaspoons stock or water

1 teaspoon sesame oil

Mix together the salt and 1 × 5 ml spoon/1 teaspoon of the cornflour (cornstarch) in a bowl. Add the pork pieces and turn to coat thoroughly. Melt about half the lard in a pan. Add the pork and stir-fry, separating all the pieces, until the meat is pale in colour. Remove from the heat.

Melt the remaining lard in a clean pan. When it is very hot, add the spring onions (shallots/scallions) and bamboo shoots and stir-fry for a few seconds, then add the pork together with the soy sauce, sherry and sugar.

Dissolve the remaining cornflour (cornstarch) in the stock or water and add to the pan. Simmer, stirring, until thickened. Add the sesame seed oil just before serving, with rice.

Stir-Fried Green Pepper with Pork (left)
Pork and Bamboo Shoot Slices (right)

Pork Slices with Bamboo Shoots and Wood (Tree) Ears

METRIC/IMPERIAL

225 g/8 oz pork fillet, thinly sliced into bite-size pieces

1 × 2.5 ml spoon/½ teaspoon salt

1 egg white, lightly beaten

2 × 5 ml spoons/2 teaspoons cornflour

50 g/2 oz lard

2 spring onions (shallots), cut into 2.5 cm/1 inch pieces

1 × 150 g/5 oz can bamboo shoots, drained and sliced

25 g/1 oz dried wood ears, soaked for 20 minutes, drained, stemmed and sliced

2 × 15 ml spoons/2 tablespoons soy sauce

1 × 15 ml spoon/1 tablespoon dry sherry

1 × 5 ml spoon/1 teaspoon sugar

2 × 5 ml spoons/2 teaspoons stock or water

1 × 5 ml spoon/1 teaspoon sesame seed oil

AMERICAN

½ lb pork tenderloin, thinly sliced into bite-size pieces

½ teaspoon salt

1 egg white, lightly beaten

2 teaspoons cornstarch

¼ cup lard

2 scallions, cut into 1 inch pieces

1 × 5 oz can bamboo shoots, drained and sliced

1 cup dried tree ears, soaked for 20 minutes, drained, stemmed and sliced

2 tablespoons soy sauce

1 tablespoon pale dry sherry

1 teaspoon sugar

2 teaspoons stock or water

1 teaspoon sesame oil

Sprinkle the pork with the salt, dip into the egg white and then coat with 1 × 5 ml spoon/ 1 teaspoon of the cornflour (cornstarch). Melt about half the lard in a pan. Add the pork and stir-fry until lightly browned. Remove from the pan.

Melt the remaining lard in the pan. Add the spring onions (shallots/scallions), bamboo shoots and mushrooms and stir-fry for 30 seconds. Add the soy sauce, sherry and sugar. Dissolve the remaining cornflour (cornstarch) in the stock or water and add to the pan. Stir-fry for about 1 minute, then add the pork and mix well. When the juices start to bubble, add the sesame seed oil and serve hot.

Soy Pork (left)
Pork Slices with Bamboo Shoots and
Wood (Tree) Ears (centre)
Spareribs in Sweet and Sour Sauce
(right)

Spareribs in Sweet and Sour Sauce

METRIC/IMPERIAL

1×2.5 ml spoon/$\frac{1}{2}$ teaspoon salt

1×15 ml spoon/1 tablespoon dry sherry

1×5 ml spoon/1 teaspoon cornflour

0.5 kg/1 lb pork spareribs, cut into 2.5 cm/1 inch squares

4×15 ml spoons/4 tablespoons oil

Sauce

50 g/2 oz sugar

3×15 ml spoons/3 tablespoons wine vinegar

2×15 ml spoons/2 tablespoons soy sauce

1×5 ml spoon/1 teaspoon cornflour

AMERICAN

$\frac{1}{2}$ teaspoon salt

1 tablespoon pale dry sherry

1 teaspoon cornstarch

1 lb pork spareribs, cut into 1 inch squares

$\frac{1}{4}$ cup oil

Sauce

$\frac{1}{4}$ cup sugar

3 tablespoons wine vinegar

2 tablespoons soy sauce

1 teaspoon cornstarch

Mix together the salt, sherry and cornflour (cornstarch) in a dish. Add the sparerib pieces, toss to coat with the mixture and leave to marinate for about 30 minutes.
Heat the oil in a pan. Add the sparerib pieces and fry over low heat for about 2 minutes. Take out with a slotted spoon and drain. Increase the heat and when the oil is really hot, return the spareribs to the pan and fry for about 30 seconds until golden. Remove with a slotted spoon and drain on absorbent kitchen paper. Keep hot.
There should be enough oil left in the pan to cook the sauce.
Mix together the sauce ingredients and add to the pan. When the sauce is bubbling, mix in the spareribs. Stir well until each piece is coated with the sauce. Serve hot.

Soy Pork

METRIC/IMPERIAL

0.5 kg/1 lb boned, rolled loin of pork

2×15 ml spoons/2 tablespoons sweet soy bean paste or hoisin sauce

3×15 ml spoons/3 tablespoons soy sauce

2×15 ml spoons/2 tablespoons dry sherry

pinch of 5-spice powder

450 ml/$\frac{3}{4}$ pint water

50 g/2 oz crystal or brown sugar

1 round lettuce, shredded

AMERICAN

1 lb boneless pork, loin or butt

2 tablespoons sweet bean sauce or hoisin sauce

3 tablespoons soy sauce

2 tablespoons pale dry sherry

pinch of 5-spice powder

1 pint water

2 oz rock sugar or $\frac{1}{3}$ cup brown sugar

1 head iceberg or Boston lettuce, shredded

Rub the pork with the sweet soy bean paste (sauce) or hoisin sauce. Leave it to marinate for 2 to 3 hours.
Put the soy sauce, sherry, 5-spice powder, pork and water in a large saucepan. Bring to the boil, then cover and simmer for 30 minutes. Add the sugar and continue cooking over low heat for 1 hour, turning the meat occasionally. When the sauce has reduced almost completely, remove the pan from the heat and allow to cool.
To serve, slice the pork and arrange neatly on a dish of shredded lettuce. Pour any remaining sauce over the meat. Serve hot, with hoisin sauce dip if liked.

Stir-Fried Mixed Vegetables

METRIC/IMPERIAL

3.5 × 15 ml spoons/3½ tablespoons vegetable oil

1 onion, thinly sliced

3 cloves garlic, crushed

1.5 × 5 ml spoons/1½ teaspoons salt

½ green pepper, cored, seeded and sliced

½ red pepper, cored, seeded and sliced

¼ cucumber, chopped

2 sticks celery, chopped

2 spring onions (shallots), chopped

3–4 lettuce leaves, chopped

225 g/½ lb bean sprouts

1.5 × 5 ml spoons/1½ teaspoons sugar

2 × 15 ml spoons/2 tablespoons soy sauce

2 × 15 ml spoons/2 tablespoons chicken stock

AMERICAN

3½ tablespoons vegetable oil

1 onion, thinly sliced

3 cloves garlic, minced

1½ teaspoons salt

½ green pepper, cored, seeded and sliced

½ red pepper, cored, seeded and sliced

¼ cucumber, chopped

2 stalks celery, chopped

2 scallions, chopped

3–4 lettuce leaves, chopped

1⅓ cups bean sprouts

1½ teaspoons sugar

2 tablespoons soy sauce

2 tablespoons chicken stock

Heat the oil in a large pan over moderate heat. Add the onion, garlic and salt and stir-fry for 30 seconds. Add all the other vegetables and toss them until well coated. Sprinkle in the sugar, soy sauce and chicken stock. Stir-fry for 1½ minutes. Serve hot.

Tung-Po Pork

METRIC/IMPERIAL

0.5 kg/1 lb belly pork, in one piece

2 × 5 ml spoons/2 teaspoons salt

2 × 15 ml spoons/2 tablespoons dark soy sauce

1 × 15 ml spoon/1 tablespoon dry sherry

2 spring onions (shallots)

2 slices root ginger

2 × 15 ml spoons/2 tablespoons water

AMERICAN

1 lb fresh pork sides, in one piece

2 teaspoons salt

2 tablespoons dark soy sauce

1 tablespoon pale dry sherry

2 scallions

2 slices ginger root

2 tablespoons water

Ask the butcher to trim the meat to a square, then tie it with string like a parcel, so it will retain its shape during cooking. Rub with the salt and let stand for 2 hours. Discard the liquid and wipe the meat dry. Blanch the pork in boiling water 2 or 3 times, using fresh water each time. Place the meat, skin side up, in a large pan. Add the soy sauce, sherry, spring onions (shallots/scallions), ginger and water. Bring to the boil, cover tightly and simmer gently for 2 hours.

Transfer the meat to a heatproof bowl, placing it skin side down. Strain over the cooking juices. Cover the bowl with foil and steam for 4 hours.

To serve, turn the meat out onto a plate with the skin side up, remove and discard string. Pour any remaining juice over it and serve hot. Handle the meat very carefully as it is so tender that it will melt in your mouth.

Steamed Pork with Ground Rice

METRIC/IMPERIAL

1 kg/2 lb belly pork
2 × 15 ml spoons/2 tablespoons dry sherry
3 × 15 ml spoons/3 tablespoons soy sauce
1 × 15 ml spoon/1 tablespoon sugar
1 × 2.5 ml spoon/½ teaspoon 5-spice powder
75 g/3 oz ground rice
1–2 lettuces, separated into leaves

AMERICAN

2 lb fresh pork sides
2 tablespoons pale dry sherry
3 tablespoons soy sauce
1 tablespoon sugar
½ teaspoon 5-spice powder
¾ cup ground rice
1–2 heads lettuce, separated into leaves

Cut the pork, through the skin and fat, into 4 cm/1½ inch squares. Mix together the sherry, soy sauce, sugar and 5-spice powder in a dish. Add the pork and leave to marinate for 30 minutes. Meanwhile, roast the ground rice in a dry pan over a low heat, stirring until lightly browned. Coat each piece of meat with ground rice.

Line the bottom of a steamer with lettuce leaves. Arrange the pork in layers on top and steam vigorously for at least 2 hours.

When ready, the meat should be very tender and aromatic. Serve it hot with the lettuce leaves, which will have absorbed all the pork fat and should taste delicious.

Stir-Fried Mixed Vegetables (left)

Tung-Po Pork (top right)
Steamed Pork with Ground Rice (below right)

Lion's Head

METRIC/IMPERIAL

1 kg/2 lb minced pork

2 spring onions (shallots), finely chopped

2 slices root ginger, finely chopped

2 × 15 ml spoons/2 tablespoons dry sherry

2 × 15 ml spoons/2 tablespoons cornflour

1 × 15 ml spoon/1 tablespoon salt

40 g/1½ oz lard

0.5 kg/1 lb Chinese cabbage, quartered lengthwise

250 ml/8 fl oz chicken stock

AMERICAN

2 lb ground pork butt

2 scallions, finely chopped

2 slices ginger root, finely chopped

2 tablespoons pale dry sherry

2 tablespoons cornstarch

1 tablespoon salt

3 tablespoons lard

1 lb Chinese cabbage (bok choy), quartered lengthwise

1 cup chicken stock

Mix together the pork, spring onions (shallots/scallions), ginger, sherry, cornflour (cornstarch) and half the salt. Shape the mixture into 6 or 8 meatballs.

Melt the lard in a deep pan. Add the cabbage and remaining salt and fry for 30 seconds. Place the meatballs on top of the cabbage and pour the stock over the top. Bring to the boil, then cover tightly and simmer gently for 30 to 45 minutes. Serve hot.

Note: Alternatively the meatballs may be fried in a little lard, with a little soy sauce and sugar added, before placing them on top of the cabbage.

Foochow Pork

METRIC/IMPERIAL

1 kg/2 lb belly pork

2 × 15 ml spoons/2 tablespoons dry sherry

2 × 15 ml spoons/2 tablespoons soy sauce

4 eggs, beaten

225 g/8 oz lard

1 × 15 ml spoon/1 tablespoon sugar

1 × 2.5 ml spoon/½ teaspoon 5-spice powder

1 lettuce, separated into leaves

1 × 15 ml spoon/1 tablespoon sesame seed oil

pepper ring and parsley sprigs to garnish

AMERICAN

2 lb fresh pork sides

2 tablespoons pale dry sherry

2 tablespoons soy sauce

4 eggs, beaten

1 cup lard

1 tablespoon sugar

½ teaspoon 5-spice powder

1 head lettuce, separated into leaves

1 tablespoon sesame oil

pepper ring and parsley sprigs to garnish

Cut the pork, through the skin and fat, into 4 cm/1½ inch squares. Place in a bowl with the sherry and soy sauce and leave to marinate for 10 minutes. Drain, reserving the marinade. Mix the pork with the beaten eggs.

Melt the lard in a deep pan. Add the pork mixture and fry until golden. Lift out with a perforated spoon and place in a large heat-proof bowl. Pour over the marinade together with the sugar and 5-spice powder. Mix well, then place in a steamer; steam for 1 hour. Place on a bed of lettuce and sprinkle with the sesame seed oil. Top with the garnish.

Lion's Head (below left)
Red-Cooked Lamb (above centre)
Foochow Pork (below centre)
Fried Lamb Slices with Onions (top right)

Fried Lamb Slices with Onions

METRIC/IMPERIAL

225 g/8 oz lean boned lamb, thinly sliced

1 × 2.5 ml spoon/½ teaspoon salt

1 × 5 ml spoon/1 teaspoon cornflour

4 × 15 ml spoons/4 tablespoons oil

225 g/8 oz onions, sliced

2 garlic cloves, crushed

2 × 15 ml spoons/2 tablespoons soy sauce

1 × 15 ml spoon/1 tablespoon dry sherry

pinch of monosodium glutamate (optional)

1 × 5 ml spoon/1 teaspoon sesame seed oil (optional)

cucumber and cherries to garnish

AMERICAN

½ lb lean boneless lamb, thinly sliced

½ teaspoon salt

1 teaspoon cornstarch

¼ cup oil

2 onions, sliced

2 garlic cloves, minced

2 tablespoons soy sauce

1 tablespoon pale dry sherry

pinch of msg (optional)

1 teaspoon sesame oil (optional)

cucumber and cherries to garnish

Mix the lamb slices with the salt and cornflour (cornstarch). Heat the oil in a pan. When it is very hot, add the lamb and stir-fry until lightly browned. Remove lamb from the pan with a slotted spoon.

Add the onions and garlic to the pan and fry until just tender. Return the lamb to the pan with the soy sauce, sherry and monosodium glutamate (msg), if using. Stir well. Add the sesame seed oil, if using, just before serving. Garnish with cucumber, cut to form a fan shape, and cherries.

Red-Cooked Lamb

METRIC/IMPERIAL

1 kg/2 lb stewing lamb

4 × 15 ml spoons/4 tablespoons dry sherry

4 slices root ginger

2 garlic cloves, crushed

1 × 2.5 ml spoon/½ teaspoon 5-spice powder

stock or water

4 × 15 ml spoons/4 tablespoons soy sauce

1 × 15 ml spoon/1 tablespoon sugar

AMERICAN

2 lb stewing lamb

¼ cup pale dry sherry

4 slices ginger root

2 garlic cloves, minced

½ teaspoon 5-spice powder

stock or water

¼ cup soy sauce

1 tablespoon sugar

Blanch the lamb in boiling water for 3 minutes. Drain and cut into small cubes. Put the lamb in a large pan and add the sherry, ginger, garlic and 5-spice powder. Cook, stirring, for 2 minutes, then add enough stock or water to just cover the meat. Bring to the boil and simmer for about 1 hour.

Add the soy sauce and sugar and continue cooking for 20 to 30 minutes, or until the sauce is reduced almost to nothing. Serve hot.

125

Fried Green Tomatoes with Eggs

METRIC/IMPERIAL

3 eggs

2 × 5 ml spoons/2 teaspoons salt

1 × 15 ml spoon/1 tablespoon dry sherry

3 × 15 ml spoons/3 tablespoons oil

0.5 kg/1 lb green tomatoes, skinned and sliced

3 × 15 ml spoons/3 tablespoons stock

AMERICAN

3 eggs

2 teaspoons salt

1 tablespoon pale dry sherry

3 tablespoons oil

1 lb green tomatoes, skinned and sliced

3 tablespoons stock

Beat the eggs with 1 × 2.5 ml spoon/½ teaspoon of the salt and the sherry in a bowl. Heat the oil in a pan. Add the tomatoes and fry for 1 to 2 minutes. Add the remaining salt, stir-fry for a few seconds, then pour the eggs over the tomatoes. When the 'omelet' begins to set, turn it over and add the stock. Cook for a further 1 to 2 minutes, then serve hot.

Pork with Bean Curd

Pork with Bean Curd

METRIC/IMPERIAL

1 kg/2 lb lean pork, diced

900 ml/1½ pints water

1 × 15 ml spoon/1 tablespoon dry sherry

1 × 5 ml spoon/1 teaspoon brown sugar

1 × 5 ml spoon/1 teaspoon salt

4 × 15 ml spoons/4 tablespoons soy sauce

2 × 15 ml spoons/2 tablespoons oil

3 cakes bean curd, cut into 5 cm/2 inch squares

1 spring onion (shallot), chopped

parsley to garnish

AMERICAN

2 lb pork tenderloin, diced

3¾ cups water

1 tablespoon pale dry sherry

1 teaspoon brown sugar

1 teaspoon salt

¼ cup soy sauce

2 tablespoons oil

3 cakes bean curd, cut into 2 inch squares

1 scallion, chopped

parsley to garnish

Place the pork in a large pan with two-thirds of the water. Bring to the boil, skim any scum from the surface, cover and simmer for 1 hour. Add the sherry, sugar, salt and half the soy sauce. Cover and cook for a further 30 minutes.

Heat the oil in another pan and fry the bean curd for 2 to 3 minutes, turning it once during cooking. Add the remaining soy sauce and water and the spring onion (shallot/scallion). Stir well and cook for 10 minutes, stirring occasionally. Mix the bean curd mixture into the pork and turn into a dish. Serve hot, garnished with parsley.

Ham with Lotus Seeds in Honey Sauce

METRIC/IMPERIAL

1 × 5 cm/2 inch thick slice of ham (about 1–1.25 kg/2–2½ lb)

3 × 15 ml spoons/3 tablespoons brown sugar

pinch of ground cinnamon

6 × 15 ml spoons/6 tablespoons water

100 g/4 oz lotus seeds or peanuts

Honey sauce

3 × 15 ml spoons/3 tablespoons clear honey

1.5 × 15 ml spoons/1½ tablespoons sugar

2 × 5 ml spoons/2 teaspoons cornflour

3 × 15 ml spoons/3 tablespoons water

AMERICAN

1 × 2 inch thick slice of Smithfield ham (about 2–2½ lb)

3 tablespoons brown sugar

pinch of ground cinnamon

6 tablespoons water

1⅔ cups lotus seeds or peanuts

Honey sauce

3 tablespoons clear honey

1½ tablespoons sugar

2 teaspoons cornstarch

3 tablespoons water

Place the ham on a heatproof dish. Put into a steamer and steam steadily for 1 hour. Cut the ham into 8 pieces, then reassemble them into the original shape.

Heat the brown sugar, cinnamon and water in a pan until the sugar is dissolved. Add the lotus seeds or peanuts and cook, stirring, for 2 minutes.

Spoon the mixture over the ham. Return the dish to the steamer and steam steadily for a further 1½ hours.

Place the ingredients for the honey sauce in a saucepan and cook, stirring continuously, until thickened. Pour over the lotus seeds. The ham should be tender enough to be broken into small bite-size pieces with chopsticks. Serve hot.

Ham with Lotus Seeds in Honey Sauce (right)

Braised Chicken with Leeks

METRIC/IMPERIAL

1 × 1.25 kg/2½ lb chicken, cut into pieces

3 × 15 ml spoons/3 tablespoons soy sauce

2 × 15 ml spoons/2 tablespoons dry sherry

225 g/8 oz leeks

50 g/2 oz lard

2–3 spring onions (shallots), finely chopped

3 slices root ginger, finely chopped

1 × 15 ml spoon/1 tablespoon sugar

2 × 5 ml spoons/2 teaspoons salt

120 ml/4 fl oz chicken stock

1 × 15 ml spoon/1 tablespoon cornflour, dissolved in 1.5 × 15 ml spoons/1½ tablespoons water

1 × 5 ml spoon/1 teaspoon sesame seed oil

AMERICAN

1 × 2½ lb chicken, cut into pieces

3 tablespoons soy sauce

2 tablespoons pale dry sherry

½ lb leeks

¼ cup lard

2–3 scallions, finely chopped

3 slices ginger root, finely chopped

1 tablespoon sugar

2 teaspoons salt

½ cup chicken stock

1 tablespoon cornstarch, dissolved in 1½ tablespoons water

1 teaspoon sesame oil

Sprinkle the chicken pieces with the soy sauce and sherry and leave to marinate for 30 minutes. Cut the leeks into diamond-shape pieces by rolling each leek half a turn every time you make a diagonal cut through.
Melt the lard in a pan. Add the chicken pieces and fry for about 1 minute. Remove from the pan with a slotted spoon. Add the spring onions (shallots/scallions) and ginger to the pan and stir-fry for 1 minute. Add the leeks, chicken pieces, sugar, salt and stock and cook together for 6 to 8 minutes over high heat, stirring constantly. Add the cornflour (cornstarch) mixture and cook, stirring, until thickened. Add the sesame seed oil and serve hot.

Braised Bamboo Shoots

METRIC/IMPERIAL

3 × 15 ml spoons/3 tablespoons oil

1 × 400 g/14 oz can bamboo shoots, drained and sliced into thin strips

1 × 15 ml spoon/1 tablespoon dry sherry

2 × 15 ml spoons/2 tablespoons soy sauce

1 × 15 ml spoon/1 tablespoon sugar

3 × 15 ml spoons/3 tablespoons boiling water

1 × 15 ml spoon/1 tablespoon sesame seed oil

AMERICAN

3 tablespoons oil

1 × 14 oz can bamboo shoots, drained and sliced into thin strips (about 4 cups)

1 tablespoon pale dry sherry

2 tablespoons soy sauce

1 tablespoon sugar

3 tablespoons boiling water

1 tablespoon sesame oil

Heat the oil in a pan. Add the bamboo shoots and stir-fry until golden. Add the sherry, soy sauce and sugar, stirring continuously. Add the boiling water and simmer for 7 to 8 minutes or until all the liquid has evaporated. Add the sesame seed oil, mix well and serve hot.
This dish can also be served cold as part of an hors d'oeuvres.

Sweet and Sour Cucumber

METRIC/IMPERIAL

1 cucumber

salt

2 × 15 ml spoons/2 tablespoons sugar

3 × 15 ml spoons/3 tablespoons wine vinegar

1 slice root ginger, finely chopped

1 × 15 ml spoon/1 tablespoon sesame seed oil

AMERICAN

1 cucumber

salt

2 tablespoons sugar

3 tablespoons wine vinegar

1 slice ginger root, finely chopped

1 tablespoon sesame oil

Split the cucumber in half lengthwise, then cut it crosswise into thin slices. Sprinkle with salt and leave for about 10 minutes. Meanwhile, dissolve the sugar in the vinegar.
Drain the cucumber and arrange on a serving plate. Top with ginger. Pour the sugar and vinegar mixture and the sesame seed oil over just before serving.

Celery Salad

METRIC/IMPERIAL

1 head celery

Salad dressing

pinch of salt

2 × 15 ml spoons/2 tablespoons soy sauce

1 × 15 ml spoon/1 tablespoon sugar

1 × 15 ml spoon/1 tablespoon sesame seed oil

AMERICAN

1 bunch celery

Salad dressing

pinch of salt

2 tablespoons soy sauce

1 tablespoon sugar

1 tablespoon sesame oil

Discard the root and leaves of the celery and cut into small diamond-shaped pieces by rolling each stalk half a turn every time you make a diagonal cut through.

Blanch the celery in boiling water for 1 minute. Drain and place on a plate. Mix the salad dressing ingredients together then pour over the celery. Chill before serving.

Braised Chicken with Leeks (left)
Braised Bamboo Shoots (centre)
Sweet and Sour Cucumber (right)
Celery Salad (top right)

Kidneys with Spring Onions (Scallions) and Cauliflower

METRIC/IMPERIAL

4 lambs' kidneys, halved and cored

2 × 15 ml spoons/2 tablespoons sherry

1 small cauliflower, broken into florets

salt

2 × 15 ml spoons/2 tablespoons oil

4 spring onions (shallots), cut into 2.5 cm/ 1 inch pieces

1 × 15 ml spoon/1 tablespoon cornflour

1 × 15 ml spoon/1 tablespoon soy sauce

2 × 15 ml spoons/2 tablespoons water

1 × 5 ml spoon/1 teaspoon brown sugar

AMERICAN

4 lamb kidneys, halved and cored

2 tablespoons pale dry sherry

1 small cauliflower, broken into florets

salt

2 tablespoons oil

4 scallions, cut into 1 inch pieces

1 tablespoon cornstarch

1 tablespoon soy sauce

2 tablespoons water

1 teaspoon brown sugar

Score the kidney halves with shallow criss-cross cuts, about 1 cm/½ inch apart. Marinate in the sherry for 10 minutes. Drain, reserving the marinade. Cook the cauliflower in boiling salted water for 3 minutes. Drain thoroughly.

Kidneys with Spring Onions (Scallions) and Cauliflower (above)

Heat the oil in a pan. Add the kidneys, spring onions (shallots/scallions) and cauliflower and fry for 2 minutes. Mix the cornflour (cornstarch) with the soy sauce, water, sugar, reserved marinade and 1 × 5 ml spoon/1 teaspoon salt. Add to the pan and cook gently for 3 minutes, stirring until the sauce is thickened. Serve hot.

Chinese Cabbage Salad

METRIC IMPERIAL

225 g/8 oz Chinese cabbage or hard white cabbage, cored and cut into strips

Salad dressing

2 × 15 ml spoons/2 tablespoons soy sauce

pinch of salt

1 × 15 ml spoon/1 tablespoon sugar

1 × 15 ml spoon/1 tablespoon sesame seed oil

AMERICAN

½ lb Chinese cabbage (bok choy) or hard white cabbage, cored and cut into strips

Salad dressing

2 tablespoons soy sauce

pinch of salt

1 tablespoon sugar

1 tablespoon sesame oil

Blanch the cabbage in boiling water for 2 to 3 minutes. Drain and place in a large bowl. Mix together the ingredients for the salad dressing. Pour over the cabbage and toss well. Serve either hot or cold.

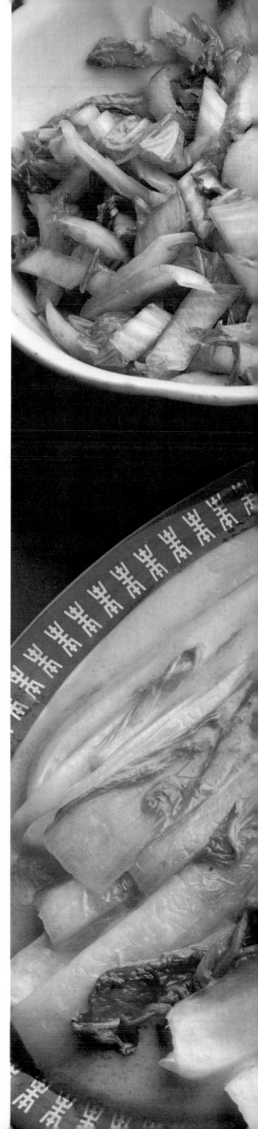

Chinese Cabbage in Cream Sauce

METRIC/IMPERIAL

0.5 kg/1 lb Chinese cabbage

5 × 15 ml spoons/5 tablespoons oil

2 × 5 ml spoons/2 teaspoons salt

1 × 5 ml spoon/1 teaspoon sugar

250 ml/8 fl oz stock or water

1 × 15 ml spoon/1 tablespoon cornflour, dissolved in 1.5 × 15 ml spoons/ 1½ tablespoons water

4 × 15 ml spoons/4 tablespoons milk

freshly ground black pepper

AMERICAN

1 lb Chinese cabbage (bok choy)

5 tablespoons oil

2 teaspoons salt

1 teaspoon sugar

1 cup stock or water

1 tablespoon cornstarch, dissolved in 1½ tablespoons water

¼ cup milk

freshly ground black pepper

Separate the cabbage into leaves, and cut each leaf in half lengthwise then crosswise. Heat 4 × 15 ml spoons/4 tablespoons of the oil in a pan. When very hot, add the cabbage and stir-fry for about 3 minutes. Add the salt and sugar and mix well. When the cabbage is just tender, remove from the heat and set to one side.

Heat the remaining oil in a clean pan. Add the stock or water and bring to the boil. Add the cornflour (cornstarch) mixture and milk and cook, stirring, for about 1 minute until thickened.

Pour half of this sauce into a jug. Add the cooked cabbage to the remaining sauce in the pan and heat thoroughly. Place the cabbage on a serving plate and pour the sauce from the jug over it. Taste and correct the seasoning if necessary, adding pepper to taste. Serve hot.

Chinese Cabbage Salad (above)
Chinese Cabbage in Cream Sauce (below)

Chicken and Noodle Soup

METRIC/IMPERIAL

pinch of salt

1 egg white

1 × 5 ml spoon/1 teaspoon cornflour

225 g/8 oz chicken breast meat, shredded

350 g/12 oz fresh egg noodles

1.2 litres/2 pints chicken stock

40 g/1½ oz lard

100 g/4 oz canned bamboo shoots, drained and shredded

50 g/2 oz mushrooms, shredded

225 g/8 oz spinach

2–3 spring onions (shallots), cut into 2.5 cm/1 inch pieces

Sauce

3 × 15 ml spoons/3 tablespoons soy sauce

1 × 15 ml spoon/1 tablespoon dry sherry

1 × 5 ml spoon/1 teaspoon salt

1 × 5 ml spoon/1 teaspoon sugar

1 × 5 ml spoon/1 teaspoon sesame seed oil

AMERICAN

pinch of salt

1 egg white

1 teaspoon cornstarch

½ lb chicken breast meat, shredded

¾ lb fresh egg noodles

2½ pints chicken stock

3 tablespoons lard

Bean Curd and Spinach Soup

METRIC/IMPERIAL

1 cake bean curd

750 ml/1¾ pints stock or clear broth (see page 15)

100 g/4 oz spinach

2 × 5 ml spoons/2 teaspoons salt

1 × 2.5 ml spoon/½ teaspoon monosodium glutamate

AMERICAN

1 cake bean curd

4¼ cups stock or clear broth (see page 15)

¼ lb spinach

2 teaspoons salt

½ teaspoon msg

Cut the bean curd into 12 small slices about 5 mm/¼ inch thick. Bring the stock or broth to the boil in a saucepan. Add the spinach and bean curd and simmer for 2 minutes. Skim the soup to make it clear, then pour it over the salt and monosodium glutamate (msg) in a large serving bowl. Stir and serve hot.

Pork Spareribs Soup (left)
Bean Curd and Spinach Soup (centre)
Chicken and Noodle Soup (right)

---

1 cup shredded canned bamboo shoots

½ cup shredded mushrooms

½ lb spinach

2-3 scallions, cut into 1 inch pieces

Sauce

3 tablespoons soy sauce

1 tablespoon pale dry sherry

1 teaspoon salt

1 teaspoon sugar

1 teaspoon sesame oil

Mix together the salt, egg white and corn-flour (cornstarch) in a bowl. Add the chicken and turn to coat thoroughly.

Cook the noodles in boiling water for about 5 minutes or until tender. Drain and place in a large serving bowl. Bring the chicken stock to the boil and pour over the noodles. Keep hot.

Melt the lard in a pan. Add the chicken, bamboo shoots, mushrooms, spinach and spring onions (shallots/scallions) and stir-fry for 2 minutes. Combine the sauce ingredients and stir into the pan. When the liquid starts to bubble, pour over the noodles and stock mixture and serve.

Pork Spareribs Soup

METRIC/IMPERIAL

50 g/2 oz lard

0.5 kg/1 lb pork spareribs, cut into 2.5 cm/ 1 inch squares

2 × 5 ml spoons/2 teaspoons salt

4 slices root ginger

1.5 litres/2½ pints water

2 spring onions (shallots), chopped

pinch of monosodium glutamate

AMERICAN

¼ cup lard

1 lb pork spareribs, cut into 1 inch squares

2 teaspoons salt

4 slices ginger root

6¼ cups water

2 scallions, chopped

pinch of msg

Melt the lard in a large pan. Add the spareribs and fry for about 10 minutes. Add the salt, ginger and water and bring to the boil. Simmer for 2 hours.

Add the spring onions (shallots/scallions) and monosodium glutamate (msg) and stir-fry for 2 to 3 minutes before serving.

Prawn (Shrimp) Noodles

METRIC/IMPERIAL

1 × 5 ml spoon/1 teaspoon cornflour

1 egg white

100 g/4 oz shelled prawns

350 g/12 oz fresh egg noodles

salt

40 g/1½ oz lard

2–3 spring onions (shallots), cut into 2.5 cm/
1 inch pieces

2 × 15 ml spoons/2 tablespoons soy sauce

1 × 15 ml spoon/1 tablespoon dry sherry

1 × 5 ml spoon/1 teaspoon sugar

1 × 5 ml spoon/1 teaspoon sesame seed oil

AMERICAN

1 teaspoon cornstarch

1 egg white

¼ lb shelled shrimp

¾ lb fresh egg noodles

salt

3 tablespoons lard

2-3 scallions, cut into 1 inch pieces

2 tablespoons soy sauce

1 tablespoon pale dry sherry

1 teaspoon sugar

1 teaspoon sesame oil

Mix the cornflour (cornstarch) with the egg white in a bowl. Add the prawns (shrimp) and toss to coat well. Cook the noodles in boiling salted water for about 5 minutes. Drain and rinse under cold running water. Melt the lard in a pan. Add the spring onions (shallots/scallions) and prawns (shrimp) and stir-fry for 1 minute. Add the soy sauce, sherry and sugar and stir well. Add the noodles and mix well. Continue cooking for 2 to 3 minutes, then add the sesame seed oil just before serving.

Golden Braised Fish

METRIC/IMPERIAL

1 × 1 kg/2 lb whole fish (bream or bass)

salt

flour for coating

2 × 15 ml spoons/2 tablespoons oil

4 dried Chinese mushrooms, soaked for 20 minutes, drained, stemmed and shredded

4 spring onions (shallots), cut into 1 cm/
½ inch pieces

1 × 5 ml spoon/1 teaspoon very finely chopped root ginger

300 ml/½ pint fish stock or water

2 × 15 ml spoons/2 tablespoons soy sauce

1 × 15 ml spoon/1 tablespoon dry sherry

6 water chestnuts, sliced

2 garlic cloves, crushed

1 whole star anise

1 × 5 ml spoon/1 teaspoon sugar

spring onions (shallots) to garnish

AMERICAN

1 × 2 lb whole fish (bass or red snapper)

salt

flour for coating

2 tablespoons oil

4 dried Chinese mushrooms, soaked for 20 minutes, drained, stemmed and shredded

4 scallions, cut into ½ inch pieces

1 teaspoon very finely chopped ginger root

1¼ cups fish stock or water

2 tablespoons soy sauce

1 tablespoon pale dry sherry

6 water chestnuts, sliced

2 garlic cloves, minced

1 whole star anise

1 teaspoon sugar

scallions to garnish

Clean the fish, leaving on the head and tail. Make two diagonal slits on each side, in the

Fried Rice with Ham and Bean Sprouts

METRIC/IMPERIAL

2 × 15 ml spoons/2 tablespoons vegetable oil

2 spring onions (shallots), finely chopped

1 garlic clove, crushed

350 g/12 oz cooked long-grain rice, well-drained

175 g/6 oz cooked ham, diced

2 × 15 ml spoons/2 tablespoons soy sauce

2 eggs

salt

freshly ground black pepper

225 g/8 oz fresh or canned bean sprouts, drained

Golden Braised Fish (above)
Fried Rice with Ham and Bean Sprouts (below)

AMERICAN

2 tablespoons vegetable oil

2 scallions, finely chopped

1 garlic clove, minced

4 cups cooked long-grain rice, well-drained

¾ cup diced cooked ham

2 tablespoons soy sauce

2 eggs

salt

freshly ground black pepper

½ lb fresh or canned bean sprouts, drained

Heat the oil in a pan. Add the spring onions (shallots/scallions) and garlic and stir-fry for 2 minutes. Add the rice and stir well. Cook gently, turning, until heated through.

Stir in the ham and soy sauce. Beat the eggs with salt and pepper to taste. Pour into the rice mixture in a thin stream, stirring all the time. Add the bean sprouts and continue cooking, stirring, until all the ingredients are hot and the eggs are set. Serve immediately.

thickest part of the body. Sprinkle fish with salt and coat with flour.

Heat the oil in a pan. Add the fish and fry on both sides until golden. Pour off excess oil and add the mushrooms to the pan with the spring onions (shallots/scallions), ginger, stock or water, soy sauce, sherry, 1 × 5 ml spoon/1 teaspoon salt, the water chestnuts, garlic, star anise and sugar. Bring to the boil, cover and simmer for about 30 minutes, turning the fish once during cooking.

Transfer the fish to a large serving platter. Decorate with spring onions (shallots/scallions) and pour the sauce over before serving.

135

Steamed Dumplings (Buns) with Meat and Vegetable Filling

METRIC/IMPERIAL

Pastry

1.5 × 15 ml spoons/1½ tablespoons dried yeast

2.5 × 5 ml spoons/2½ teaspoons sugar

3 × 15 ml spoons/3 tablespoons lukewarm water

0.5 kg/1 lb plain flour

300 ml/½ pint lukewarm milk

Filling

0.5 kg/1 lb pork fillet, diced

2–3 spring onions (shallots), finely chopped

3 × 15 ml spoons/3 tablespoons soy sauce

1 × 15 ml spoon/1 tablespoon sesame seed oil

0.5 kg/1 lb cabbage, cored and finely chopped

1 × 5 ml spoon/1 teaspoon salt

AMERICAN

Pastry

1½ packages active dry yeast

2½ teaspoons sugar

3 tablespoons lukewarm water

4 cups all-purpose flour

1¼ cups lukewarm milk

Filling

1 lb pork tenderloin, diced

2-3 scallions, finely chopped

3 tablespoons soy sauce

1 tablespoon sesame oil

1 lb cabbage, cored and finely chopped

1 teaspoon salt

Dissolve the yeast and sugar in the water. Leave in a warm place for 15 minutes until frothy. Sift the flour into a mixing bowl. Gradually pour in the yeast mixture and milk and mix to a smooth, firm dough.

Put the dough on a lightly floured surface and knead well for 10 minutes. Leave in a warm place for 1½ to 2 hours, or until the dough has doubled in bulk.

Meanwhile, prepare the filling. Mix together the pork, spring onions (shallots/scallions), soy sauce and sesame seed oil. Mix the cabbage with the salt and leave for 5 minutes, then squeeze dry, discarding the salty water. Add the cabbage to the pork and mix well.

Knead the dough for about 5 minutes, then form into a long sausage shape, 5 cm/2 inches in diameter. Slice the roll into about twenty-four 2.5 cm/1 inch thick rounds. Flatten each round with the palm of the hand, then with a rolling pin, roll out each piece until it is 10 cm/4 inches in diameter.

Place 2 × 15 ml spoons/2 tablespoons of the pork filling in the centre of each round. Gather the sides over the filling to meet at the top, then twist the top to close tightly. Let the dumplings rest for 20 to 30 minutes.

Place the dumplings on a damp cloth on the bottom of a steamer, leaving 2.5 cm/1 inch space between each. Steam vigorously for 20 minutes. Serve hot.

Chestnuts in Syrup (left)
Steamed Dumplings (Buns) with Meat and Vegetable Filling (right)

Peas Pudding

METRIC/IMPERIAL

225 g/8 oz dried peas, soaked overnight in 1.2 litres/2 pints water

75 g/3 oz sugar

2 × 15 ml spoons/2 tablespoons cornflour

AMERICAN

1⅛ cups dried peas, soaked overnight in 2½ pints water

6 tablespoons sugar

2 tablespoons cornstarch

Put the peas and their soaking water in a saucepan and bring to the boil. Simmer for 2½ hours or until soft. Press the peas with any remaining cooking liquid through a fine sieve or purée in an electric blender. Return to the pan and add the sugar and cornflour (cornstarch). Mix well.

Over a low heat, bring the mixture back to the boil, stirring continuously. Continue cooking for 15 minutes or until the mixture is quite thick. Pour into a shallow pan so that the pea mixture is about 2.5 cm/1 inch deep. Chill until set, then cut into 2.5 cm/1 inch squares to serve.

Chestnuts in Syrup

METRIC/IMPERIAL

225 g/8 oz chestnuts, shelled and skinned

1.2 litres/2 pints water

100 g/4 oz crystal sugar

AMERICAN

½ lb chestnuts, shelled and skinned

2½ pints water

½ cup rock sugar

Put the chestnuts and water in a saucepan and bring to the boil. Skim off any particles floating on the surface. Add the sugar and simmer for 20 minutes, stirring occasionally. Serve hot or cold.

Western China
Szechuan and Yunnan

Mary Ma Stavonhagen

Szechuan, in the west of China, is a great mountain-ringed basin. Because of its rich fertile soil and mild climate, Szechuan has always been one of the most prosperous regions of China and its hearty and flavoursome food is well known in the West. The source of its appeal lies in the way in which spices and herbs are used liberally, yet in perfect proportion, to attain a perfect blend of flavours. Hot spicy food is certainly popular and chilli peppers are a characteristic ingredient of the Szechuan cuisine. Perhaps it was the Chinese who migrated from the arid north and central plains who felt a need for such food to encourage a sweat and so to counteract the *chang chi* (jungle dampness) of the Szechuan summer.

Food preservation techniques, including salting, drying, smoking, pickling and spicing with chilli, are commonly used in Western China. Yunnan, to the south of Szechuan, is famous for its cured, smoked raw ham which imparts a highly distinctive flavour to dishes. Szechuan hot pickle is another popular ingredient in this part of China.

There are traditionally seven flavours and eight methods of preparation associated with Szechuan cooking. The flavours, which are imparted to food during the cooking process or by means of an accompanying sauce, are as follows:

Sweet, or *tien*, from sugar or honey
Salty, or *xien*, from soy sauce or salt
Sour, or *suan*, from vinegar
Bitter, or *ku*, from spring onion (shallot/scallion) or leek
Fragrant, or *xiang*, from garlic or ginger
Sesame/nutty, or *ma*, from sesame seed oil or seeds
Hot/chilli, or *la*, from red chilli peppers.

The eight methods of preparation are:

Hang-you: This is a sauce made from chilli oil, sugar, spring onion (shallot/scallion), ginger, garlic, sesame seed paste and soy sauce, and is poured over a dish just before serving.

Tiao-ma: Szechuan peppercorns and sesame seed paste dominate this sauce, which also includes soy sauce, ginger, sugar and spring onion (shallot/scallion). Szechuan peppercorns make the sauce aromatic and slightly tart. It is poured over a cooked dish before serving.

Ma-la: This sauce is peppery and hot because it contains Szechuan peppercorns and red chilli peppers. Ginger, spring onion (shallot/scallion), soy sauce and sugar are the other ingredients, and this sauce will permeate foods so they become light brown in colour.

Guai-wei: This sauce incorporates sweet, sour, hot and spicy flavours, in such a way that they are perfectly blended and no single flavour predominates. It is made from Szechuan peppercorns, sesame seed oil, sesame seed paste, garlic, spring onion (shallot/scallion), vinegar, sugar, chilli oil and soy sauce.

Tiang-zu: This sauce consists of root ginger, either grated or chopped, mixed with soy sauce, vinegar and sesame seed oil; it is eaten cold.

Gan-chao: In this 'Dry-frying', food is fried with a little oil over a high heat with no additional liquid. The food is cooked for longer than the normal stir-frying time and is therefore well-cooked, often crispy and deeply coloured.

Gan-shao: In this method, meat or vegetables are cooked in clear broth, with wine and spices added, until the liquid has reduced to a thick sauce with a rich flavour. Dishes cooked by the *Gan-shao* method are usually not too hot or spicy.

Yu-xiang: Dishes cooked in this way are either spicy or sweet and sour. The food is first stir-fried or deep-fried, then cooked with liberal quantities of chopped garlic, ginger, hot soy bean paste (sauce) and spices, giving a deep reddish-brown colour.

Many of the dishes from Western China are now well known in other parts of the world. The most characteristic Szechuan dishes have plenty of zest, mainly due to the use of chilli peppers, hot pepper oil, and Szechuan peppercorns. These peppercorns, which can now be found in most Chinese foodstores, are a piquant spice with a delayed reaction. Use them with caution!

Pork and Cucumber Soup

This is a strong-tasting soup, as the Szechuan pickle (kohlrabi) makes it rather 'hot' and salty.

METRIC/IMPERIAL

pinch of salt

1 egg white

1 × 5 ml spoon/1 teaspoon cornflour

225 g/8 oz pork fillet, thinly sliced and cut into bite-sized pieces

1.2 litres/2 pints water

75 g/3 oz Szechuan hot pickles, cut into bite-sized pieces (optional)

100 g/4 oz cucumber, peeled and sliced

AMERICAN

pinch of salt

1 egg white

1 teaspoon cornstarch

½ lb pork tenderloin, thinly sliced and cut into bite-sized pieces

5 cups water

½ cup chopped Szechuan kohlrabi (optional)

1 cup peeled and sliced cucumber

Mix together the salt, egg white and cornflour (cornstarch). Add the pork and leave to marinate for 10 minutes.
Bring the water to the boil. Add the pork and when the water returns to the boil, add the Szechuan pickle (kohlrabi), if used, and cucumber. Simmer for about 5 minutes. Check the seasoning. Serve hot.

Deep-Fried Spiced Fish

METRIC/IMPERIAL

0.75 kg/1½ lb whole fish (sole, cod, halibut, snapper, bream, etc), cleaned and scaled

1 × 5 ml spoon/1 teaspoon grated root ginger

3 spring onions (shallots), chopped

2 × 5 ml spoons/2 teaspoons salt

2 × 15 ml spoons/2 tablespoons dry sherry

oil for deep frying

1 × 5 ml spoon/1 teaspoon ground Szechuan or black peppercorns

2 × 15 ml spoons/2 tablespoons sesame seed oil

lemon slices to garnish

AMERICAN

1½ lb whole fish (sole, cod, halibut), cleaned and scaled

1 teaspoon minced ginger root

3 scallions, chopped

2 teaspoons salt

2 tablespoons pale dry sherry

oil for deep frying

1 teaspoon ground Szechuan or black peppercorns

2 tablespoons sesame oil

lemon slices to garnish

Score the fish by making diagonal slashes on each side. Place the ginger, spring onions (shallots/scallions), 1 × 5 ml spoon/1 teaspoon of the salt and the sherry in a dish and add the fish. Leave to marinate for 30 minutes.

Heat the oil to 180°C/350°F. Deep-fry the fish until golden brown. Drain on absorbent kitchen paper and place on a dish. Sprinkle with the ground peppercorns and the remaining salt. Heat the sesame seed oil and pour over the fish. Serve hot, garnished with the lemon slices.

Sautéed Prawns (Shrimp) with Pepper Sauce

METRIC/IMPERIAL

1 × 2.5 ml spoon/½ teaspoon salt

2 × 5 ml spoons/2 teaspoons dry sherry

1 egg white

1 × 15 ml spoon/1 tablespoon cornflour

0.5 kg/1 lb Pacific or Dublin Bay prawns, shelled, deveined and cut into 2.5 cm/1 inch pieces

5 × 15 ml spoons/5 tablespoons oil

1 × 2.5 ml spoon/½ teaspoon crushed garlic

3 spring onions (shallots), cut into 2.5 cm/1 inch pieces

1 × 15 ml spoon/1 tablespoon soy sauce

1 × 5 ml spoon/1 teaspoon sugar

1 × 15 ml spoon/1 tablespoon red wine vinegar

dash of Tabasco sauce

AMERICAN

½ teaspoon salt

2 teaspoons pale dry sherry

1 egg white

1 tablespoon cornstarch

1 lb jumbo shrimp, shelled, deveined and cut into 1 inch pieces

5 tablespoons oil

½ teaspoon minced garlic

3 scallions, cut into 1 inch pieces

1 tablespoon soy sauce

1 teaspoon sugar

1 tablespoon red wine vinegar

dash of Tabasco sauce

Mix together the salt, sherry, egg white and cornflour (cornstarch). Add the prawns (shrimp) and toss to coat with the batter. Heat the oil in a pan. Add the garlic, prawns (shrimp) and spring onions (shallots/scallions) and stir-fry for 2 minutes.
Add the remaining ingredients and stir well. Serve hot.

Pork and Cucumber Soup (left)

Sautéed Prawns (Shrimp) with Pepper Sauce (top right)
Deep-Fried Spiced Fish (bottom right)

Stir-Fried Chicken with Green Peppers and Chillies

METRIC/IMPERIAL

1 × 15 ml spoon/1 tablespoon dry sherry

2 × 15 ml spoons/2 tablespoons soy sauce

1 small egg white

2 × 15 ml spoons/2 tablespoons cornflour

0.5 kg/1 lb chicken meat, cut into 2.5 cm/
1 inch cubes

1 × 15 ml spoon/1 tablespoon red wine
vinegar

1 × 5 ml spoon/1 teaspoon salt

1 × 15 ml spoon/1 tablespoon sugar

2 × 5 ml spoons/2 teaspoons sesame seed oil

6 × 15 ml spoons/6 tablespoons oil

2 garlic cloves, crushed

2 red chilli peppers, seeded and chopped, or
2 × 5 ml spoons/2 teaspoons cayenne pepper

2 green peppers, cored, seeded and cut into
2.5 cm/1 inch pieces

AMERICAN

1 tablespoon pale dry sherry

2 tablespoons soy sauce

1 small egg white

2 tablespoons cornstarch

1 lb chicken meat, cut into 1 inch cubes

1 tablespoon red wine vinegar

1 teaspoon salt

1 tablespoon sugar

2 teaspoons sesame oil

6 tablespoons oil

2 garlic cloves, minced

2 fresh chili peppers, seeded and chopped, or
2 teaspoons cayenne pepper

2 green peppers, cored, seeded and cut into
1 inch pieces

Mix together the sherry, soy sauce, egg white and cornflour (cornstarch). Add the chicken cubes and turn to coat well. Leave to marinate for 3 minutes. Mix together the vinegar, salt, sugar and sesame seed oil in a small bowl.

Heat the oil in a pan. Add the garlic, chilli peppers or cayenne, and chicken. Stir-fry until the chicken is golden brown, then add the green peppers and vinegar mixture. Stir-fry until the sauce starts bubbling and thickens. Serve hot.

Stir-Fried Chicken with Green Peppers and Chillies (left)
Sautéed Chicken with Onion (centre)
Scallop Fu-Yung (right)

Sautéed Chicken with Onion

METRIC/IMPERIAL

6 × 15 ml spoons/6 tablespoons oil

0.5 kg/1 lb boned chicken, cut into 2.5 cm/
1 inch squares

1 onion, cut into 6 sections

1 × 5 ml spoon/1 teaspoon ground Szechuan
or black peppercorns

1 × 15 ml spoon/1 tablespoon dry sherry

1 × 5 ml spoon/1 teaspoon grated root ginger

1 × 5 ml spoon/1 teaspoon sugar

1 × 2.5 ml spoon/½ teaspoon salt

2 × 15 ml spoons/2 tablespoons soy sauce

1 × 15 ml spoon/1 tablespoon cornflour,
dissolved in 2 × 15 ml spoons/2 tablespoons
water

onion rings to garnish

AMERICAN

6 tablespoons oil

1 lb boneless frying chicken, cut into 1 inch
squares

1 onion, cut into 6 sections

1 teaspoon ground Szechuan or black
peppercorns

1 tablespoon pale dry sherry

1 teaspoon minced ginger root

1 teaspoon sugar

½ teaspoon salt

2 tablespoons soy sauce

1 tablespoon cornstarch, dissolved in 2
tablespoons water

onion rings to garnish

Heat the oil in a pan. Add the chicken and onion and stir-fry for 2 minutes. Add the pepper, sherry, ginger, sugar, salt and soy sauce. Stir well. Add just enough water to cover the chicken and bring to the boil. Cover and simmer for 15 minutes or until the chicken is tender. Add the cornflour (cornstarch) mixture and simmer, stirring, until thickened. Serve hot, garnished with onion rings.

Scallop Fu-Yung

METRIC/IMPERIAL

1 × 15 ml spoon/1 tablespoon dry sherry

1 × 5 ml spoon/1 teaspoon salt

2 × 15 ml spoons/2 tablespoons cornflour

225 g/8 oz fresh scallops, cut into 5 mm/
¼ inch thick slices

225 g/8 oz chicken breast meat, cut into
5 mm/¼ inch thick slices

9 × 15 ml spoons/9 tablespoons oil

5 egg whites

250 ml/8 fl oz chicken stock

large pinch of white pepper

2 × 15 ml spoons/2 tablespoons chopped
cooked ham

2 × 15 ml spoons/2 tablespoons chopped
parsley

AMERICAN

1 tablespoon pale dry sherry

1 teaspoon salt

2 tablespoons cornstarch

½ lb scallops, cut into ¼ inch thick slices

½ lb chicken breast meat, cut into ¼ inch thick
slices

9 tablespoons oil

5 egg whites

1 cup chicken stock

large pinch of white pepper

2 tablespoons chopped cooked ham

2 tablespoons chopped parsley

Mix together the sherry, 1 × 2.5 ml spoon/
½ teaspoon of the salt and 1 × 15 ml spoon/
1 tablespoon of the cornflour (cornstarch). Add the scallops and chicken and turn to coat in the mixture. Heat 4 × 15 ml spoons/
4 tablespoons of the oil in a pan. Add the scallops and chicken and stir-fry for 1 minute. Remove from the heat.

Whisk the egg whites until stiff, then fold in the remaining cornflour (cornstarch) and salt, the stock, pepper, scallops and chicken. Heat the remaining oil in the pan. Add the egg white mixture and stir-fry until firm. Serve immediately, sprinkled with the chopped ham and parsley.

Note: For a delicate garnish, top with a red pepper, cut to form a flower head shape, and place parsley sprigs in the centre.

Aubergines (Eggplant) with Garlic Sauce

METRIC/IMPERIAL

oil for deep frying

1 kg/2 lb aubergines, peeled and cut into 2.5 cm/1 inch cubes

2 × 15 ml spoons/2 tablespoons oil

1 × 5 ml spoon/1 teaspoon crushed garlic

100 g/4 oz minced pork or beef

1 × 2.5 ml spoon/½ teaspoon salt

2 × 5 ml spoons/2 teaspoons sugar

2 × 15 ml spoons/2 tablespoons soy sauce

250 ml/8 fl oz stock or water

2 × 5 ml spoons/2 teaspoons red wine vinegar

1 × 15 ml spoon/1 tablespoon chopped spring onion (shallot)

AMERICAN

oil for deep frying

2 lb eggplant, peeled and cut into 1 inch cubes

2 tablespoons oil

1 teaspoon minced garlic

¼ lb ground pork or beef

½ teaspoon salt

2 teaspoons sugar

2 tablespoons soy sauce

1 cup stock or water

2 teaspoons red wine vinegar

1 tablespoon chopped scallion

Heat oil to 180°C/350°F. Deep-fry the aubergine (eggplant) cubes until soft. Drain on absorbent kitchen paper.

Heat the 2 × 15 ml spoons/2 tablespoons oil in a pan. Add the garlic and meat and stir-fry for a few seconds. Add the salt, sugar, soy sauce and stock or water and bring to the boil. Add the aubergines (eggplant) and cook for 1 minute. Stir in the vinegar and spring onion (shallot/scallion). Serve hot.

Dry-Cooked Green Beans

METRIC/IMPERIAL

oil for deep frying

0.5 kg/1 lb runner (green) beans

2 × 15 ml spoons/2 tablespoons oil

100 g/4 oz minced beef or pork

1 × 5 ml spoon/1 teaspoon salt

1 × 5 ml spoon/1 teaspoon chopped root ginger

1 × 15 ml spoon/1 tablespoon sugar

5 × 15 ml spoons/5 tablespoons water

1 × 15 ml spoon/1 tablespoon soy sauce

AMERICAN

oil for deep frying

1 lb string beans

2 tablespoons oil

¼ lb ground beef or pork

1 teaspoon salt

1 teaspoon minced ginger root

1 tablespoon sugar

5 tablespoons water

1 tablespoon soy sauce

Heat the oil to 180°C/350°F. Deep-fry the beans until they are wrinkled. Drain on

Pickled Salad

METRIC/IMPERIAL

0.5 kg/1 lb cucumber, peeled

0.5 kg/1 lb cabbage, cored and chopped

2 × 5 ml spoons/2 teaspoons salt

1 × 5 ml spoon/1 teaspoon crushed garlic

1 × 5 ml spoon/1 teaspoon ground Szechuan or black peppercorns

1 × 5 ml spoon/1 teaspoon sugar

1 × 15 ml spoon/1 tablespoon soy sauce

2 × 15 ml spoons/2 tablespoons sesame seed oil

1 × 15 ml spoon/1 tablespoon red wine vinegar

Aubergines (Eggplant) with Garlic Sauce (above left)
Dry-Cooked Green Beans (below left)
Pickled Salad (below right)

AMERICAN

2 large cucumbers, peeled

1 lb cabbage, cored and chopped

2 teaspoons salt

1 teaspoon minced garlic

1 teaspoon ground Szechuan or black peppercorns

1 teaspoon sugar

1 tablespoon soy sauce

2 tablespoons sesame oil

1 tablespoon red wine vinegar

Crush the cucumbers until cracks appear on the surface. Quarter lengthwise, then cut into pieces. Place in a bowl, with the cabbage. Sprinkle with salt and leave for 2 hours. Rinse the vegetables and drain well on absorbent kitchen paper. Mix together the garlic, pepper, sugar, soy sauce, oil and vinegar. Pour this mixture over the vegetables and allow to stand for at least 3 hours before serving on a bed of cabbage, if liked.

absorbent kitchen paper. Arrange in a dish. Heat the 2 × 15 ml spoons/2 tablespoons oil in a pan. Add the meat, salt, ginger, sugar, water and soy sauce and stir-fry until the meat begins to turn brown. Cook over a high heat until all the liquid in the sauce has completely evaporated. Serve the beans with the meat sauce on top.

Omelette with Meat Sauce

METRIC/IMPERIAL

8 eggs

1 × 5 ml spoon/1 teaspoon salt

1 × 15 ml spoon/1 tablespoon cornflour, dissolved in 1 × 15 ml spoon/1 tablespoon water

6 × 15 ml spoons/6 tablespoons oil

Sauce

2 × 15 ml spoons/2 tablespoons oil

1 × 5 ml spoon/1 teaspoon grated root ginger

1 × 5 ml spoon/1 teaspoon crushed garlic or garlic powder (optional)

100 g/4 oz minced pork or beef

1 × 15 ml spoon/1 tablespoon dry sherry

2 × 15 ml spoons/2 tablespoons soy sauce

1 × 2.5 ml spoon/½ teaspoon salt

1 × 5 ml spoon/1 teaspoon sugar

175 ml/6 fl oz stock

1 × 15 ml spoon/1 tablespoon cornflour, dissolved in 1 × 15 ml spoon/1 tablespoon water

1 × 15 ml spoon/1 tablespoon red wine vinegar

Garnish

2 × 15 ml spoons/2 tablespoons chopped spring onion (shallot) or celery

AMERICAN

8 eggs

1 teaspoon salt

1 tablespoon cornstarch, dissolved in 1 tablespoon water

6 tablespoons oil

Sauce

2 tablespoons oil

1 teaspoon minced ginger root

1 teaspoon minced garlic or garlic powder (optional)

¼ lb ground pork or beef

1 tablespoon pale dry sherry

2 tablespoons soy sauce

½ teaspoon salt

1 teaspoon sugar

¾ cup stock

1 tablespoon cornstarch, dissolved in 1 tablespoon water

1 tablespoon red wine vinegar

Garnish

2 tablespoons chopped scallion or celery

Beat the eggs with the salt and add the cornflour (cornstarch) mixture. Beat until smooth. Heat the oil in a pan. Add the eggs and fry over moderate heat until golden brown underneath, then turn over and fry the other side until firm. Transfer to a plate and keep hot.

To make the sauce, heat the oil in a saucepan. Add the ginger, garlic, if used, and meat and stir-fry until browned. Add the sherry, soy sauce, salt, sugar and stock and bring to the boil. Add the cornflour (cornstarch) mixture with the vinegar. Simmer, stirring, until the sauce has thickened.

Pour the meat sauce over the omelette and sprinkle with the spring onion (shallot/scallion) or celery. Serve hot.

Complex Szechuan Sauce

METRIC/IMPERIAL

2 × 15 ml spoons/2 tablespoons sesame seed paste

4 × 15 ml spoons/4 tablespoons water

2 × 15 ml spoons/2 tablespoons chopped spring onion (shallot)

2 × 5 ml spoons/2 teaspoons crushed garlic

2 × 5 ml spoons/2 teaspoons grated root ginger

1 × 5 ml spoon/1 teaspoon ground Szechuan peppercorns

1 × 15 ml spoon/1 tablespoon sugar

1 × 15 ml spoon/1 tablespoon red wine vinegar

1 × 15 ml spoon/1 tablespoon hot pepper oil

1 × 15 ml spoon/1 tablespoon sesame seed oil

4 × 15 ml spoons/4 tablespoons soy sauce

To serve

4 chicken pieces, cooked and cooled

AMERICAN

2 tablespoons sesame paste

¼ cup water

2 tablespoons chopped scallion

2 teaspoons minced garlic

2 teaspoons minced ginger root

1 teaspoon ground Szechuan peppercorns

1 tablespoon sugar

1 tablespoon red wine vinegar

1 tablespoon hot oil

1 tablespoon sesame oil

¼ cup soy sauce

Omelette with Meat Sauce *(left)*
Complex Szechuan Sauce *(right)*

To serve

4 chicken pieces, cooked and cooled

Mix the sesame seed paste with the water, then add the remaining ingredients and mix well.

Arrange the chicken pieces on a plate and pour the sauce over.

Note: Peanut butter can be used instead of sesame paste. Alternatively, toast sesame seeds in a pan, grind finely and add sesame seed oil to form a fairly thick paste.

Duck with Almonds

METRIC/IMPERIAL

0.5 kg/1 lb duck meat, cut into bite-size pieces

2 slices root ginger, shredded

1 × 5 ml spoon/1 teaspoon salt

3 × 15 ml spoons/3 tablespoons oil

2 spring onions (shallots), cut into 1 cm/ ½ inch pieces

1 × 5 ml spoon/1 teaspoon sugar

2.5 × 15 ml spoons/2½ tablespoons soy sauce

5 × 15 ml spoons/5 tablespoons green peas

5 × 15 ml spoons/5 tablespoons toasted almonds

2 × 5 ml spoons/2 teaspoons cornflour

3 × 15 ml spoons/3 tablespoons stock

2 × 15 ml spoons/2 tablespoons dry sherry

AMERICAN

1 lb duck meat, cut into bite-size pieces

2 slices ginger root, shredded

1 teaspoon salt

3 tablespoons oil

2 scallions, cut into ½ inch pieces

1 teaspoon sugar

2½ tablespoons soy sauce

5 tablespoons green peas

5 tablespoons toasted almonds

2 teaspoons cornstarch

3 tablespoons stock

2 tablespoons pale dry sherry

Duck with Almonds

Rub the duck with the ginger, salt and 1 × 15 ml spoon/1 tablespoon of the oil. Leave for 30 minutes.

Heat the remaining oil in a pan over high heat. Add the duck and spring onions (shallots/scallions) and stir-fry for 1½ minutes. Add the sugar and soy sauce and stir-fry for 30 seconds. Add the peas and almonds. Stir-fry for a further 1 minute. Dissolve the cornflour (cornstarch) in the stock and sherry. Add to the pan, stirring until the sauce thickens. Simmer for a final 30 seconds. Serve hot.

Note: Braised celery and fried rice are suitable accompaniments to this dish.

Sautéed Beef with Mushrooms

METRIC/IMPERIAL

1 egg white

2.5 × 15 ml spoons/2½ tablespoons soy sauce

1 × 5 ml spoon/1 teaspoon cornflour

0.5 kg/1 lb lean beef, shredded

7 × 15 ml spoons/7 tablespoons oil

100 g/4 oz canned bamboo shoots, drained and shredded

50 g/2 oz dried Chinese mushrooms, soaked for 20 minutes, drained, stemmed and shredded

1 × 15 ml spoon/1 tablespoon red wine

1 × 5 ml spoon/1 teaspoon sugar

1 × 2.5 ml spoon/½ teaspoon salt

AMERICAN

1 egg white

2½ tablespoons soy sauce

1 teaspoon cornstarch

1 lb flank steak, shredded

7 tablespoons oil

1 cup shredded canned bamboo shoots

1 cup dried Chinese mushrooms, soaked for 20 minutes, drained, stemmed and shredded

1 tablespoon red wine

1 teaspoon sugar

½ teaspoon salt

Mix together the egg white, 1 × 15 ml spoon/1 tablespoon of the soy sauce and the cornflour (cornstarch) in a bowl. Add the beef and leave to marinate for 5 minutes.

Heat 4 × 15 ml spoons/4 tablespoons oil in a pan. Add the beef and stir-fry over high heat until the colour changes. Remove from the pan. Heat the remaining oil in the pan. Add the bamboo shoots and mushrooms and stir-fry over high heat until well coated with oil. Return the beef to the pan with the remaining ingredients including the rest of the soy sauce. Stir-fry for 1 minute. Serve hot.

Note: Fresh mushrooms may be substituted for the dried Chinese mushrooms. The dish may be garnished with red pepper strips and coriander (Chinese parsley) leaves, arranged to form a flower head.

Corn Soup

METRIC/IMPERIAL

1.2 litres/2 pints clear broth (see page 15) or stock

1 × 440 g/15 oz can cream-style sweetcorn

1 × 5 ml spoon/1 teaspoon salt

1 × 15 ml spoon/1 tablespoon dry sherry

pinch of pepper

2 × 15 ml spoons/2 tablespoons cornflour, dissolved in 2 × 15 ml spoons/2 tablespoons water

2 eggs, beaten

1–2 spring onions (shallots), chopped

AMERICAN

2½ pints clear broth (see page 15) or stock

1 × 15 oz can cream-style corn

1 teaspoon salt

1 tablespoon pale dry sherry

pinch of pepper

2 tablespoons cornstarch, dissolved in 2 tablespoons water

2 eggs, beaten

1–2 scallions, chopped

Bring the broth or stock to the boil in a saucepan. Stir in the corn, then add the salt, sherry and pepper to taste. Add the cornflour (cornstarch) mixture and simmer, stirring continuously, until thickened.

Reduce the heat to low and add the beaten eggs in a thin stream, stirring continuously; the soup should not be boiling when the eggs are added. Sprinkle with the spring onion (shallot/scallion) and serve hot.

Corn Soup (above)
Sautéed Beef with Mushrooms (below)

Liver Soup

METRIC/IMPERIAL

275 g/10 oz pig's, chicken or calves' liver, finely chopped

1 × 5 ml spoon/1 teaspoon grated root ginger

1 × 2.5 ml spoon/½ teaspoon pepper

2 spring onions (shallots), chopped

4 eggs, beaten

600 ml/1 pint clear broth (see page 15) or stock

1 × 15 ml spoon/1 tablespoon dry sherry

1 × 2.5 ml spoon/½ teaspoon salt

1 × 15 ml spoon/1 tablespoon chopped cooked ham

1 × 15 ml spoon/1 tablespoon chopped parsley

AMERICAN

10 oz pork, chicken or veal liver, finely chopped

1 teaspoon minced ginger root

½ teaspoon pepper

2 scallions, chopped

4 eggs, beaten

2½ cups clear broth (see page 15) or stock

1 tablespoon pale dry sherry

½ teaspoon salt

1 tablespoon chopped cooked ham

1 tablespoon chopped parsley

Finely mince (grind) the liver or purée in a blender. Mix with the ginger, pepper, spring onions (shallots/scallions) and eggs. Turn into a heatproof bowl and steam for 30 minutes.

Meanwhile, bring the broth or stock to the boil. Add the sherry and salt. Place the steamed liver mixture in a serving dish. Pour the soup over and garnish with the ham and parsley. Serve hot.

Dry-Fried Shredded Beef

METRIC/IMPERIAL

9 × 15 ml spoons/9 tablespoons oil

3 large celery stalks, finely chopped

3 carrots, finely chopped

1 × 5 ml spoon/1 teaspoon salt

0.5 kg/1 lb sirloin steak, shredded

1 × 5 ml spoon/1 teaspoon crushed garlic

1 × 5 ml spoon/1 teaspoon red wine vinegar

1 × 5 ml spoon/1 teaspoon sugar

1 × 5 ml spoon/1 teaspoon soy sauce

1 × 15 ml spoon/1 tablespoon sesame seed oil

1 × 15 ml spoon/1 tablespoon hot soy bean paste or hot pepper oil

shredded raw carrot to garnish

AMERICAN

9 tablespoons oil

1 cup finely chopped celery

1 cup finely chopped carrots

1 teaspoon salt

1 lb flank steak, shredded

1 teaspoon minced garlic

1 teaspoon red wine vinegar

1 teaspoon sugar

1 teaspoon soy sauce

1 tablespoon sesame oil

1 tablespoon hot bean sauce or hot oil

shredded raw carrot to garnish

Heat 3 × 15 ml spoons/3 tablespoons of the oil in a pan. Add the celery, carrots and salt and stir-fry over high heat until partially cooked. Remove from the pan and set aside. Heat the remaining oil in the pan. Add the steak and stir-fry for about 10 minutes or until it has turned dark brown and is dry-looking. Stir in the garlic, vinegar, sugar, soy sauce, sesame seed oil and bean paste (sauce) or oil. When the smell of garlic and bean paste (sauce) is noticeable, add the vegetables. Continue to stir-fry until the vegetables are hot. Taste and check seasoning; add more hot bean paste (sauce) or pepper oil if desired. Serve hot. Surround with a ring of shredded raw carrot to garnish.

Liver Soup (below left)
Dry-Fried Shredded Beef (centre)
Beef Steak with Mange-Tout (Snow Peas) (below right)

Beef Steak with Mange-Tout (Snow Peas)

METRIC/IMPERIAL

1 × 15 ml spoon/1 tablespoon oil

0.5 kg/1 lb mange-tout

salt

2 × 15 ml spoons/2 tablespoons beef dripping or oil

1 kg/2 lb fillet or rump steak, cut into 4 pieces

2 × 5 ml spoons/2 teaspoons crushed garlic

1 × 15 ml spoon/1 tablespoon soy sauce

coriander leaves to garnish

AMERICAN

1 tablespoon oil

1 lb snow peas

salt

2 tablespoons beef drippings or oil

2 lb sirloin steak, cut into 4 pieces

2 teaspoons minced garlic

1 tablespoon soy sauce

Chinese parsley leaves to garnish

Heat the 1 × 15 ml spoon/1 tablespoon oil in a pan. Add the mange-tout (snow peas) and stir-fry for about 1 minute. Add salt to taste. Transfer to a serving plate and keep hot. Heat the dripping or oil in a heavy pan over moderate heat. Add the steak to the pan and sear for 1 minute or until blood rises on the uncooked surface. Turn and sear the other side for another 1 minute. Remove the steak and cut into 1 cm/½ inch thick strips. Return the steak to the pan with the garlic and soy sauce. Reduce the heat and continue cooking until the steak is cooked to your taste. Serve hot with the mange-tout (snow peas), garnished with the coriander (Chinese parsley) leaves.

Szechuan Peppery Hot Sauce

This sauce is brown in colour and has the fragrant, strong taste of chilli.

METRIC/IMPERIAL

2 × 15 ml spoons/2 tablespoons chopped spring onion (shallot)

1 × 15 ml spoon/1 tablespoon sesame seed oil

1 × 15 ml spoon/1 tablespoon sesame seeds

2 × 15 ml spoons/2 tablespoons red wine vinegar

3 × 15 ml spoons/3 tablespoons soy sauce

3 × 15 ml spoons/3 tablespoons chicken stock

1 × 5 ml spoon/1 teaspoon ground Szechuan peppercorns

2 × 5 ml spoons/2 teaspoons hot pepper oil

To serve

0.5 kg/1 lb bean sprouts, parboiled for 2 minutes and drained

0.5 kg/1 lb cooked chicken, sliced

few coriander leaves

AMERICAN

2 tablespoons chopped scallion

1 tablespoon sesame oil

1 tablespoon sesame seeds

2 tablespoons red wine vinegar

3 tablespoons soy sauce

3 tablespoons chicken stock

1 teaspoon ground Szechuan peppercorns

2 teaspoons hot oil

To serve

1 lb bean sprouts, parboiled for 2 minutes and drained

1 lb cooked chicken, sliced

few Chinese parsley leaves

Mix all the sauce ingredients together in a bowl. Arrange the bean sprouts and chicken on a serving plate and pour over the sauce. Garnish with coriander (Chinese parsley).

Szechuan Peppery Hot Sauce (below)

Stir-Fried Diced Chicken

METRIC/IMPERIAL

1 egg white

1 × 2.5 ml spoon/½ teaspoon salt

2 × 5 ml spoons/2 teaspoons cornflour

0.5 kg/1 lb chicken meat, diced

1 × 15 ml spoon/1 tablespoon dry sherry

3 × 15 ml spoons/3 tablespoons soy sauce

1 × 2.5 ml spoon/½ teaspoon sugar

4 × 15 ml spoons/4 tablespoons oil

4 red chilli peppers, seeded and shredded

1 × 15 ml spoon/1 tablespoon water

AMERICAN

1 egg white

½ teaspoon salt

2 teaspoons cornstarch

1 lb chicken meat, diced

1 tablespoon pale dry sherry

3 tablespoons soy sauce

½ teaspoon sugar

¼ cup oil

4 red chili peppers, seeded and shredded

1 tablespoon water

Whisk the egg white lightly with the salt and 1 × 5 ml spoon/1 teaspoon of the cornflour (cornstarch). Add the chicken and turn to coat. In another bowl, mix together the sherry, soy sauce and sugar.

Heat the oil in a pan. Add the chilli peppers and stir-fry for a few seconds. Add the chicken and stir-fry until the chicken turns golden. Stir in the sherry mixture.

Dissolve the remaining cornflour (cornstarch) in the water and add to the pan. Stir continuously until thickened. Serve hot.

Sizzling Rice Soup (left)
Stir-Fried Diced Chicken (right)

Sizzling Rice Soup

METRIC/IMPERIAL

1.2 litres/2 pints clear broth (see page 15) or water

225 g/8 oz prawns, shelled and deveined

100 g/4 oz mushrooms, halved

1 × 2.5 ml spoon/½ teaspoon salt

1 × 15 ml spoon/1 tablespoon soy sauce

1 × 15 ml spoon/1 tablespoon dry sherry

pinch of pepper

oil for deep frying

150 g/5 oz moist cooked rice (see note), broken into 7.5 cm/3 inch pieces

AMERICAN

5 cups clear broth (see page 15) or water

½ lb shrimp, shelled and deveined

¼ lb mushrooms, halved

½ teaspoon salt

1 tablespoon soy sauce

1 tablespoon pale dry sherry

pinch of pepper

oil for deep frying

1 cup rice paddies (see note), broken into 3 inch pieces

Bring the broth or water to the boil in a saucepan. Add the prawns (shrimp), mushrooms, salt, soy sauce, sherry and pepper and stir well. Cover and simmer until the ingredients are heated through, then pour into a warmed soup tureen. Keep hot while preparing the rice.

Heat the oil to 180°C/350°F. Deep-fry the pieces of rice (rice paddies) for about 30 seconds until crisp but not brown. Drain and arrange on a warmed plate.

To serve, place the rice in individual bowls and, at the table, pour the stock mixture over the rice. The resulting sizzling gives this dish its name and is one of its great attractions.

Note: Prepare the moist cooked rice (rice paddies) by spreading an even layer of cooked rice on a baking sheet; press firmly to make the layer uniform, and dry in the sun or in a very slow oven until brittle.

Beef and Tomato Soup

METRIC/IMPERIAL

1×15 ml spoon/1 tablespoon dry sherry

1×15 ml spoon/1 tablespoon soy sauce

pinch of pepper

2×5 ml spoons/2 teaspoons cornflour

100 g/4 oz lean beef, thinly sliced and cut into bite-size pieces

1×15 ml spoon/1 tablespoon oil

1.2 litres/2 pints chicken stock

2×5 ml spoons/2 teaspoons salt

2 tomatoes, skinned and roughly chopped

2 eggs, beaten

1×15 ml spoon/1 tablespoon chopped spring onion (shallot)

Beef and Tomato Soup (below left)
Steamed Beef with Semolina (Rice Powder) (top right)
Szechuan Peppercorn Sauce (bottom right)

AMERICAN

1 tablespoon pale dry sherry

1 tablespoon soy sauce

pinch of pepper

2 teaspoons cornstarch

$\frac{1}{4}$ lb flank steak, thinly sliced and cut into bite-size pieces

1 tablespoon oil

5 cups chicken stock

2 teaspoons salt

2 tomatoes, skinned and roughly chopped

2 eggs, beaten

1 tablespoon chopped scallion

In a bowl, mix together the sherry, soy sauce, pepper and cornflour (cornstarch). Add the beef and turn to coat well.

Heat the oil in a saucepan. Add the beef and stir-fry until it changes colour. Add the stock and salt and bring to the boil. Add the tomato pieces.

Reduce the heat and slowly pour in the beaten eggs, without stirring, so they resemble clouds floating on top of the soup. Garnish with the chopped spring onion (shallot/scallion). Serve hot.

Steamed Beef with Semolina (Rice Powder)

METRIC/IMPERIAL

1×15 ml spoon/1 tablespoon dry sherry

4×15 ml spoons/4 tablespoons soy sauce

1×2.5 ml spoon/$\frac{1}{2}$ teaspoon salt

1×5 ml spoon/1 teaspoon grated root ginger

1×5 ml spoon/1 teaspoon sugar

1×5 ml spoon/1 teaspoon cayenne pepper

0.5 kg/1 lb lean beef, thinly sliced and cut into bite-size pieces

225 g/8 oz cabbage, cored and shredded

175 g/6 oz semolina or ground rice

250 ml/8 fl oz water or chicken stock

2×15 ml spoons/2 tablespoons chopped spring onion (shallot)

AMERICAN

1 tablespoon pale dry sherry

$\frac{1}{4}$ cup soy sauce

$\frac{1}{2}$ teaspoon salt

1 teaspoon minced ginger root

1 teaspoon sugar

1 teaspoon cayenne pepper

1 lb flank steak, thinly sliced and cut into bite-size pieces

$\frac{1}{2}$ lb cabbage, cored and shredded

1 cup rice powder or cream of wheat cereal

1 cup water or chicken stock

2 tablespoons chopped scallion

Mix together the sherry, soy sauce, salt, ginger, sugar and cayenne pepper in a bowl. Add the beef strips and leave to marinate for 30 minutes.

Spread the cabbage in a steamer basket. Dissolve the semolina or ground rice (rice powder or cream of wheat) in the water or stock and stir into the beef mixture. Place on the cabbage.

Steam for about 50 minutes or until the beef is tender. Serve hot, sprinkled with the spring onion (shallot/scallion).

Szechuan Peppercorn Sauce

Peppercorn has a fascinating sweet/bitter chilli taste unknown in Western cooking.

METRIC/IMPERIAL

2 × 5 ml spoons/2 teaspoons black Szechuan peppercorns

2 × 15 ml spoons/2 tablespoons chopped spring onion (shallot)

2 × 5 ml spoons/2 teaspoons chopped root ginger

1 × 2.5 ml spoon/½ teaspoon salt

3 × 15 ml spoons/3 tablespoons soy sauce

2 × 15 ml spoons/2 tablespoons sesame seed oil

1 × 15 ml spoon/1 tablespoon chicken stock

1 × 5 ml spoon/1 teaspoon red wine vinegar

1 × 5 ml spoon/1 teaspoon sugar

To serve

1 small Webb's Wonder lettuce, shredded

0.75 kg/1½ lb cooked chicken meat, cut into bite-size pieces

AMERICAN

2 teaspoons black Szechuan peppercorns

2 tablespoons chopped scallion

2 teaspoons chopped ginger root

½ teaspoon salt

3 tablespoons soy sauce

2 tablespoons sesame oil

1 tablespoon chicken stock

1 teaspoon red wine vinegar

1 teaspoon sugar

To serve

1 small head iceberg lettuce, shredded

1½ lb cooked chicken meat, cut into bite-size pieces

Remove the seeds from the peppercorns (good quality peppercorns usually have no seeds or very few tiny ones). Crush the peppercorns and mix with the remaining ingredients.

Make a bed of shredded lettuce on a serving plate and pile the chicken on top. Pour the sauce over the chicken before serving.

Double-Cooked Pork

METRIC/IMPERIAL

0.75 kg/1½ lb belly pork

3.5 × 15 ml spoons/3½ tablespoons oil

2 dried chilli peppers, seeded and thinly sliced, or 2 × 5 ml spoons/2 teaspoons chilli sauce

1.5 × 15 ml spoons/1½ tablespoons dried wood ears, soaked for 20 minutes, drained and stemmed

4 garlic cloves, crushed

1 × 15 ml spoon/1 tablespoon soy bean paste

2 × 15 ml spoons/2 tablespoons soy sauce

1 × 15 ml spoon/1 tablespoon hoisin sauce, or sweet soy bean paste

2 × 15 ml spoons/2 tablespoons tomato purée

2 × 5 ml spoons/2 teaspoons sugar

3 × 15 ml spoons/3 tablespoons clear broth (see page 15)

4 spring onions (shallots), cut into 4 cm/1½ inch pieces

1.5 × 15 ml spoons/1½ tablespoons dry sherry

1 × 15 ml spoon/1 tablespoon sesame seed oil

AMERICAN

1½ lb fresh pork sides

3½ tablespoons oil

2 dried chili peppers, seeded and thinly sliced, or 2 teaspoons chili sauce

1½ tablespoons dried tree ears, soaked for 20 minutes, drained and stemmed

4 garlic cloves, minced

1 tablespoon bean sauce

2 tablespoons soy sauce

1 tablespoon hoisin sauce, or sweet bean sauce

2 tablespoons tomato paste

2 teaspoons sugar

3 tablespoons clear broth (see page 15)

4 scallions, cut into 1½ inch pieces

1½ tablespoons pale dry sherry

1 tablespoon sesame oil

Put the pork into a saucepan of boiling water. Bring back to the boil and simmer for 25 minutes. Leave to cool, then cut through the fat and skin into slices, 4 × 5 cm/1½ × 2 inches.

Heat the oil in a pan. Add the chilli peppers, if used, and mushrooms and stir-fry for 1 minute. Add the garlic, soy bean paste (sauce), soy sauce, hoisin sauce, tomato purée (paste), sugar, broth and chilli sauce, if used. Stir-fry for 30 seconds or until the mixture becomes smooth.

Add the pork pieces and increase the heat to high. Stir continuously until the pork is well coated and the sauce begins to thicken. Sprinkle in the spring onions (shallots/ scallions), sherry and sesame seed oil and stir-fry for a further few seconds. Serve hot.

Deep-Fried Scallops (right)
Stewed Beef (far right)
Double-Cooked Pork (below)

Stewed Beef

METRIC/IMPERIAL

0.75 kg/1½ lb stewing beef

1-2 spring onions (shallots), chopped

3 slices root ginger

3 whole star anise

1 × 15 ml spoon/1 tablespoon whole peppercorns

1 × 15 ml spoon/1 tablespoon dry sherry

5 × 15 ml spoons/5 tablespoons soy sauce

2 × 5 ml spoons/2 teaspoons cornflour, dissolved in 2 × 5 ml spoons/2 teaspoons water

AMERICAN

1½ lb beef rump

1-2 scallions, chopped

3 slices ginger root

3 whole star anise

1 tablespoon whole peppercorns

1 tablespoon pale dry sherry

5 tablespoons soy sauce

2 teaspoons cornstarch, dissolved in 2 teaspoons water

Put the beef in a saucepan and add the spring onions (shallots/scallions), ginger, anise, peppercorns, sherry and soy sauce. Bring to the boil, then add just enough water to cover the beef. Cover and simmer for about 2 hours or until the beef is tender.

Remove the beef from the pan and cut into 1 cm/½ inch thick slices. Keep hot. Add the cornflour (cornstarch) mixture to the pan. Simmer, stirring, until thickened. Pour over the beef and serve hot.

Deep-Fried Scallops

METRIC/IMPERIAL

10 fresh scallops, cut into bite-size pieces

1 × 2.5 ml spoon/½ teaspoon ginger juice (see page 35)

1 egg

1 × 5 ml spoon/1 teaspoon dry white wine

1 × 2.5 ml spoon/½ teaspoon salt

3 × 15 ml spoons/3 tablespoons self-raising flour

oil for deep frying

AMERICAN

10 fresh scallops, cut into bite-size pieces

½ teaspoon ginger juice (see page 35)

1 egg

1 teaspoon dry white wine

½ teaspoon salt

3 tablespoons self-rising flour

oil for deep-frying

Parboil the scallops for 1 minute and drain. Sprinkle with the ginger juice. Beat the egg in a bowl. Add the wine, salt and flour, and beat until smooth. Fold in the scallops and toss until evenly coated with batter.

Heat the oil to 160°C/325°F. Deep-fry the scallops until golden brown. Drain on absorbent kitchen paper.

Serve hot with tomato ketchup (sauce) or hoisin sauce.

Dry-Cooked Bamboo Shoots

Fresh bamboo shoots are at their best in early spring when the shoots are young and tender.

METRIC/IMPERIAL

0.5 kg/1 lb fresh or canned bamboo shoots

2 red peppers (optional)

oil for deep frying

2 × 15 ml spoons/2 tablespoons oil

1 × 5 ml spoon/1 teaspoon chopped root ginger

2 × 15 ml spoons/2 tablespoons dried shrimps, soaked for 15 minutes, drained and chopped

50 g/2 oz Szechuan hot pickles, chopped

2 × 15 ml spoons/2 tablespoons soy sauce

1 × 15 ml spoon/1 tablespoon sugar

1 × 2.5 ml spoon/½ teaspoon salt

pinch of pepper

120 ml/4 fl oz clear broth (see page 15) or water

1 × 15 ml spoon/1 tablespoon sesame seed oil

2 × 15 ml spoons/2 tablespoons chopped spring onion (shallot)

AMERICAN

4 cups fresh or canned bamboo shoots

2 red peppers (optional)

oil for deep frying

2 tablespoons oil

1 teaspoon minced ginger root

2 tablespoons dried shrimp, soaked for 15 minutes, drained and chopped

½ cup chopped Szechuan kohlrabi

2 tablespoons soy sauce

1 tablespoon sugar

½ teaspoon salt

pinch of pepper

½ cup clear broth (see page 15) or water

1 tablespoon sesame oil

2 tablespoons chopped scallion

If using fresh bamboo shoots, remove the tough outer skin and cook in boiling water with the red peppers for 40 minutes. Drain. Heat the oil to 180°C/350°F. Add the bamboo shoots and deep-fry until the edges turn yellow. Drain and cut into slices.

Heat the 2 × 15 ml spoons/2 tablespoons oil in a pan. Add the ginger, shrimps and pickles (kohlrabi) and stir-fry for 1 minute. Add the soy sauce, sugar, salt, pepper, broth or water. Mix well and bring to the boil. Simmer until the liquid has completely evaporated. Add the sesame seed oil and spring onion (shallot/scallion) and stir well.

Arrange the bamboo shoots on a serving dish and place the shrimp mixture on top. Serve hot.

Stir-Fried Pork with 'Hot Sauce'

METRIC/IMPERIAL

2 × 15 ml spoons/2 tablespoons soy sauce

1.5 × 5 ml spoons/1½ teaspoons dry sherry

1.5 × 5 ml spoons/1½ teaspoons cornflour

225 g/8 oz pork fillet, cut into 5 cm/2 inch strips

1 × 15 ml spoon/1 tablespoon hot soy bean paste or Tabasco sauce

large pinch of black pepper

1 × 2.5 ml spoon/½ teaspoon salt

1 × 5 ml spoon/1 teaspoon sugar

1 × 15 ml spoon/1 tablespoon red wine vinegar

7 × 15 ml spoons/7 tablespoons oil

1 × 15 ml spoon/1 tablespoon shredded root ginger

1 × 2.5 ml spoon/½ teaspoon crushed garlic

4 dried Chinese mushrooms, soaked for 20 minutes, drained, stemmed and shredded

100 g/4 oz canned bamboo shoots or water chestnuts, drained and shredded

Dry-Cooked Bamboo Shoots (above)
Stir-Fried Pork with 'Hot Sauce'
(below)

AMERICAN

2 tablespoons soy sauce

1½ teaspoons pale dry sherry

1½ teaspoons cornstarch

½ lb pork tenderloin, cut into 2 inch strips

1 tablespoon hot bean sauce or Tabasco sauce

large pinch of black pepper

½ teaspoon salt

1 teaspoon sugar

1 tablespoon red wine vinegar

7 tablespoons oil

1 tablespoon shredded ginger root

½ teaspoon minced garlic

½ cup dried Chinese mushrooms, soaked for 20 minutes, drained, stemmed and shredded

½ cup shredded canned bamboo shoots or water chestnuts

Mix together 1 × 15 ml spoon/1 tablespoon of the soy sauce, the sherry and cornflour (cornstarch). Add the pork and leave to marinate for 15 minutes. Mix together the hot soy bean paste (sauce) or Tabasco sauce, pepper, salt, sugar, remaining soy sauce and the vinegar in a small serving bowl.

Heat 4 × 15 ml spoons/4 tablespoons of the oil in a pan. Add the shredded pork and stir-fry until lightly browned. Transfer to a plate. Heat the remaining oil in the pan and add the ginger and garlic. Stir-fry over high heat for 20 seconds. Add the mushrooms and bamboo shoots or water chestnuts and stir-fry for another 30 seconds. Add the pork and seasoning mixture and stir briefly. Serve hot, accompanied by the 'hot sauce'.

Note: The dish may be garnished with additional water chestnuts, sliced, and topped with spring onion (shallot/scallion) slices.

Hot Ma Po Mashed Bean Curd with Minced (Ground) Beef

METRIC/IMPERIAL

5–6 dried Chinese mushrooms

300 ml/½ pint water

4 × 15 ml spoons/4 tablespoons oil

2 × 5 ml spoons/2 teaspoons salted black beans, soaked for 10 minutes and drained

5–6 × 15 ml spoons/5–6 tablespoons minced beef

3 spring onions (shallots), thinly sliced

4 garlic cloves, crushed

2 × 15 ml spoons/2 tablespoons soy sauce

2 × 15 ml spoons/2 tablespoons hoisin sauce

2 × 5 ml spoons/2 teaspoons chilli sauce

1 × 5 ml spoon/1 teaspoon sugar

2–3 cakes bean curd, diced

4 × 15 ml spoons/4 tablespoons clear broth (see page 15)

2 × 5 ml spoons/2 teaspoons cornflour, dissolved in 3 × 15 ml spoons/3 tablespoons water

1 × 15 ml spoon/1 tablespoon sesame seed oil

AMERICAN

5–6 dried Chinese mushrooms

1¼ cups water

¼ cup oil

2 teaspoons salted black beans, soaked for 10 minutes and drained

5–6 tablespoons ground beef

3 scallions, thinly sliced

4 garlic cloves, minced

2 tablespoons soy sauce

2 tablespoons hoisin sauce

2 teaspoons chili sauce

1 teaspoon sugar

2–3 cakes bean curd, diced

¼ cup clear broth (see page 15)

2 teaspoons cornstarch, dissolved in 3 tablespoons water

1 tablespoon sesame oil

Hot Ma Po Mashed Bean Curd with Minced (Ground) Beef

Soak the mushrooms in the water for 20 minutes. Drain, reserving the water. Stem the mushrooms and cut into quarters.

Heat the oil in a pan. Add the black beans. Stir-fry for 20 seconds. Add the beef, half the spring onions (shallots/scallions) and the mushrooms. Stir-fry for 3 to 4 minutes. Add the garlic, 3–4 × 15 ml spoons/3–4 tablespoons of the mushroom water, the soy sauce, hoisin sauce, chilli sauce, sugar, bean curd and broth. Bring to the boil and simmer for 3 to 4 minutes.

Sprinkle in the cornflour (cornstarch) mixture, the remaining spring onions (shallots/scallions) and the sesame seed oil. Cook, stirring, until thickened. Serve hot.

Sautéed Frogs' Legs

METRIC/IMPERIAL

1 egg white

1 × 5 ml spoon/1 teaspoon salt

2 × 15 ml spoons/2 tablespoons cornflour

0.5 kg/1 lb frogs' legs, cut into bite-size pieces

oil for deep frying

2 × 15 ml spoons/2 tablespoons oil

1 green pepper, cored, seeded and diced

2 red chilli peppers, seeded and chopped

2 × 15 ml spoons/2 tablespoons salted black beans, soaked for 10 minutes and drained

1 × 15 ml spoon/1 tablespoon soy sauce

3 × 15 ml spoons/3 tablespoons chicken stock

2 × 5 ml spoons/2 teaspoons sugar

AMERICAN

1 egg white

1 teaspoon salt

2 tablespoons cornstarch

1 lb frogs' legs, cut into bite-size pieces

oil for deep frying

2 tablespoons oil

1 green pepper, cored, seeded and diced

2 red chili peppers, seeded and chopped

2 tablespoons salted black beans, soaked for 10 minutes and drained

1 tablespoon soy sauce

3 tablespoons chicken stock

2 teaspoons sugar

Mix together the egg white, 1 × 2.5 ml spoon/½ teaspoon of the salt and the cornflour (cornstarch) in a bowl. Add the frogs' legs and turn to coat in the batter. Heat the oil to 180°C/350°F. Deep-fry the frogs' legs until lightly browned but not completely cooked through. Drain on absorbent kitchen paper. Heat the 2 × 15 ml spoons/2 tablespoons oil in a pan. Add the green pepper, chilli peppers and black beans and stir-fry for 1 minute. Add the frogs' legs, soy sauce, stock, remaining salt and the sugar. Fry for another 2 minutes or until the ingredients are well mixed. Serve hot.

Sautéed Frogs' Legs

Sesame Seed Biscuits

METRIC/IMPERIAL

225 g/8 oz self-raising flour, sifted

25 g/1 oz sugar

2 × 15 ml spoons/2 tablespoons sesame seeds

15 g/½ oz lard

4 × 15 ml spoons/4 tablespoons water

oil for deep frying

AMERICAN

2 cups self-rising flour, sifted

¼ cup sugar

2 tablespoons sesame seeds

1 tablespoon lard

¼ cup water

oil for deep frying

Mix together the flour, sugar, sesame seeds, lard and water and knead well to yield a soft dough. Place on a floured board and roll out to 3 mm/⅛ inch thickness. Cut into 1.5 × 5 cm/¾ × 2 inch rectangles and make a slit in the centre of each. Bring one end of the rectangle through the slit to form a twist. Heat the oil to 160°C/325°F. Deep-fry the biscuits until golden brown. Drain on absorbent kitchen paper and serve either hot or cold.

Steamed Lobster with Assorted Szechuan Sauces

Steamed Lobster with Assorted Szechuan Sauces (left)
Szechuan Garlic Pork (centre)
Shredded Chicken with Spiced Sesame Sauce (right)

Szechuan Garlic Pork

METRIC/IMPERIAL

1 × 0.75–1.25 kg/1½–2½ lb lobster or
0.5 kg/1 lb lobster meat, diced

1 Webb's Wonder lettuce, shredded

1 × 2.5 ml spoon/½ teaspoon salt

To serve

Szechuan Peppercorn Sauce (see page 155)

Szechuan Peppery Hot Sauce (see page 152)

Complex Szechuan sauce (see page 146)

AMERICAN

1 × 1½–2½ lb lobster or 2 cups diced lobster meat

2 cups shredded iceberg lettuce

½ teaspoon salt

To serve

Szechuan Peppercorn Sauce (see page 155)

Szechuan Peppery Hot Sauce (see page 152)

Complex Szechuan Sauce (see page 146)

Rinse the lobster thoroughly then split in half lengthwise through the head and tail along the centre line of the shell. Discard the grey sac in the head and the dark intestinal vein in the body. Remove the meat from the shells and cut into 2 cm/¾ inch cubes. Arrange the shredded lettuce on a platter and sprinkle with salt. Pile the cubed lobster meat carefully in the centre and place the head and tail at either end. Serve with the Szechuan sauces.

Note: Tomato shells make attractive 'dishes' for the sauces.

In China, this dish is called 'White Cloud Pork' as the layers of fat and lean do resemble layers of clouds. At first glance the meat might look too fatty, but much of the fat is boiled out.

METRIC/IMPERIAL

0.5 kg/1 lb belly pork, skinned

1 slice root ginger, chopped

1 spring onion (shallot), chopped

1 × 15 ml spoon/1 tablespoon crushed garlic

large pinch of salt

2 × 15 ml spoons/2 tablespoons soy sauce

1 whole star anise

1 × 15 ml spoon/1 tablespoon dry sherry

1 × 15 ml spoon/1 tablespoon sugar

1 × 5 ml spoon/1 teaspoon red wine vinegar

1 × 15 ml spoon/1 tablespoon hot pepper oil

AMERICAN

1 lb pork sides (boneless), skinned

1 slice ginger root, minced

1 scallion, chopped

1 tablespoon minced garlic

large pinch of salt

2 tablespoons soy sauce

1 whole star anise

1 tablespoon pale dry sherry

1 tablespoon sugar

1 teaspoon red wine vinegar

1 tablespoon hot oil

Put the pork in a saucepan and pour over water to cover. Bring to the boil, cover and simmer for 30 minutes. Drain, reserving 3 × 15 ml spoons/3 tablespoons of the cooking liquid.

Allow the cooked pork to cool slightly, then cut into paper-thin slices across the grain. Arrange the slices on a warmed serving plate and keep hot.

Place the ginger, spring onion (shallot/ scallion), garlic, salt, soy sauce, anise, sherry, sugar, vinegar and reserved cooking liquid in a saucepan. Bring to the boil and simmer for 5 minutes. Strain over the pork, then sprinkle with the hot pepper oil. Serve hot.

Shredded Chicken with Spiced Sesame Sauce

METRIC/IMPERIAL

$\frac{1}{2} \times 2$ kg/$4\frac{1}{2}$ lb chicken, or 1 kg/2 lb chicken breasts

2 spring onions (shallots)

2 slices root ginger

Sauce

2 × 15 ml spoons/2 tablespoons sesame seed paste

2 × 15 ml spoons/2 tablespoons water

3 × 15 ml spoons/3 tablespoons soy sauce

1 × 15 ml spoon/1 tablespoon sesame seed oil

2 × 15 ml spoons/2 tablespoons chopped spring onion (shallot)

1 × 5 ml spoon/1 teaspoon red wine vinegar

2 × 5 ml spoons/2 teaspoons sugar

1 × 5 ml spoon/1 teaspoon hot pepper oil

1 × 2.5 ml spoon/$\frac{1}{2}$ teaspoon salt

2 × 5 ml spoons/2 teaspoons crushed garlic

1 × 5 ml spoon/1 teaspoon grated root ginger

1 × 5 ml spoon/1 teaspoon ground Szechuan peppercorns

Garnish

$\frac{1}{2}$ cucumber, peeled and thinly sliced

AMERICAN

$\frac{1}{2} \times 4\frac{1}{2}$ lb chicken or 2 lb chicken breasts

2 scallions

2 slices ginger root

Sauce

2 tablespoons sesame paste

2 tablespoons water

3 tablespoons soy sauce

1 tablespoon sesame oil

2 tablespoons chopped scallion

1 teaspoon red wine vinegar

2 teaspoons sugar

1 teaspoon hot oil

$\frac{1}{2}$ teaspoon salt

2 teaspoons minced garlic

1 teaspoon minced ginger root

1 teaspoon ground Szechuan peppercorns

Garnish

$\frac{1}{2}$ cucumber, peeled and thinly sliced

Steam the chicken or cook in boiling water, with the spring onions (shallots/scallions) and ginger, for 30 minutes. Discard the ginger and spring onions (shallots/scallions). Put the chicken immediately under cold running water for about 1 minute, so that the meat will be firm. Remove the meat from the bones and cut into strips, 1.5 cm/$\frac{3}{4}$ inch thick, 5 mm/$\frac{1}{4}$ inch wide and 2.5 cm/1 inch long.

Mix the sesame paste with the water, then add the remaining sauce ingredients and mix well.

Arrange the cucumber on a serving plate and pile the shredded chicken on top. Pour over the sauce. Toss well at the table.

163

Ham and Peppers

METRIC/IMPERIAL

3 red peppers, cored, seeded and cut into 2.5 cm/1 inch strips

1 × 15 ml spoon/1 tablespoon cornflour

2 × 15 ml spoons/2 tablespoons soy sauce

1 × 15 ml spoon/1 tablespoon dry sherry

1 × 5 ml spoon/1 teaspoon sugar

2 × 15 ml spoons/2 tablespoons stock or water

350 g/12 oz cooked ham, cut into 2.5 cm/1 inch cubes

2 × 15 ml spoons/2 tablespoons oil

AMERICAN

3 red peppers, cored, seeded and cut into 1 inch strips

1 tablespoon cornstarch

2 tablespoons soy sauce

1 tablespoon pale dry sherry

1 teaspoon sugar

2 tablespoons stock or water

¾ lb cooked ham, cut into 1 inch cubes

2 tablespoons oil

Blanch the peppers in boiling water for 1 minute. Drain. Place the cornflour (cornstarch) in a bowl and stir in the soy sauce, sherry, sugar and stock or water. Add the ham and toss until thoroughly coated.

Heat the oil in a pan. Add the pepper strips and stir-fry for 2 minutes over a high heat. Remove from the pan and reserve. Add the ham to the pan together with the liquid and stir-fry for 1 minute. Replace the peppers in the pan and stir-fry for a further 1 minute. Serve hot.

Braised Pork with Pumpkin

METRIC/IMPERIAL

2 × 15 ml spoons/2 tablespoons dry sherry

5 × 15 ml spoons/5 tablespoons soy sauce

350 g/12 oz belly pork, skinned and cut into small 1 cm/½ inch thick pieces

3 × 15 ml spoons/3 tablespoons oil

0.5 kg/1¼ lb pumpkin, peeled, seeded and cut into 5 cm/2 inch cubes

300 ml/½ pint clear broth (see page 15)

2 × 5 ml spoons/2 teaspoons sugar

AMERICAN

2 tablespoons pale dry sherry

5 tablespoons soy sauce

¾ lb fresh pork sides (boneless), cut into small ½ inch thick pieces

3 tablespoons oil

1¼ lb pumpkin, peeled, seeded and cut into 2 inch cubes

½ pint clear broth (see page 15)

2 teaspoons sugar

Mix together half of the sherry and 1 × 15 ml spoon/1 tablespoon of the soy sauce in a bowl. Add the pork pieces and turn to coat thoroughly. Heat the oil in a pan and add the pork. Stir-fry until evenly browned. Add the pumpkin pieces. Stir well, then add the broth, sugar and remaining sherry and soy sauce. Bring to the boil and simmer for 15 minutes or until the pumpkin is tender. Serve hot.

Braised Beef with Turnips

METRIC/IMPERIAL

1.25 kg/2½ lb stewing beef, in 2 pieces

3 slices root ginger

2 whole star anise

1 × 5 ml spoon/1 teaspoon whole peppercorns

120 ml/4 fl oz soy sauce

1 × 15 ml spoon/1 tablespoon sugar

2 × 15 ml spoons/2 tablespoons dry sherry

1 kg/2 lb turnips, cut into 1 cm/½ inch thick slices

2 × 5 ml spoons/2 teaspoons cornflour, dissolved in 2 × 15 ml spoons/2 tablespoons water

parsley sprig to garnish

AMERICAN

2½ lb beef rump, in 2 pieces

3 slices ginger root

2 whole star anise

1 teaspoon whole peppercorns

½ cup soy sauce

1 tablespoon sugar

2 tablespoons pale dry sherry

2 lb turnips, cut into ½ inch thick slices

2 teaspoons cornstarch, dissolved in 2 tablespoons water

parsley sprig to garnish

Put the beef in a saucepan with the ginger, anise, peppercorns, soy sauce, sugar and sherry. Add enough water to just cover the meat and bring to the boil. Cover and simmer for 1 hour or until tender. Meanwhile, parboil the turnips for 2 minutes. Drain.

Remove the beef from the pan and cut into 1 cm/½ inch thick slices. Put into a deep heatproof bowl and arrange the turnips on top. Pour the liquid from the pan over the turnips and steam for 30 minutes.

Drain the liquid from the bowl into a saucepan. Invert the beef and turnips onto a warmed serving plate and keep hot. Discard the ginger and anise from the pan. Add the cornflour (cornstarch) mixture to the liquid and simmer, stirring, until thickened. Pour over the beef and turnips. Serve hot, garnished with the parsley.

Ham and Peppers (left)

Braised Pork with Pumpkin (above right)

Braised Beef with Turnips (below right)

Poached Kidneys with Hot Sauce

Kidneys are considered a delicacy in China. They are scored to facilitate cooking by creating more surface area. As they cook, the scored pieces open slightly to resemble flowers; therefore, the Chinese word *hua*, or flower, appears in the Chinese name for this dish.

Poached Kidneys with Hot Sauce (left)
Braised Fish with Hot Soy Bean Paste (Sauce)
Stir-Fried Pork with Mushrooms (right)

METRIC/IMPERIAL	AMERICAN
350 g/12 oz pig's kidneys	¾ lb pork kidneys
salt	salt
100 g/4 oz courgettes or cucumber, sliced	1 cup sliced zucchini or cucumber
1 × 15 ml spoon/1 tablespoon sesame seed paste, mixed with 2 × 15 ml spoons/2 tablespoons water	1 tablespoon sesame paste, mixed with 2 tablespoons water
2 × 15 ml spoons/2 tablespoons soy sauce	2 tablespoons soy sauce
1 × 15 ml spoon/1 tablespoon red wine vinegar	1 tablespoon red wine vinegar
1 × 5 ml spoon/1 teaspoon sugar	1 teaspoon sugar
2 × 5 ml spoons/2 teaspoons hot pepper oil	2 teaspoons hot oil
2 × 5 ml spoons/2 teaspoons grated root ginger	2 teaspoons minced ginger root
2 × 5 ml spoons/2 teaspoons crushed garlic	2 teaspoons minced garlic
1 × 5 ml spoon/1 teaspoon ground Szechuan peppercorns	1 teaspoon ground Szechuan peppercorns
parsley sprigs to garnish	parsley sprigs to garnish

Skin, halve and core the kidneys. Score the surface of the kidneys with 1 cm/½ inch deep cuts, about 1 cm/½ inch apart, in a criss-cross pattern. Then cut each one into 2.5 cm/1 inch cubes. Soak in cold salted water for at least 20 minutes. Drain.

Sprinkle the courgettes (zucchini) or cucumber with salt and leave for 20 minutes. Pat dry with absorbent kitchen paper and arrange on a serving dish. Place the sesame seed paste mixture in a bowl. Add the soy sauce, vinegar, sugar, pepper oil, ginger, garlic and ground peppercorns, mix well.

Cook the kidney pieces in a little boiling water for 3 to 4 minutes or until they turn white. Drain and rinse under cold running water. Arrange the kidney pieces on top of the courgettes (zucchini) or cucumber. Just before serving, pour the sesame seed paste mixture over the kidneys. Serve cold, garnished with parsley.

Note: 2 × 15 ml spoons/2 tablespoons peanut butter may be used instead of sesame seed paste, if unobtainable.

Braised Fish with Hot Soy Bean Paste (Sauce)

METRIC/IMPERIAL

1 kg/2 lb whole white fish (sole, plaice, snapper, cod, etc), cleaned

oil for shallow frying

2 × 15 ml spoons/2 tablespoons crushed garlic

1 × 15 ml spoon/1 tablespoon chopped root ginger

2 × 15 ml spoons/2 tablespoons chopped spring onion (shallot)

1.5 × 15 ml spoon/1½ tablespoons hot soy bean paste

2 × 15 ml spoons/2 tablespoons dry sherry

3 × 15 ml spoons/3 tablespoons soy sauce

1 × 2.5 ml spoon/½ teaspoon salt

1 × 5 ml spoon/1 teaspoon sugar

1 × 15 ml spoon/1 tablespoon red wine vinegar

2 × 5 ml spoons/2 teaspoons cornflour, dissolved in 4 × 15 ml spoons/4 tablespoons water

shredded spring onion (shallot) to garnish

AMERICAN

2 lb whole white fish, (sole, sea bass, cod, etc), cleaned

oil for shallow frying

2 tablespoons minced garlic

1 tablespoon chopped ginger root

2 tablespoons chopped scallion

1½ tablespoons hot bean sauce

2 tablespoons pale dry sherry

3 tablespoons soy sauce

½ teaspoon salt

1 teaspoon sugar

1 tablespoon red wine vinegar

2 teaspoons cornstarch, dissolved in ¼ cup water

shredded scallion to garnish

Score the fish on both sides with diagonal cuts, 1 cm/½ in deep and 1.5 cm/¾ inch apart. Heat just enough oil in a pan to make a thin film. Place the whole fish in the pan and fry until light brown on both sides. Transfer to a warmed plate.

Add 4 × 15 ml spoons/4 tablespoons oil to the pan and heat. Add the garlic, ginger and spring onion (shallot/scallion) and stir-fry over high heat for a few seconds. Put the fish on top and add the soy bean paste (bean sauce), sherry, soy sauce, salt, sugar and vinegar. Bring to the boil and simmer for 10 minutes.

Add the cornflour (cornstarch) mixture and simmer, stirring, until the sauce has thickened. Serve hot, garnished with the shredded spring onion (shallot/scallion).

Stir-Fried Pork with Mushrooms

METRIC/IMPERIAL

2 × 15 ml spoons/2 tablespoons soy sauce

1.5 × 15 ml spoons/1½ tablespoons hoisin sauce

1 × 15 ml spoon/1 tablespoon dry sherry

1 × 5 ml spoon/1 teaspoon sugar

1.5 × 15 ml spoons/1½ tablespoons tomato purée

1 × 5 ml spoon/1 teaspoon chilli sauce

3.5 × 15 ml spoons/3½ tablespoons oil

0.5 kg/1 lb lean pork, cut into 4 × 2.5 cm/1½ × 1 inch slices

6–8 dried Chinese mushrooms, soaked for 20 minutes, drained, stemmed and quartered

1.5 × 5 ml spoons/1½ teaspoons cornflour, dissolved in 3 × 15 ml spoons/3 tablespoons water

tomato wedges and parsley sprigs to garnish

AMERICAN

2 tablespoons soy sauce

1½ tablespoons hoisin sauce

1 tablespoon pale dry sherry

1 teaspoon sugar

1½ tablespoons tomato paste

1 teaspoon chili sauce

3½ tablespoons oil

1 lb lean pork, cut into 1½ × 1 inch slices

6–8 dried Chinese mushrooms, soaked for 20 minutes, drained, stemmed and quartered

1½ teaspoons cornstarch, dissolved in 3 tablespoons water

tomato wedges and parsley sprigs to garnish

Mix the soy sauce, hoisin sauce, sherry, sugar, tomato purée (paste) and chilli sauce with 1.5 × 15 ml spoons/1½ tablespoons of the oil. Pour half of this mixture into a dish, add the pork and leave to marinate for 30 minutes.

Heat the remaining oil in a pan over high heat. Add the pork with the marinade and stir-fry for 2 minutes. Add the mushrooms and the remaining soy sauce mixture. Stir-fry for 1½ minutes. Stir in the cornflour (cornstarch) mixture and cook, stirring, until the sauce thickens.

Transfer to a serving dish and garnish with the tomato wedges and parsley. Serve hot.

Braised Chicken with Peppers

METRIC/IMPERIAL

3 × 15 ml spoons/3 tablespoons oil

3 red peppers, cored, seeded and sliced into rings

1 × 5 ml spoon/1 teaspoon salt

2 × 15 ml spoons/2 tablespoons water

0.5 kg/1 lb chicken meat, cut into 2.5 cm/1 inch pieces

25 g/1 oz root ginger, finely chopped

pinch of brown sugar

2 × 5 ml spoons/2 teaspoons dry sherry

1 × 5 ml spoon/1 teaspoon cornflour

2 × 5 ml spoons/2 teaspoons soy sauce

AMERICAN

3 tablespoons oil

3 red peppers, cored, seeded and sliced into rings

1 teaspoon salt

2 tablespoons water

1 lb chicken meat, cut into 1 inch pieces

2 tablespoons finely chopped ginger root

pinch of brown sugar

2 teaspoons pale dry sherry

1 teaspoon cornstarch

2 teaspoons soy sauce

Heat 1 × 15 ml spoon/1 tablespoon of the oil in a pan. Add the pepper rings and salt; stir-fry for 1 minute. Add the water and simmer until the liquid has evaporated. Remove the peppers from the pan and set aside.

Heat the remaining oil in the pan. Add the chicken and ginger and stir-fry for 1 minute. Stir in the sugar and sherry.

Dissolve the cornflour (cornstarch) in the soy sauce and add to the pan. Simmer, stirring, until thickened. Add the pepper rings and cook for 1 minute. Serve hot.

Prawns (Shrimp) with Tomato Sauce

METRIC/IMPERIAL

1 × 5 ml spoon/1 teaspoon salt

1 egg white

4 × 5 ml spoons/4 teaspoons cornflour

0.5 kg/1 lb prawns, shelled and deveined

6 × 15 ml spoons/6 tablespoons oil

3 spring onions (shallots), finely chopped

2 slices root ginger, finely chopped

2 × 15 ml spoons/2 tablespoons tomato ketchup (sauce)

1 × 5 ml spoon/1 teaspoon sugar

1 × 5 ml spoon/1 teaspoon red wine vinegar or lemon juice

3 × 15 ml spoons/3 tablespoons water

AMERICAN

1 teaspoon salt

1 egg white

4 teaspoons cornstarch

1 lb shrimp, shelled and deveined

6 tablespoons oil

Braised Chicken with peppers

3 scallions, finely chopped

2 slices ginger root, finely chopped

2 tablespoons tomato ketchup

1 teaspoon sugar

1 teaspoon red wine vinegar or lemon juice

3 tablespoons water

Mix together the salt, egg white and 1 × 15 ml spoon/1 tablespoon of the cornflour (cornstarch). Add the prawns (shrimp) and turn to coat with the batter.

Heat the oil in a pan. When very hot, add two-thirds of the spring onions (shallots/scallions), the ginger and tomato ketchup (sauce) and stir-fry for 30 seconds. Add the prawns (shrimp), sugar, a pinch of salt, and the wine vinegar or lemon juice. Stir well.

Dissolve the remaining cornflour (cornstarch) in the water and add to the pan. Simmer, stirring, until thickened. Serve hot, garnished with the remaining spring onion (shallot/scallion).

Chicken with Hot Oil Sauce

This hot sauce is typical of Szechuan. Its rich colour is not only pleasing to the eye, it also stimulates the appetite.

METRIC/IMPERIAL

1 kg/2 lb chicken breasts or thighs

2 spring onions (shallots)

2 slices root ginger

oil for deep frying

225 g/8 oz cashew nuts or peanuts

Sauce

1 spring onion (shallot), chopped

3 × 15 ml spoons/3 tablespoons soy sauce

2 × 15 ml spoons/2 tablespoons hot pepper oil

2 × 15 ml spoons/2 tablespoons sesame seed oil

1 × 15 ml spoon/1 tablespoon sesame seed paste

1 × 5 ml spoon/1 teaspoon ground Szechuan peppercorns

1 × 2.5 ml spoon/½ teaspoon sugar

AMERICAN

2 lb chicken breasts or thighs

2 scallions

2 slices ginger root

oil for deep frying

1 cup cashew nuts or peanuts

Sauce

1 scallion, chopped

3 tablespoons soy sauce

2 tablespoons hot oil

2 tablespoons sesame oil

1 tablespoon sesame paste

1 teaspoon ground Szechuan peppercorns

½ teaspoon sugar

*Chicken with Hot Oil Sauce (left)
Prawns (Shrimp) with Tomato Sauce
(right)*

Put the chicken in a saucepan with the spring onions (shallots/scallions) and ginger and add just enough water to cover. Bring to the boil, cover and simmer for 30 minutes or until the chicken is tender. Drain the chicken, reserving 2 × 15 ml spoons/2 tablespoons of the cooking liquid.

Hold the chicken under cold running water for about 1 minute, so that the flesh will be firm. Remove the meat from the bones and cut into bite-size pieces. Arrange the meat on a serving plate. Place all the ingredients for the sauce in a bowl. Add the reserved cooking liquid and mix well.

Heat the oil to 180 C/350 F. Deep-fry the nuts until golden brown. Drain and cool. Sprinkle the nuts over the chicken, then pour over the sauce.

Courgettes (Zucchini) with Tomatoes

In China, *Huang gua*, a type of marrow (squash), is used in this dish. It is very similar to the courgette (zucchini) which is therefore an ideal substitute. For maximum flavour, the courgettes (zucchini) and tomatoes should be fresh from the garden.

METRIC/IMPERIAL

0.5 kg/1 lb courgettes

6 × 15 ml spoons/6 tablespoons oil

1 × 5 ml spoon/1 teaspoon salt

4–5 tomatoes, skinned and quartered

250 ml/8 fl oz chicken stock

1 × 15 ml spoon/1 tablespoon cornflour, dissolved in 2 × 15 ml spoons/2 tablespoons water

AMERICAN

1 lb zucchini

6 tablespoons oil

1 teaspoon salt

4–5 tomatoes, skinned and quartered

1 cup chicken stock

1 tablespoon cornstarch, dissolved in 2 tablespoons water

Cut the courgettes (zucchini) lengthwise into quarters, and then crosswise into 1 cm/½ inch pieces.

Heat 3 × 15 ml spoons/3 tablespoons of the oil in a pan. Add the courgettes (zucchini) and half the salt and stir-fry over high heat until slightly softened. Transfer to a plate and keep hot. Heat the remaining oil in the pan and stir-fry the tomatoes for 30 seconds. Add to the courgettes (zucchini).

Add the stock to the pan with the remaining salt and bring to the boil. Stir in the cornflour (cornstarch) mixture and simmer, stirring, until thickened.

Place the courgettes (zucchini) in the centre of a warmed serving plate and arrange the tomatoes around them. Pour the stock over the courgettes (zucchini) and serve hot.

Prawn (Shrimp) Toast

METRIC/IMPERIAL

1 × 5 ml spoon/1 teaspoon dry sherry

1 × 5 ml spoon/1 teaspoon salt

1 egg white

1 × 5 ml spoon/1 teaspoon cornflour

0.5 kg/1 lb prawns, shelled, deveined and finely chopped

7 slices of white bread from a large sliced loaf, with the crusts removed

2 × 15 ml spoons/2 tablespoons sesame seeds

2 × 15 ml spoons/2 tablespoons chopped cooked ham

oil for deep frying

parsley sprigs to garnish

AMERICAN

1 teaspoon pale dry sherry

1 teaspoon salt

1 egg white

1 teaspoon cornstarch

1 lb shrimp, shelled, deveined and finely chopped

7 slices of white bread from a large sliced loaf, with the crusts removed

2 tablespoons sesame seeds

2 tablespoons chopped cooked ham

oil for deep frying

parsley sprigs to garnish

Place the sherry, salt, egg white and cornflour (cornstarch) in a bowl and mix until smooth. Stir in the prawns (shrimp). Divide this mixture between the bread slices. Sprinkle with the sesame seeds and ham and press the topping firmly into the bread, using the back of a spoon.

Heat oil to 180°C/350°F. Deep-fry the toasts, a few at a time, with the prawn (shrimp) side down. When the edges of the bread turn golden, turn to the other side. Fry until golden brown. Drain on absorbent kitchen paper and cut each slice of bread into 4 squares. Arrange on a serving plate, garnish with parsley and serve hot.

Paper-Wrapped Fish

METRIC/IMPERIAL

0.5 kg/1 lb fish fillets (sole, plaice, bream)

1 × 5 ml spoon/1 teaspoon salt

1 × 5 ml spoon/1 teaspoon dry sherry

1 × 15 ml spoon/1 tablespoon oil

1 × 15 ml spoon/1 tablespoon shredded root ginger

1 × 15 ml spoon/1 tablespoon shredded spring onion (shallot)

oil for deep frying

8 spring onion (shallot) flowers to garnish (see note)

AMERICAN

1 lb fish fillets (sole, flounder, etc)

1 teaspoon salt

1 teaspoon pale dry sherry

1 tablespoon oil

1 tablespoon shredded ginger root

1 tablespoon shredded scallion

oil for deep frying

8 scallion flowers to garnish (see note)

Cut each fish fillet into 2.5 cm/1 inch squares, about 5 mm/¼ inch thick. Sprinkle with the salt and sherry and leave to marinate for 10 minutes.

Cut a 15 cm/6 inch square piece of grease-proof paper or non-stick parchment for each piece of fish. Brush with oil. Place one slice of fish and two pieces of shredded ginger and spring onion (shallot/scallion) on each oiled square. Fold into envelopes, tucking in the flaps to secure.

Heat oil to 180 C/350 F. Deep-fry the wrapped fish for 3 minutes. Drain on absorbent kitchen paper, arrange on a serving plate and garnish with the spring onion (shallot/scallion) flowers. The paper wrapping is opened by the guests.

Note: To prepare the garnish, shred the spring onion (shallot/scallion) tops to within 2.5 cm/1 inch of the base. Leave in a bowl of iced water to open; drain.

Prawn (Shrimp) Toast (above)
Courgettes (Zucchini) with Tomatoes (below left)
Paper-Wrapped Fish (right)

Sweet and Sour Cabbage Salad

METRIC/IMPERIAL

0.75 kg/1½ lb white cabbage, cored and separated into leaves

salt

3 × 15 ml spoons/3 tablespoons oil

1 red pepper, cored, seeded and chopped

3 × 15 ml spoons/3 tablespoons soy sauce

3 × 15 ml spoons/3 tablespoons sugar

3 × 15 ml spoons/3 tablespoons red wine vinegar

AMERICAN

1½ lb cabbage, cored and separated into leaves

salt

3 tablespoons oil

1 red pepper, cored, seeded and chopped

3 tablespoons soy sauce

3 tablespoons sugar

3 tablespoons red wine vinegar

Cook the cabbage in boiling salted water for about 10 minutes, or until just tender but still crisp. Drain. Roll the cabbage leaves from the stalk towards the end of the leaf, folding in the two sides as the leaf widens. Squeeze out any excess water, then cut the rolls crosswise into 2 cm/¾ inch slices. Arrange on a serving plate.

Heat the oil in a pan. Add the pepper and stir-fry for a few seconds. Add the remaining ingredients and bring to the boil. Immediately pour over the cabbage rolls. Cool and chill before serving.

Coin Purse Eggs

METRIC/IMPERIAL

6–8 × 15 ml spoons/6–8 tablespoons oil

6 eggs

3 spring onions (shallots), cut into 2.5 cm/1 inch pieces

4 dried Chinese mushrooms, soaked for 20 minutes, drained, stemmed and quartered

100 g/4 oz canned bamboo shoots, drained and cut into 5 mm/¼ inch slices

250 ml/8 fl oz clear broth (see page 15) or water

2 × 15 ml spoons/2 tablespoons soy sauce

1 × 15 ml spoon/1 tablespoon dry sherry

2 × 5 ml spoons/2 teaspoons cornflour, dissolved in 2 × 15 ml spoons/2 tablespoons water

AMERICAN

6–8 tablespoons oil

6 eggs

3 scallions, cut into 1 inch pieces

4 dried Chinese mushrooms, soaked for 20 minutes, drained, stemmed and quartered

1 cup canned bamboo shoots, cut into ¼ inch thick slices

1 cup clear broth (see page 15) or water

2 tablespoons soy sauce

1 tablespoon pale dry sherry

2 teaspoons cornstarch, dissolved in 2 tablespoons water

Heat 1 × 15 ml spoon/1 tablespoon of the oil in a pan. Break an egg into it and fry until the edges are set. Turn over carefully and fry the other side until the egg is completely set. Transfer to a serving plate and keep hot. Fry the remaining eggs in the same way, adding more oil to the pan as necessary.

Heat 2 × 15 ml spoons/2 tablespoons of oil in a pan. Add the spring onions (shallots/scallions) and stir-fry until fragrant. Add the mushrooms and bamboo shoots and stir-fry for a few seconds. Stir in the broth or water, soy sauce and sherry and bring to the boil. Add the cornflour (cornstarch) mixture and simmer, stirring, until thickened. Spoon the sauce over the eggs and serve hot.

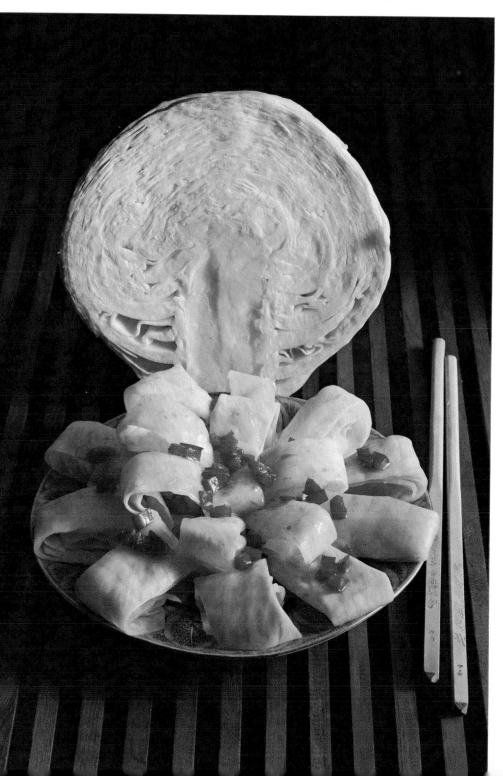

Sweet and Sour Cabbage Salad (left)

Coin Purse Eggs (right)

Stir-Fried Pork with Szechuan Hot Pickle

METRIC/IMPERIAL

2 × 15 ml spoons/2 tablespoons soy sauce

1 × 15 ml spoon/1 tablespoon dry sherry

1 × 5 ml spoon/1 teaspoon cornflour

225 g/8 oz lean pork, shredded

5 × 15 ml spoons/5 tablespoons oil

100 g/4 oz canned bamboo shoots, drained and coarsely shredded

100 g/4 oz Szechuan hot pickle, coarsely shredded, soaked for 5 minutes and drained

1 × 15 ml spoon/1 tablespoon sugar

AMERICAN

2 tablespoons soy sauce

1 tablespoon pale dry sherry

1 teaspoon cornstarch

½ lb lean pork, shredded

5 tablespoons oil

1 cup canned coarsely shredded bamboo shoots

1 cup coarsely shredded Szechuan kohlrabi, soaked for 5 minutes and drained

1 tablespoon sugar

Mix together 1 × 15 ml spoon/1 tablespoon of the soy sauce, the sherry and cornflour (cornstarch) in a bowl. Add the pork and leave to marinate for 10 minutes.

Heat the oil in a pan over high heat. Add the pork and stir-fry until lightly browned. Add the bamboo shoots, pickle (kohlrabi), sugar and the rest of the soy sauce. Stir-fry for a further 4 to 5 minutes. Serve hot.

Note: For an attractive finish, arrange strips of spring onion (shallot/scallion) to make flower heads with cherries to form the centres, on top of the dish.

Stir-Fried Diced Pork with Cucumber

METRIC/IMPERIAL

2 × 15 ml spoons/2 tablespoons soy sauce

2 × 5 ml spoons/2 teaspoons cornflour

225 g/8 oz pork fillet, cut into 1 cm/½ inch cubes

4 × 15 ml spoons/4 tablespoons oil

2 fresh or dried red chilli peppers, or 2 × 5 ml spoons/2 teaspoons Tabasco sauce

1 × 2.5 ml spoon/½ teaspoon salt

1 × 5 ml spoon/1 teaspoon sugar

2 × 5 ml spoons/2 teaspoons red wine vinegar

100 g/4 oz cucumber, diced

2 green peppers, cored, seeded and diced

1 × 15 ml spoon/1 tablespoon water

1 × 15 ml spoon/1 tablespoon sesame seed oil

AMERICAN

2 tablespoons soy sauce

2 teaspoons cornstarch

½ lb pork tenderloin, cut into ½ inch cubes

¼ cup oil

2 fresh or dried chili peppers, or 2 teaspoons Tabasco sauce

½ teaspoon salt

1 teaspoon sugar

2 teaspoons red wine vinegar

1 cup diced cucumber

1 cup diced green pepper

1 tablespoon water

1 tablespoon sesame oil

Mix together 1 × 15 ml spoon/1 tablespoon of the soy sauce and 1 × 5 ml spoon/1 teaspoon of the cornflour (cornstarch) in a bowl. Add the pork cubes and turn to coat with the mixture. Heat the oil in a pan over high heat. Add the chilli peppers, if used, stir-fry for 30 seconds, then remove from the pan. Add the pork to the pan and stir-fry until lightly browned.

Add the salt, sugar, vinegar, Tabasco, if used, and remaining soy sauce; stir-fry for 30 seconds. Add the cucumber and green peppers and stir-fry for a few seconds.

Dissolve the remaining cornflour (cornstarch) in the water and stir into the pan. Simmer, stirring, until thickened. Stir in the sesame seed oil. Serve hot.

Stir-Fried Pork with Noodles

METRIC/IMPERIAL

40 g/1½ oz transparent pea-starch noodles

4 × 15 ml spoons/4 tablespoons oil

225 g/8 oz minced pork

3 spring onions (shallots), chopped

1 × 15 ml spoon/1 tablespoon hot soy bean paste

2 × 15 ml spoons/2 tablespoons soy sauce

1 × 15 ml spoon/1 tablespoon dry sherry

1 × 2.5 ml spoon/½ teaspoon sugar

120 ml/4 fl oz water

AMERICAN

1½ oz cellophane noodles

¼ cup oil

½ lb ground pork

3 scallions, chopped

1 tablespoon hot bean sauce

2 tablespoons soy sauce

1 tablespoon pale dry sherry

½ teaspoon sugar

½ cup water

Soak the noodles in lukewarm water for 15 minutes. Drain and cut into 7.5 cm/3 inch pieces.

Heat the oil in a pan, add the pork and stir-fry over high heat until lightly browned. Add the noodles, stir-fry for a few seconds, then add the remaining ingredients. Bring to the boil and simmer until all the liquid has evaporated. Serve hot.

Note: 1 × 2.5 ml spoon/½ teaspoon of Tabasco sauce or 1 × 15 ml spoon/1 tablespoon chopped red chilli pepper may be substituted for the hot soy bean paste (sauce).

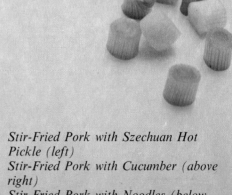

Stir-Fried Pork with Szechuan Hot Pickle (left)
Stir-Fried Pork with Cucumber (above right)
Stir-Fried Pork with Noodles (below right)

Bean Curd with Chilli Sauce

METRIC/IMPERIAL

2 cakes bean curd

4 × 15 ml spoons/4 tablespoons oil

5 × 15 ml spoons/5 tablespoons finely chopped onion

1 × 2.5 ml spoon/½ teaspoon crushed garlic

100 g/4 oz minced beef

3 chilli peppers, seeded and chopped

1 × 2.5 ml spoon/½ teaspoon sugar

3 × 15 ml spoons/3 tablespoons soy sauce

2 × 5 ml spoons/2 teaspoons cornflour, dissolved in 4 × 15 ml spoons/4 tablespoons water

AMERICAN

2 cakes bean curd

¼ cup oil

5 tablespoons finely chopped onion

½ teaspoon minced garlic

¼ lb ground beef

3 chili peppers, seeded and chopped

½ teaspoon sugar

3 tablespoons soy sauce

2 teaspoons cornstarch, dissolved in ¼ cup water

Blanch the bean curd in boiling water for 1 minute. Drain and cut into 5 mm/¼ inch cubes.

Heat the oil in a pan and add the onion and garlic. Stir-fry for 1 minute, then add the beef. Stir-fry until the beef is evenly browned. Add the bean curd, chilli peppers, sugar and soy sauce. Bring to the boil.

Add the cornflour (cornstarch) mixture and simmer, stirring, until the sauce has thickened. Serve hot.

Dan Dan Noodles, or Noodles with Sesame Paste Sauce

METRIC/IMPERIAL

0.5 kg/1 lb fresh noodles

900 ml/1½ pints clear broth (see page 15) or stock

Sauce

2 × 15 ml spoons/2 tablespoons sesame seed paste

4 × 15 ml spoons/4 tablespoons water

4 × 15 ml spoons/4 tablespoons chopped spring onions (shallots)

1 × 5 ml spoon/1 teaspoon crushed garlic

Dan Dan Noodles, or Noodles with Sesame Paste Sauce (left)
Bean Curd with Chilli Sauce (right)

1 × 15 ml spoon/1 tablespoon soy sauce

2 × 5 ml spoons/2 teaspoons red wine vinegar

2 × 5 ml spoons/2 teaspoons hot pepper oil

1 × 5 ml spoon/1 teaspoon salt

AMERICAN

1 lb fresh noodles

3¾ cups clear broth (see page 15) or stock

Sauce

2 tablespoons sesame paste

¼ cup water

¼ cup chopped scallions

1 teaspoon minced garlic

1 tablespoon soy sauce

2 teaspoons red wine vinegar

2 teaspoons hot oil

1 teaspoon salt

Cook the noodles in plenty of boiling salted water until just tender. Bring the stock or broth to the boil in another pan.

To make the sauce, mix the sesame seed paste with the water, then add the remaining ingredients.

When the noodles are cooked, drain well. Divide the boiling stock or broth between four individual soup bowls, add the cooked noodles and top with the sauce. Each person tosses the contents of his bowl before eating.

Red-Cooked Pork with Chestnuts

METRIC/IMPERIAL

1.5–2 kg/3–4 lb belly pork

1.5 × 5 ml spoons/1½ teaspoons sugar

120 ml/4 fl oz water

5.5 × 15 ml spoons/5½ tablespoons soy sauce

225 g/8 oz chestnuts

5 × 15 ml spoons/5 tablespoons dry sherry

225 g/8 oz chestnuts

AMERICAN

3–4 lb fresh pork sides

1½ teaspoons sugar

½ cup water

5½ tablespoons soy sauce

½ lb chestnuts

5 tablespoons pale dry sherry

Cut the pork, through the skin, lean and fat, into 4 cm/1½ inch pieces. Combine the sugar, water and 4.5 × 15 ml spoons/4½ tablespoons of the soy sauce.

Put the pork pieces into a flameproof casserole and pour over just enough boiling water to cover. Simmer for 15 minutes, then drain off all the water. Pour in the soy sauce mixture. Stir the pork pieces in the sauce until well coated. Transfer to a preheated cool oven (150 C/300 F, Gas Mark 2) and cook for 1 hour, stirring twice.

Meanwhile, cook the chestnuts in boiling water for 30 minutes. Drain; remove the shells and skin.

Add the chestnuts to the pork with the sherry and the remaining soy sauce. Stir well and return to the oven for a further 1 hour. Serve hot, on cooked shredded cabbage, if liked.

Red-Cooked Pork with Chestnuts

Southern China
Canton

Julia Chih Cheng

There is an old Chinese saying: 'Die in Liu-Chow, but eat in Kwang-Chow'. This is because Liu-Chow is famous for its coffins, and Kwang-Chow (or Canton) in southeast China, is renowned for its excellent cuisine.

Because of its geographic location, Kwangtung province enjoys four seasons of agricultural produce, as well as a multitude of fresh seafood all year round. No wonder, then, that for centuries the people of this region have been noted for their novel and original cuisine. Of the four culinary regions, this has the most varied repertoire, which is partly due to the abundant natural resources and partly to an event in 1644. In that year, the Ming Dynasty was overthrown and the chefs of the Imperial household in Peking fled south to Canton, the capital city of Kwangtung province. Cantonese cooking, which is derived not only from Canton but also from the country districts around that seaport and trading city, is well known in the West. This is because the first Chinese to emigrate in large numbers in the 19th Century came from this region.

The cooking of Southern China is versatile and colourful. Steaming is the favourite method of preparation because it retains natural flavours and colours. Dumplings, meat patties and the smaller fresh fish which are readily available are cooked in this way. Chicken steamed with ginger, star anise and other flavourings is a particularly delicious speciality. Roasting and barbecuing – using a well-tried process, bring flavours and texture to meat which are almost unexcelled. Cantonese or Cha shao roasting involves marinating meat, especially pork, for a long time and then roasting for a short time. This is in contrast to the method used in Northern China where meat is roasted for a long time and not marinated beforehand.

As would be expected, seafood plays an important part in the cooking of Southern China. Prawns (shrimp), abalone, scallops and sea cucumber are in plentiful supply. These fruits of the sea are stir-fried or steamed, often with root ginger to offset their 'fishiness'. Cantonese lobster and crab – flavoured with ginger and onion, are very popular, as is the typically Cantonese way of cooking meat with fish. Fried beef with oyster sauce (*page 190*) is a typical example.

Cantonese cooking does not depend nearly so much on hot spicy ingredients as its neighbour Szechuan, but soy sauce is still widely used. However, light-coloured soy sauce is preferred to the dark variety because it does not detract from the colours of the other ingredients in a dish. Other popular sauces are oyster, hoisin, black bean, lobster and plum.

The abundant tender fresh vegetables grown in this region are extensively used in many favourite recipes. Cantonese cooks specialize in the quick-stir-fry method of vegetable preparation, which helps to retain nutrients, colour and flavour. These vegetables are often served alone, or just with oyster sauce. Vegetables are also combined with meat or fish to make dishes such as Beef with broccoli (*page 202*); Fried prawns (shrimp) with broad (lima) beans (*page 184*); Pork and mustard green soup (*page 187*). Winter melon, spinach, Chinese cabbage (bok choy) and dried Chinese mushrooms are also widely used. The valleys of this semi-tropical region also produce sugar-cane and fruit, particularly tangerines or mandarin oranges, pomelos – a type of grapefruit, and loquats. As with fish, fruit is sometimes used combined with poultry and meat in dishes and in the very popular sweet and sour sauce.

The Cantonese are famous for *dim sum*, which means 'to please the heart'. These snack foods or titbits are usually served in tea houses in the afternoon. In the West they are welcome at cocktail parties or served as hors d'œuvres.

The unique cooking of Southern China, with its colourful and sophisticated dishes, redolent with delightful aromas, has done much to spread the popularity of Chinese cooking all over the world.

Shrimp Wonton Soup

METRIC/IMPERIAL

40 sheets wonton wrappings

1.2 litres/2 pints clear broth (see page 15)

1 spring onion (shallot), chopped

Filling

1 egg

1 × 5 ml spoon/1 teaspoon dry sherry

1 × 5 ml spoon/1 teaspoon salt

pinch of pepper

2 × 5 ml spoons/2 teaspoons oil

1 × 2.5 ml spoon/½ teaspoon sugar

1 × 15 ml spoon/1 tablespoon cornflour

225 g/8 oz prawns, shelled, deveined and finely chopped

100 g/4 oz fresh or canned water chestnuts, drained and chopped

AMERICAN

½ package wonton skins (about 40 sheets)

2½ pints clear broth (see page 15)

1 scallion, chopped

Filling

1 egg

1 teaspoon pale dry sherry

1 teaspoon salt

pinch of pepper

2 teaspoons oil

½ teaspoon sugar

1 tablespoon cornstarch

½ lb shrimp, shelled, deveined and finely chopped

½ cup fresh or canned chopped water chestnuts

For the filling, combine the egg, sherry, salt, pepper, oil, sugar and cornflour (cornstarch) in a bowl. Add the prawns (shrimp) and water chestnuts and stir until the mixture holds together.

Place 1 × 2.5 ml spoon/½ teaspoon filling in centre of each wonton wrapping (skin). Moisten the edges with water, fold corner to corner into a triangle and seal. Then seal the bottom corners together like a nun's hat.

Fill a saucepan with water and bring to the boil. Add the wonton, a few at a time, and cook until they float to the surface. Lift out with a slotted spoon and place in the hot broth in another saucepan. Keep hot while cooking the remaining wonton in the same way.

Sprinkle with chopped spring onion (shallot/scallion) and serve hot.

Note: Any leftover wonton wrappings can be used to make Date Crisps (see page 188).

Sweet Peanut Cream

METRIC/IMPERIAL

50 g/2 oz smooth peanut butter

1 litre/1¾ pints milk or water

4 × 15 ml spoons/4 tablespoons sugar

4 × 5 ml spoons/4 teaspoons rice flour or cornflour, dissolved in 4 × 15 ml spoons/ 4 tablespoons water

AMERICAN

¼ cup smooth peanut butter

4½ cups milk or water

¼ cup sugar

4 teaspoons rice flour or cornstarch, dissolved in ¼ cup water

Put the peanut butter into a saucepan and gradually stir in the milk or water to make a smooth paste. Add the sugar and bring to the boil, stirring constantly. Add the dissolved rice flour or cornflour (cornstarch) and cook, stirring, until the mixture thickens. Transfer to a bowl and serve warm, as a dessert.

Deep-Fried Sweet Potato Balls

METRIC/IMPERIAL

0.5 kg/1 lb sweet potatoes (yams)

100 g/4 oz glutinous rice flour

50 g/2 oz brown sugar

50 g/2 oz sesame seeds

oil for deep frying

AMERICAN

1 lb sweet potatoes

1 cup glutinous or sweet rice flour

⅓ cup brown sugar

½ cup sesame seeds

oil for deep frying

Put the potatoes in a saucepan, cover with water and bring to the boil. Reduce the heat and simmer for 15 to 20 minutes or until the potatoes are tender. Drain and peel. Mash the potatoes, then beat in the glutinous rice flour and sugar.

With dampened hands, form the mixture into walnut-sized balls. Roll each ball in sesame seeds until well coated.

Heat the oil to 160°C/325°F. Deep-fry the potato balls until golden brown. Drain on absorbent kitchen paper.

Serve hot as a dessert.

Deep-Fried Sweet Potato Balls (right)
Sweet Peanut Cream (far right)

Shrimp Wonton Soup (below)

Fried Whole Chicken
Spinach and Bean Curd Soup (below left)
Deep-Fried Pork Spareribs with Tomato Sauce (below right)

Fried Whole Chicken

METRIC/IMPERIAL

1×1.25 kg/$2\frac{1}{2}$ lb oven-ready chicken

3 whole star anise

1×5 ml spoon/1 teaspoon black or red Szechuan peppercorns

2 slices root ginger

3×15 ml spoons/3 tablespoons dry sherry

1×2.5 ml spoon/$\frac{1}{2}$ teaspoon ground cinnamon

1×5 ml spoon/1 teaspoon salt

1×5 ml spoon/1 teaspoon white vinegar

3×15 ml spoons/3 tablespoons honey or golden syrup

cornflour for coating

oil for deep-frying

prawn crackers to garnish

AMERICAN

$1 \times 2\frac{1}{2}$ lb oven-ready chicken

3 whole star anise

1 teaspoon black or red Szechuan peppercorns

2 slices ginger root

3 tablespoons pale dry sherry

$\frac{1}{2}$ teaspoon ground cinnamon

1 teaspoon salt

1 teaspoon white vinegar

3 tablespoons honey or corn syrup

cornstarch for coating

oil for deep-frying

shrimp chips to garnish

Put the chicken in a pan of boiling water with the star anise, peppercorns, ginger, sherry, cinnamon and salt. Simmer for 20 minutes. Remove the chicken, cool and pat dry inside and out, then brush with the vinegar and honey or syrup and sprinkle with cornflour (cornstarch). Hang the chicken in a well-ventilated place to dry for 2 to 3 hours.

Heat the oil to 160°C/325°F. Deep-fry the chicken, basting with oil constantly, until the skin becomes brown and crisp. Drain on absorbent kitchen paper. Cut into bite-sized pieces and arrange on a plate. Serve hot, garnished with prawn crackers (shrimp chips).

Spinach and Bean Curd Soup

METRIC/IMPERIAL

750 ml/1¼ pints chicken or beef stock

225 g/8 oz spinach, torn into small pieces

4 cakes bean curd, cut into 2.5 cm/1 inch cubes

1 spring onion (shallot), chopped

salt

freshly ground black pepper

AMERICAN

3 cups chicken or beef stock

½ lb spinach, torn into small pieces

4 cakes bean curd, cut into 1 inch cubes

1 scallion, chopped

salt

freshly ground black pepper

Bring the stock to the boil in a saucepan. Add the spinach and bean curd. Bring back to the boil, then add the spring onion (shallot/scallion) and salt and pepper to taste. Simmer for about 10 minutes; do not overcook or the spinach will lose its green colour and the bean curd become tough. Serve hot.

Deep-Fried Pork Spareribs with Tomato Sauce

METRIC/IMPERIAL

1 kg/2 lb pork spareribs

oil for deep frying

Marinade

3 × 15 ml spoons/3 tablespoons soy sauce

2 × 15 ml spoons/2 tablespoons dry sherry

1 × 15 ml spoon/1 tablespoon ginger juice (see page 35)

100 g/4 oz plain flour

2 × 15 ml spoons/2 tablespoons cornflour

Sauce

1.5 × 15 ml spoons/1½ tablespoons oil

1.5 × 5 ml spoons/1½ teaspoons salt

2 × 15 ml spoons/2 tablespoons Worcestershire sauce

4 × 15 ml spoons/4 tablespoons tomato ketchup (sauce)

6 × 15 ml spoons/6 tablespoons sugar

1 × 15 ml spoon/1 tablespoon cornflour

Garnish

6-8 spring onion (shallot) flowers (see note)

AMERICAN

2 lb pork spareribs or country-style spareribs

oil for deep frying

Marinade

3 tablespoons soy sauce

2 tablespoons pale dry sherry

1 tablespoon ginger juice (see page 35)

1 cup all-purpose flour

2 tablespoons cornstarch

Sauce

1½ tablespoons oil

1½ teaspoons salt

2 tablespoons Worcestershire sauce

¼ cup tomato ketchup

6 tablespoons sugar

1 tablespoon cornstarch

Garnish

6-8 scallion flowers (see note)

Cut the meat into strips, 2.5 cm/1 inch wide and 5 cm/2 inches long. Put into a saucepan, cover with boiling water and boil until the meat changes colour. Drain well.

Mix together the ingredients for the marinade in a bowl. Add the spareribs and leave for 30 minutes. Drain, reserving the marinade.

Heat the oil to 180°C/350°F. Deep-fry the spareribs until golden brown. Drain on absorbent kitchen paper, arrange on a serving plate and keep warm.

To make the sauce, place the ingredients, with the reserved marinade, in a saucepan. Bring to the boil and simmer, stirring constantly, until the sauce thickens. Pour over the spareribs and serve hot, garnished with spring onion (shallot/scallion) flowers.

Note: To prepare the garnish, shred the spring onion (shallot/scallion) tops to within 1 cm/½ inch of the base. Leave in a bowl of iced water until open, then drain.

Hairy Melon Stuffed with Meat

METRIC/IMPERIAL

225 g/8 oz minced pork

225 g/8 oz prawns, shelled, deveined and chopped

2 medium dried Chinese mushrooms, soaked for 20 minutes, drained, stemmed and chopped

1 spring onion (shallot), chopped

1 × 5 ml spoon/1 teaspoon ginger juice (see page 35)

1 × 15 ml spoon/1 tablespoon dry sherry

1.5 × 5 ml spoons/1½ teaspoons salt

2 × 15 ml spoons/2 tablespoons soy sauce

1 × 5 ml spoon/1 teaspoon sugar

1 × 5 ml spoon/1 teaspoon sesame seed oil

50 g/2 oz cornflour

1 kg/2 lb hairy melon or courgettes, peeled and cut into 2.5 cm/1 inch slices

3 × 15 ml spoons/3 tablespoons oil

50 g/2 oz transparent pea-starch noodles, soaked in hot water for 5 minutes, drained and cut into 10 cm/4 inch lengths (optional)

250 ml/8 fl oz water

AMERICAN

½ lb ground pork

½ lb shrimp, shelled, deveined and chopped

2 medium dried Chinese mushrooms, soaked for 20 minutes, drained, stemmed and chopped

1 scallion, chopped

1 teaspoon ginger juice (see page 35)

1 tablespoon pale dry sherry

1½ teaspoons salt

2 tablespoons soy sauce

1 teaspoon sugar

1 teaspoon sesame oil

½ cup cornstarch

2 lb hairy melon or zucchini, peeled and cut into 1 inch slices

3 tablespoons oil

2 oz cellophane noodles, soaked in hot water for 5 minutes, drained and cut into 4 inch lengths (optional)

1 cup water

Mix together the pork, prawns (shrimp), mushrooms, spring onion (shallot/scallion), ginger juice, sherry and half the salt, soy sauce, sugar and sesame seed oil in a bowl. Add 1 × 15 ml spoon/1 tablespoon of the cornflour (cornstarch). Stir until the mixture holds together. Sprinkle a little cornflour (cornstarch) onto each melon or courgette (zucchini) slice, and spread with the meat mixture.

Heat the oil in a pan. Add the melon or courgette (zucchini) slices and fry both sides until the meat turns brown. Add the remaining salt, soy sauce, sugar and sesame seed oil and stir. Add the softened noodles and all but 1 × 15 ml spoon/1 tablespoon of the water. Cover and cook for 10 to 15 minutes or until the meat and noodles are tender.

Mix the remaining cornflour (cornstarch) with the remaining water and stir into the pan. Simmer, stirring, until thickened. Serve hot.

Quick-Fried Pork with Bean Sprouts and Spring Onions (Scallions)

METRIC/IMPERIAL

0.5 kg/1 lb lean pork, thinly sliced

2 × 15 ml spoons/2 tablespoons soy sauce

4 × 15 ml spoons/4 tablespoons oil

1 × 5 ml spoon/1 teaspoon salt

pinch of pepper

350 g/12 oz fresh or canned bean sprouts, drained

4 spring onions (shallots), cut into 2.5 cm/1 inch pieces

1 × 5 ml spoon/1 teaspoon sugar

2 × 15 ml spoons/2 tablespoons boiling water

1.5 × 15 ml spoons/1½ tablespoons dry sherry

0.5 kg/1 lb hot cooked rice

AMERICAN

1 lb lean pork, thinly sliced

2 tablespoons soy sauce

¼ cup oil

1 teaspoon salt

pinch of pepper

2 cups fresh or canned bean sprouts, drained

4 scallions, cut into 1 inch pieces

1 teaspoon sugar

2 tablespoons boiling water

1½ tablespoons pale dry sherry

6 cups hot cooked rice

Cut the pork slices into 2.5 cm/1 inch pieces. Rub the pork with half the soy sauce and 1 × 15 ml spoon/1 tablespoon of the oil. Sprinkle with the salt and pepper.

Heat the remaining oil in a pan over high heat. Add the pork and stir-fry for 2 minutes, then remove from the pan, using a slotted spoon. Add the bean sprouts and spring onions (shallots/scallions) to the pan and stir-fry for 1 minute. Sprinkle in the remaining soy sauce, the sugar and water. Stir-fry for 30 seconds. Return the pork to the pan. Add the sherry and stir-fry for a further 1 minute.

Place the cooked rice in a warmed serving dish and arrange the pork and bean sprout mixture on top. Serve hot.

Fried Prawns (Shrimp) with Broad (Lima) Beans

METRIC/IMPERIAL

150 g/5 oz baby broad beans

3.5 × 5 ml spoons/3½ teaspoons dry sherry

2.5 × 5 ml spoons/2½ teaspoons salt

pinch of pepper

1 small egg white

2 × 5 ml spoons/2 teaspoons cornflour

0.5 kg/1 lb raw prawns, shelled and deveined

1 × 2.5 ml spoon/½ teaspoon sugar

1 × 15 ml spoon/1 tablespoon water

2 × 15 ml spoons/2 tablespoons oil

1 small spring onion (shallot), chopped

AMERICAN

1 cup baby lima beans

3½ teaspoons pale dry sherry

2½ teaspoons salt

pinch of pepper

1 small egg white

2 teaspoons cornstarch

1 lb raw shrimp, shelled and deveined

½ teaspoon sugar

1 tablespoon water

2 tablespoons oil

1 small scallion, chopped

Cook the beans in boiling salted water until just tender. Drain well. Mix together 1 × 15 ml spoon/1 tablespoon of the sherry, 1 × 5 ml spoon/1 teaspoon of the salt, the pepper, egg white and 1 × 5 ml spoon/1 teaspoon of the cornflour (cornstarch) in a bowl. Add the prawns (shrimp) and leave to marinate for 30 minutes.

Mix together the remaining sherry, salt and cornflour (cornstarch) with the sugar and water.

Heat the oil in a pan. Add the prawns (shrimp) and stir-fry for about 1½ minutes or until they become pink. Transfer to a serving dish.

Add the beans to the pan and stir-fry for a few seconds. Add the spring onion (shallot/scallion). Stir-fry for 30 seconds, then add the sugar mixture. Simmer, stirring, until thickened. Add to the prawns (shrimp) and serve hot.

Quick-Fried Pork with Bean Sprouts and Spring Onions (Scallions)

Curried Chicken with Coconut Juice

METRIC/IMPERIAL

2 × 15 ml spoons/2 tablespoons oil

1 × 1 kg/2 lb chicken, cut into serving pieces

1 × 15 ml spoon/1 tablespoon dry sherry

2 × 15 ml spoons/2 tablespoons soy sauce

1 × 5 ml spoon/1 teaspoon salt

pinch of pepper

2 onions, cut into quarters

3 spring onions (shallots), chopped

3 garlic cloves, chopped

2 × 15 ml spoons/2 tablespoons curry paste

2 × 5 ml spoons/2 teaspoons curry powder

300 ml/1½ pints water

3 medium potatoes, cut into 2.5 cm/1 inch pieces

2 medium carrots, cut into 2.5 cm/1 inch pieces

4 × 15 ml spoons/4 tablespoons coconut juice

2 × 15 ml spoons/2 tablespoons plain flour

2 × 5 ml spoons/2 teaspoons sugar

few strips of green pepper to garnish

AMERICAN

2 tablespoons oil

1 × 2 lb frying chicken, cut into serving pieces

1 tablespoon pale dry sherry

2 tablespoons soy sauce

1 teaspoon salt

pinch of pepper

2 onions, cut into quarters

3 scallions, chopped

3 garlic cloves, chopped

2 tablespoons curry paste

2 teaspoons curry powder

1¼ cups water

3 medium potatoes, cut into 1 inch pieces

2 medium carrots, cut into 1 inch pieces

¼ cup coconut juice

2 tablespoons all-purpose flour

2 teaspoons sugar

few strips of green pepper to garnish

Curried Chicken with Coconut Juice (above)
Fried Prawns (Shrimp) with Broad (Lima) Beans (below)

Heat 1 × 15 ml spoon/1 tablespoon of the oil in a pan. Add the chicken and stir-fry until lightly browned. Add the sherry, soy sauce, salt and pepper. Stir-fry for 2 seconds, then add the onions. Stir-fry for 30 seconds, then transfer the mixture to a saucepan.

Heat the remaining oil in the pan. Add the spring onions (shallots/scallions) and garlic and stir-fry for 1 second. Add the curry paste and curry powder. Stir-fry for 30 seconds, then stir in the water. Pour this sauce over the chicken and add the potatoes and carrots. Bring to the boil, cover and simmer for 20 minutes, or until the chicken is tender. Combine the coconut juice with the flour and sugar and stir into the pan. Cook, stirring, until the sauce is thickened.

Serve hot, garnished with strips of green pepper.

Note: A few drops of Tabasco or chilli sauce may be added with the curry paste to enhance the hot flavour, if liked.

Deep-Fried Chicken Legs (left)
Pork and Mustard Green Soup (centre)
Stir-Fried Lettuce with Oyster Sauce (right)

Deep-Fried Chicken Legs

METRIC/IMPERIAL

4 chicken legs, each cut into 2 pieces

2 × 15 ml spoons/2 tablespoons dry sherry

2 × 15 ml spoons/2 tablespoons soy sauce

1 × 5 ml spoon/1 teaspoon sugar

2 garlic cloves, crushed

1 × 2.5 ml spoon/½ teaspoon grated root ginger

2 eggs, beaten

2 × 15 ml spoons/2 tablespoons cornflour

25 g/1 oz plain flour

oil for deep frying

Garnish

lettuce leaves

baby tomatoes

lemon slice

AMERICAN

4 chicken legs, each cut into 2 pieces

2 tablespoons pale dry sherry

2 tablespoons soy sauce

1 teaspoon sugar

2 garlic cloves, minced

½ teaspoon minced ginger root

2 eggs, beaten

2 tablespoons cornstarch

¼ cup all-purpose flour

oil for deep frying

Garnish

lettuce leaves

cherry tomatoes

lemon slice

Mix the chicken leg pieces with the sherry, soy sauce, sugar, garlic, ginger and eggs in a bowl. Leave to marinate for at least 30 minutes. Add the cornflour (cornstarch) and flour to the marinade and toss until the chicken is thoroughly coated.

Heat the oil to 160°C/325°F. Deep-fry the chicken pieces for 10 minutes. Drain and place on a baking sheet. Put into a preheated cool oven (150°C/300°F, Gas Mark 2) and bake for about 10 minutes. Turn the legs over and bake for another 10 minutes or until tender.

Arrange the chicken on a serving platter and garnish with lettuce leaves, tomatoes and the lemon slice. Serve hot.

Pork and Mustard Green Soup

METRIC/IMPERIAL

2 × 5 ml spoons/2 teaspoons dry sherry

1 × 15 ml spoon/1 tablespoon soy sauce

1 × 5 ml spoon/1 teaspoon cornflour

4 × 5 ml spoons/4 teaspoons oil

100 g/4 oz pork fillet, thinly sliced

750 ml/1¼ pints clear broth (see page 15)

2 slices root ginger

1 small spring onion (shallot), chopped

100 g/4 oz mustard green, chopped

salt

freshly ground black pepper

AMERICAN

2 teaspoons pale dry sherry

1 tablespoon soy sauce

1 teaspoon cornstarch

4 teaspoons oil

¼ lb pork tenderloin, thinly sliced

3 cups clear broth (see page 15)

2 slices ginger root

1 small scallion, chopped

¼ lb mustard green, chopped

salt

freshly ground black pepper

Mix together the sherry, soy sauce, cornflour (cornstarch) and 1 × 5 ml spoon/1 teaspoon of the oil in a bowl. Add the pork and leave to marinate.

Bring the broth to the boil. Add the ginger, spring onion (shallot/scallion) and remaining oil. Stir in the meat with the marinade. Lower the heat and simmer for 15 minutes. Add the mustard green and simmer for a further 15 minutes. Add salt and pepper to taste. Discard the ginger. Serve hot as a main dish.

Note: Other vegetables, such as Chinese cabbage (bok choy) or spinach, may be used instead of mustard green.

Stir-Fried Lettuce with Oyster Sauce

METRIC/IMPERIAL

2 Cos lettuces

2 × 15 ml spoons/2 tablespoons oil

2 garlic cloves, crushed

2 × 5 ml spoons/2 teaspoons dry sherry

1 × 5 ml spoon/1 teaspoon salt

1 × 2.5 ml spoon/½ teaspoon sugar

2 × 15 ml spoons/2 tablespoons oyster sauce, or soy sauce

AMERICAN

2 heads Romaine lettuce

2 tablespoons oil

2 garlic cloves, minced

2 teaspoons pale dry sherry

1 teaspoon salt

½ teaspoon sugar

2 tablespoons oyster sauce, or soy sauce

Separate the lettuce into leaves and break into 5 cm/2 inch pieces.

Heat the oil in a pan and add the garlic, sherry, salt, sugar and then the lettuce leaves. Cover and cook for 1 minute. Drain the lettuce and arrange on a serving dish. Pour the oyster sauce (or soy sauce) on top of the lettuce and serve hot as a main dish, or cold as a salad.

Note: Broccoli or Chinese cabbage (bok choy) may be used in place of lettuce.

Prawns (Shrimp) in Shell with Spiced Sauce

METRIC/IMPERIAL

0.5 kg/1 lb large raw prawns

3 × 15 ml spoons/3 tablespoons oil

1 × 15 ml spoon/1 tablespoon dry sherry

1 × 5 ml spoon/1 teaspoon salt

pinch of pepper

2 garlic cloves, chopped

1 slice root ginger, chopped

1 spring onion (shallot), chopped

4 × 15 ml spoons/4 tablespoons tomato ketchup (sauce)

1 × 15 ml spoon/1 tablespoon Worcestershire sauce

dash of Tabasco sauce

2 × 5 ml spoons/2 teaspoons sugar

1 × 5 ml spoon/1 teaspoon cornflour, dissolved in 1 × 15 ml spoon/1 tablespoon water

AMERICAN

1 lb large raw shrimp

3 tablespoons oil

1 tablespoon pale dry sherry

1 teaspoon salt

pinch of pepper

2 garlic cloves, chopped

1 slice ginger root, chopped

1 scallion, chopped

¼ cup tomato ketchup

1 tablespoon Worcestershire sauce

dash of Tabasco sauce

2 teaspoons sugar

1 teaspoon cornstarch, dissolved in 1 tablespoon water

Do not shell the prawns (shrimp); if necessary cut off the legs, make a slit along the back of each and devein.

Heat the oil in a pan. Add the prawns (shrimp), sherry, salt and pepper and stir-fry until the prawns (shrimp) are pink. Remove prawns (shrimp) from the pan, using a slotted spoon. Add the garlic, ginger and spring onion (shallot/scallion) to the pan and stir-fry for a few seconds. Add the tomato ketchup (sauce), Worcestershire sauce, Tabasco and sugar and stir-fry for about 1 minute.

Stir in the cornflour (cornstarch) mixture and simmer, stirring, until thickened. Return the prawns (shrimp) to the pan and toss in the sauce until heated through. Serve hot.

Date Crisps

METRIC/IMPERIAL

30 dates, stoned

30 walnut halves

30 wonton wrappings

1.5 × 15 ml spoons/1½ tablespoons brown sugar

oil for deep frying

3 × 15 ml spoons/3 tablespoons icing sugar

AMERICAN

30 dates, pitted

30 walnut halves

30 wonton skins

1½ tablespoons brown sugar

oil for deep frying

3 tablespoons confectioners' sugar

Fill each date with a walnut half. Place each date on a wonton wrapping (skin) and add a pinch of sugar. Moisten the edges of the wrappings, roll and seal by twisting the ends. Heat the oil to 160°C/325°F. Deep-fry the rolls until golden brown; do not overcook. Drain on absorbent kitchen paper and sprinkle with icing (confectioners') sugar. Allow to cool before serving as a dessert.

Note: Use Chinese red dates (jujubes) if available.

Cha Shao Quick Roast Pork

METRIC/IMPERIAL

1 kg/2 lb pork fillet

Marinade

1.5 × 15 ml spoons/1½ tablespoons soy sauce

1.5 × 5 ml spoons/1½ teaspoons red bean curd cheese

1.5 × 15 ml spoons/1½ tablespoons dry sherry

1 × 15 ml spoon/1 tablespoon sweet soy bean paste or hoisin sauce

1 × 2.5 ml spoon/½ teaspoon salt

1.5 × 5 ml spoon/1½ teaspoons sugar or honey

1 × 15 ml spoon/1 tablespoon oil

AMERICAN

2 lb pork tenderloin

Marinade

1½ tablespoons soy sauce

1½ teaspoons red bean curd

1½ tablespoons pale dry sherry

1 tablespoon sweet bean sauce or hoisin sauce

½ teaspoon salt

1½ teaspoons sugar or honey

1 tablespoon oil

Place the pork fillet (tenderloin) in a shallow dish. Combine the marinade ingredients and pour over the pork. Turn the meat in the marinade until well coated. Leave to marinate for 2 hours, turning the pork every 20 minutes.

Put the pork on a wire rack in a roasting pan and place in the top of a preheated hot oven (220°C/425°F, Gas Mark 7). Roast for 12 minutes, turning the pork halfway through cooking.

Remove the pork from the oven and cut across the grain into 5 mm/¼ inch thick slices. Arrange on a serving platter.

Note: The high heat causes the marinade to become almost encrusted on the surface of the pork, forming a dark rim around each slice of pork, while the centre of the slice is still quite fresh and juicy. This combination gives the *Cha Shao* pork a special character and appeal.

Prawns (Shrimp) in Shell with Spiced Sauce (above)

Cha Shao Quick Roast Pork (right)

Fried Beef with Oyster Sauce

METRIC/IMPERIAL

1 × 15 ml spoon/1 tablespoon dry sherry

1 × 15 ml spoon/1 tablespoon soy sauce

1 × 15 ml spoon/1 tablespoon cornflour

1 × 2.5 ml spoon/½ teaspoon sugar

1 × 2.5 ml spoon/½ teaspoon bicarbonate of soda

4 × 15 ml spoons/4 tablespoons water

pinch of pepper

6 × 15 ml spoons/6 tablespoons oil

0.5 kg/1 lb lean beef fillet, thinly sliced across the grain into bite-size pieces

2 spring onions (shallots), chopped

1 slice root ginger, chopped

2 × 15 ml spoons/2 tablespoons oyster sauce

AMERICAN

1 tablespoon pale dry sherry

1 tablespoon soy sauce

1 tablespoon cornstarch

½ teaspoon sugar

½ teaspoon baking soda

¼ cup water

pinch of pepper

6 tablespoons oil

1 lb beef tenderloin, thinly sliced across the grain into bite-size pieces

2 scallions, chopped

1 slice ginger root, chopped

2 tablespoons oyster sauce

Mix together the sherry, soy sauce, cornflour (cornstarch), sugar, soda, water, pepper and 2 × 15 ml spoons/2 tablespoons oil in a bowl. Add the beef and leave to marinate for 1 hour.

Heat the remaining oil in a pan. Add the beef and stir-fry for about 1½ minutes or until partially cooked. Remove with a perforated spoon. Add half the spring onion (shallot/scallion), the ginger and oyster sauce to the pan and stir-fry for 1 minute. Add the beef and stir-fry for about 1 minute. Serve hot, garnished with the remaining spring onion (shallot/scallion).

Fried Fish with Celery

METRIC/IMPERIAL

1 kg/2 lb white fish fillets, cut into 1 × 5 cm/ ½ × 2 inch pieces

3 celery stalks, sliced diagonally

6 × 15 ml spoons/6 tablespoons oil

Marinade

2 × 5 ml spoons/2 teaspoons salt

1 × 15 ml spoon/1 tablespoon dry sherry

1 × 5 ml spoon/1 teaspoon ground ginger

1 egg white

2 × 15 ml spoons/2 tablespoons cornflour

pinch of pepper

Sauce

2 × 15 ml spoons/2 tablespoons sesame seed oil

1 × 5 ml spoon/1 teaspoon garlic salt

1 × 15 ml spoon/1 tablespoon dry sherry

1 × 5 ml spoon/1 teaspoon sugar

1 × 15 ml spoon/1 tablespoon cornflour, dissolved in 120 ml/4 fl oz water

Garnish

halved tomato slices

AMERICAN

2 lb white fish fillets, cut into ½ × 2 inch pieces

3 celery stalks, sliced diagonally

6 tablespoons oil

Marinade

2 teaspoons salt

1 tablespoon pale dry sherry

1 teaspoon ground ginger

1 egg white

2 tablespoons cornstarch

pinch of pepper

Sauce

2 tablespoons sesame oil

1 teaspoon garlic salt

1 tablespoon pale dry sherry

1 teaspoon sugar

1 tablespoon cornstarch, dissolved in ½ cup water

Garnish

halved tomato slices

Mix together the ingredients for the marinade in a bowl. Add the fish and leave to marinate for 10 to 15 minutes. Parboil the celery in salted water for 1 minute; drain. Heat 4 × 15 ml spoons/4 tablespoons of the oil in a pan. Add the fish pieces and fry on both sides until they become white. Drain and pile in the centre of a serving dish.

Heat the remaining oil in the pan. Add the celery and sprinkle with a little salt. Stir-fry for 2 seconds. Arrange the celery around the fish. Keep hot.

Put all the sauce ingredients in a saucepan and cook, stirring continuously, until thickened. Pour over the fish and serve hot, garnished with tomato slices.

Chopped Squab with Lettuce

METRIC/IMPERIAL

5 × 15 ml spoons/5 tablespoons oil

2 garlic cloves, chopped

2 chicken livers, blanched and diced

0.5 kg/1 lb squab meat, diced

1 × 15 ml spoon/1 tablespoon dry sherry

1 × 2.5 ml spoon/½ teaspoon salt

pinch of pepper

3 medium dried Chinese mushrooms, soaked for 20 minutes, drained, stemmed and chopped

1 × 125 g/5 oz can bamboo shoot or water chestnuts, drained and chopped

1 × 15 ml spoon/1 tablespoon oyster sauce

1 × 5 ml spoon/1 teaspoon sugar

1 × 5ml spoon/1 teaspoon cornflour, dissolved in 2 × 15 ml spoons/2 tablespoons water

1 lettuce, separated into leaves

4 × 15 ml spoons/4 tablespoons hoisin sauce

AMERICAN

5 tablespoons oil

2 garlic cloves, chopped

2 chicken livers, blanched and diced

1 lb squab meat, diced

1 tablespoon pale dry sherry

½ teaspoon salt

pinch of pepper

3 medium dried Chinese mushrooms, soaked for 20 minutes, drained, stemmed and chopped

1 × 5 oz can bamboo shoot or water chestnuts, drained and chopped

1 tablespoon oyster sauce

1 teaspoon sugar

1 teaspoon cornstarch, dissolved in 2 tablespoons water

1 head lettuce, separated into leaves

4 tablespoons hoisin sauce

Heat 3 × 15 ml spoons/3 tablespoons of the oil in a pan. Add the garlic, chicken livers and meat and stir-fry until the meat changes colour. Add the sherry, salt and pepper. Stir-fry for 1 minute. Remove from the heat and keep warm.

Heat the remaining oil in another pan. Add the mushrooms and bamboo shoot or water chestnuts and stir-fry for 2 seconds. Add the cooked meat mixture, oyster sauce and sugar. Stir-fry for 1 minute. Stir in the cornflour (cornstarch) mixture and cook, stirring, until thickened.

To serve, arrange the lettuce on a serving plate. Place the meat mixture on top and serve the hoisin sauce in a separate dish.
Note: Chicken or game hen may be substituted for the squab.

Deep-Fried Chicken Livers and Giblets

METRIC/IMPERIAL

1 × 15 ml spoon/1 tablespoon soy sauce

1 × 15 ml spoon/1 tablespoon dry sherry

1 × 5 ml spoon/1 teaspoon garlic salt

2 × 5 ml spoons/2 teaspoons sugar

2 × 5 ml spoons/2 teaspoons ground ginger

0.5 kg/1 lb chicken livers, lobes separated

0.5 kg/1 lb chicken giblets, scored in a criss-cross pattern

2 × 15 ml spoons/2 tablespoons cornflour

2 × 15 ml spoons/2 tablespoons plain flour

oil for deep frying

AMERICAN

1 tablespoon soy sauce

1 tablespoon pale dry sherry

1 teaspoon garlic salt

2 teaspoons sugar

2 teaspoons ground ginger

1 lb chicken livers, lobes separated

Fried Beef with Oyster Sauce (left)
Fried Fish with Celery (centre)
Chopped Squab with Lettuce (right)

1 lb chicken giblets, scored in a criss-cross pattern

2 tablespoons cornstarch

2 tablespoons all-purpose flour

oil for deep frying

Mix together the soy sauce, sherry, garlic salt, sugar and ginger in a bowl. Add the livers and giblets and turn to coat. Leave to marinate for 15 to 20 minutes. Add the cornflour (cornstarch) and flour and toss until the livers and giblets are well-coated.

Heat the oil to 160°C/325°F. Deep-fry the livers and giblets separately until crisp. Drain and serve hot or cold as an appetizer with Peppercorn-Salt Dip.

Peppercorn-Salt Dip

Toast 1 × 15 ml spoon/1 tablespoon black Szechuan peppercorns in a pan over high heat, shaking until the peppercorns begin to crackle. Remove and grind very finely. Sift and discard the large pieces, then mix with 3 × 15 ml spoons/3 tablespoons salt. This dip will keep for a long time in a screw-top jar and can be used for fried or roast dishes.

Lemon Chicken

METRIC/IMPERIAL

1×1.5–2 kg/3–4 lb chicken, boned and cut into bite-size pieces

1.5×5 ml spoons/$1\frac{1}{2}$ teaspoons salt

freshly ground black pepper

5×15 ml spoons/5 tablespoons oil

15 g/$\frac{1}{2}$ oz lard

4 slices root ginger, chopped

1 red pepper, cored, seeded and shredded

5–6 dried Chinese mushrooms, soaked for 20 minutes, drained, stemmed and shredded

shredded rind of 2 lemons

5 spring onions (shallots), thinly sliced

4×15 ml spoons/4 tablespoons dry sherry

1.5×5 ml spoons/$1\frac{1}{2}$ teaspoons sugar

2×15 ml spoons/2 tablespoons soy sauce (preferably light)

1×5 ml spoon/1 teaspoon cornflour, dissolved in 1×15 ml spoon/1 tablespoon water

1-2×15 ml spoons/1-2 tablespoons lemon juice

AMERICAN

1×3-4 lb chicken, boned and cut into bite-size pieces

$1\frac{1}{2}$ teaspoons salt

freshly ground black pepper

5 tablespoons oil

1 tablespoon lard

4 slices ginger root, chopped

1 red pepper, cored, seeded and shredded

5–6 dried Chinese mushrooms, soaked for 20 minutes, drained, stemmed and shredded

shredded rind of 2 lemons

5 scallions, thinly sliced

$\frac{1}{4}$ cup pale dry sherry

$1\frac{1}{2}$ teaspoons sugar

2 tablespoons soy sauce (preferably light)

1 teaspoon cornstarch, dissolved in 1 tablespoon water

1–2 tablespoons lemon juice

Rub the chicken all over with the salt, pepper and 1.5×15 ml spoons/$1\frac{1}{2}$ tablespoons of the oil. Heat the remaining oil in a pan over high heat. Add the chicken and stir-fry for 2 minutes then remove and keep warm.
Add the lard to the pan. When the fat has melted, add the ginger, red pepper and mushrooms. Stir-fry for 1 minute. Add the lemon rind and spring onions (shallots/scallions). Stir-fry for 30 seconds.
Sprinkle in the sherry, sugar and soy sauce. When the mixture comes to the boil, stir in the cornflour (cornstarch) mixture. Return the chicken to the pan and cook, stirring, for 1 minute. Sprinkle in the lemon juice and serve hot.

Fried Beef with Scrambled Egg

METRIC/IMPERIAL

1×2.5 ml spoon/$\frac{1}{2}$ teaspoon grated root ginger

1×15 ml spoon/1 tablespoon dry sherry

1×5 ml spoon/1 teaspoon sugar

2×5 ml spoons/2 teaspoons soy sauce

1×15 ml spoon/1 tablespoon cornflour

5×15 ml spoons/5 tablespoons oil

225 g/8 oz beef fillet, thinly sliced across the grain into bite-size pieces

4 large eggs

salt

freshly ground black pepper

oil for deep frying

1 spring onion (shallot), chopped

AMERICAN

$\frac{1}{2}$ teaspoon minced ginger root

1 tablespoon pale dry sherry

1 teaspoon sugar

2 teaspoons soy sauce

1 tablespoon cornstarch

5 tablespoons oil

$\frac{1}{2}$ lb beef tenderloin, thinly sliced across the grain into bite-size pieces

4 large eggs

salt

freshly ground black pepper

oil for deep frying

1 scallion, chopped

Combine the ginger, sherry, sugar, soy sauce, cornflour (cornstarch) and 1×15 ml spoon/1 tablespoon of the oil in a bowl. Add the beef and leave to marinate while preparing the eggs.
Beat the eggs with 1×15 ml spoon/1 tablespoon of the oil and salt and pepper to taste until light and fluffy.
Heat oil to $160°C/325°F$. Deep-fry the beef for a few seconds until the colour changes. Drain.
Heat the remaining 3×15 ml spoons/3 tablespoons oil in a pan. Add the deep-fried beef and eggs and stir-fry briskly over high heat. Add the spring onion (shallot/scallion) and stir for a few seconds until the eggs are cooked. Serve hot.

Lemon Chicken (left)

Fried Beef with Scrambled Egg (below)

Steamed Fish with Black Beans

METRIC/IMPERIAL

1 × 0.75 kg/1½ lb whole sea bass, snapper or bream, cleaned

1 × 2.5 ml spoon/½ teaspoon salt

pinch of pepper

2 × 15 ml spoons/2 tablespoons cornflour

1 × 15 ml spoon/1 tablespoon salted black beans, soaked for 10 minutes, drained and minced

2 garlic cloves, crushed

1 × 5 ml spoon/1 teaspoon finely chopped root ginger

1 spring onion (shallot), finely chopped

2 × 15 ml spoons/2 tablespoons oil

1 × 15 ml spoon/1 tablespoon soy sauce

2 × 15 ml spoons/2 tablespoons dry sherry

shredded spring onions (shallots) to garnish

AMERICAN

1 × 1½ lb whole sea bass, cleaned

½ teaspoon salt

pinch of pepper

2 tablespoons cornstarch

1 tablespoon salted black beans, soaked for 10 minutes, drained and minced

2 garlic cloves, minced

1 teaspoon minced ginger root

1 scallion, finely chopped

2 tablespoons oil

1 tablespoon soy sauce

2 tablespoons pale dry sherry

shredded scallions to garnish

Rub the fish, inside and out, with salt and pepper, then coat with the cornflour (cornstarch). Place the fish on a heatproof plate. Mix the black beans with the garlic, ginger and spring onion (shallot/scallion). Spoon over the fish and sprinkle with the oil, soy sauce and sherry. Place in a steamer and steam for 20 to 25 minutes.

Transfer the fish to a serving plate. Spoon the sauce over and garnish with the spring onions (shallots/scallions). Serve hot.

Stir-Fried Chinese Cabbage

METRIC/IMPERIAL

3 × 15 ml spoons/3 tablespoons oil

1 garlic clove, crushed

1 × 5 ml spoon/1 teaspoon salt

0.5 kg/1 lb Chinese cabbage, cut into 2.5 cm/ 1 inch pieces

1 × 15 ml spoon/1 tablespoon dry sherry

1 × 5 ml spoon/1 teaspoon sugar

1 × 5 ml spoon/1 teaspoon cornflour, dissolved in 1 × 15 ml spoon/1 tablespoon water

AMERICAN

3 tablespoons oil

1 garlic clove, minced

1 teaspoon salt

1 lb Chinese cabbage (bok choy), cut into 1 inch pieces

1 tablespoon pale dry sherry

1 teaspoon sugar

1 teaspoon cornstarch, dissolved in 1 tablespoon water

Heat the oil in a pan. Add the garlic and stir-fry until brown. Add the salt and cabbage and stir-fry briskly for 1 minute. Add the sherry and sugar, cover and cook for 1 minute.

Add the cornflour (cornstarch) mixture and cook, stirring, until thickened. Serve hot.

Stir-Fried Pork with Bitter Melon (top)
Tomatoes Stuffed with Meat (far right)
Steamed Fish with Black Beans (centre)
Stir-Fried Chinese Cabbage (bottom left)

Stir-Fried Pork with Bitter Melon

METRIC/IMPERIAL

1 × 15 ml spoon/1 tablespoon dry sherry

1 × 5 ml spoon/1 teaspoon soy sauce

1 × 5 ml spoon/1 teaspoon cornflour

6 × 15 ml spoons/6 tablespoons oil

225 g/8 oz pork fillet, cut into 2.5 × 5 cm/ 1 × 2 inch thin strips

0.5 kg/1 lb bitter melon, seeded and thinly sliced

1 × 2.5 ml spoon/½ teaspoon salt

2 garlic cloves, crushed

2 × 15 ml spoons/2 tablespoons salted black beans, soaked for 10 minutes and drained

2 × 5 ml spoons/2 teaspoons sugar

250 ml/8 fl oz water

AMERICAN

1 tablespoon pale dry sherry

1 teaspoon soy sauce

1 teaspoon cornstarch

6 tablespoons oil

½ lb pork tenderloin or butt, cut into 1 × 2 inch thin strips

1 lb bitter melon, seeded and thinly sliced

½ teaspoon salt

2 garlic cloves, minced

2 tablespoons salted black beans, soaked for 10 minutes and drained

2 teaspoons sugar

1 cup water

Mix together the sherry, soy sauce, cornflour (cornstarch) and 1 × 15 ml spoon/1 tablespoon of the oil in a bowl. Add the pork and turn to coat thoroughly. Set aside.

Sprinkle the melon slices with the salt. Set aside for 2 minutes, then squeeze out the water.

Heat 3 × 15 ml spoons/3 tablespoons of the remaining oil in a pan. Add the meat and stir-fry until it changes colour. Remove from the pan, using a slotted spoon.

Heat the remaining oil in the pan. Add the garlic and stir-fry until brown. Add the black beans. Stir-fry for 1 second, then add the bitter melon and stir-fry for 1 minute. Stir in the sugar and water. Cover and cook for 3 minutes or until the melon is tender. Add the meat and stir-fry for a few seconds. Serve hot.

Note: If preferred, the pan juices may be thickened with 1 × 5 ml spoon/1 teaspoon cornflour (cornstarch) dissolved in 1 × 15 ml spoon/1 tablespoon water before serving.

Tomatoes Stuffed with Meat

METRIC/IMPERIAL

0.5 kg/1 lb minced pork or beef

50 g/2 oz canned water chestnuts, drained and chopped

2 spring onions (shallots), chopped

1 × 15 ml spoon/1 tablespoon dry sherry

2 × 15 ml spoons/2 tablespoons soy sauce

1 × 5 ml spoon/1 teaspoon salt

4 × 5 ml spoons/4 teaspoons sugar

pinch of pepper

2 × 15 ml spoons/2 tablespoons cornflour

8 tomatoes, skinned, halved and seeded

5 × 15 ml spoons/5 tablespoons oil

parsley sprigs and chopped spring onion (shallot) to garnish

AMERICAN

1 lb ground pork or beef

¼ cup canned water chestnuts, drained and chopped

2 scallions, chopped

1 tablespoon pale dry sherry

2 tablespoons soy sauce

1 teaspoon salt

4 teaspoons sugar

pinch of pepper

2 tablespoons cornstarch

8 tomatoes, skinned, halved and seeded

5 tablespoons oil

parsley sprigs and chopped scallion to garnish

Mix together the meat, water chestnuts, spring onions (shallots/scallions), sherry, 1 × 15 ml spoon/1 tablespoon of the soy sauce, the salt, 2 × 5 ml spoons/2 teaspoons of the sugar, the pepper and cornflour (cornstarch). Stuff the tomato halves with this mixture.

Heat the oil in a pan. Place the stuffed tomatoes, meat side down, in the pan. Fry until the meat turns brown. Transfer to a casserole and arrange, meat side up.

Mix together the remaining soy sauce and sugar and sprinkle over the tomatoes. Bake in a preheated cool oven (150°C/300°F, Gas Mark 2) for 15 to 20 minutes. Serve hot, garnished with parsley sprigs and chopped spring onion (shallot/scallion).

Stir-Fried Chicken Livers with Prawns (Shrimp) and Broccoli

METRIC/IMPERIAL

350 g/12 oz broccoli, broken into small florets

225 g/8 oz shelled prawns

1 × 5 ml spoon/1 teaspoon salt

4 × 15 ml spoons/4 tablespoons oil

225 g/8 oz chicken livers

1.5 × 15 ml spoons/1½ tablespoons soy sauce

2 slices root ginger, shredded

1 × 5 ml spoon/1 teaspoon sugar

2 × 15 ml spoons/2 tablespoons dry sherry

AMERICAN

2 cups broccoli, broken in small florets

½ lb shelled shrimp

1 teaspoon salt

¼ cup oil

½ lb chicken livers

1½ tablespoons soy sauce

2 slices ginger root, shredded

1 teaspoon sugar

2 tablespoons sherry

Parboil the broccoli for 3 minutes, then drain. Sprinkle the prawns (shrimp) with the salt and 1 × 15 ml spoon/1 tablespoon of the oil. Cut each liver into four pieces. Sprinkle with half the soy sauce and another 1 × 15 ml spoon/1 tablespoon of the oil.

Heat the remaining oil in a pan over high heat. Add the ginger and stir-fry for 20 seconds. Add the prawns (shrimp) and chicken livers and stir-fry for 1½ minutes. Add the broccoli, sugar and sherry and bring to the boil. Sprinkle with remaining soy sauce. Stir-fry for 2 minutes. Serve hot.

Star-Anise Stewed Beef Tongue

METRIC/IMPERIAL

1 × 0.75 kg/1½ lb veal or ox tongue

1 slice root ginger

2 × 15 ml spoons/2 tablespoons dry sherry

2 × 15 ml spoons/2 tablespoons soy sauce

1 × 2.5 ml spoon/½ teaspoon salt

3 whole star anise

5 peppercorns

1 × 15 ml spoon/1 tablespoon sugar

Stir-Fried Chicken Livers with Prawns (Shrimp) and Broccoli

Onion and Ginger Crab with Egg

AMERICAN

1 × 1½ lb veal or beef tongue

1 slice ginger root

2 tablespoons pale dry sherry

2 tablespoons soy sauce

½ teaspoon salt

3 whole star anise

5 peppercorns

1 tablespoon sugar

Put the tongue in a pan, cover with cold water and bring to the boil. Drain and cover the tongue with fresh water. Bring to the boil, cover and simmer for 1 hour.

Remove the tongue, reserving the broth. Put the tongue in cold water and pull off the skin from the thick end to the tip. Put the tongue back in the broth, and add the ginger, sherry, soy sauce, salt, star anise and peppercorns. Bring to the boil, then cover and simmer for about 30 minutes or until the tongue is tender. Transfer the tongue to a serving plate.

Add the sugar to the pan and continue simmering until the liquid has reduced to about 120 ml/4 fl oz (½ cup). Serve the tongue, hot or cold, with the strained sauce.

Onion and Ginger Crab with Egg

METRIC/IMPERIAL

2–3 crabs

2 × 5 ml spoons/2 teaspoons salt

4–5 slices root ginger, shredded

2 × 15 ml spoons/2 tablespoons soy sauce

1 × 15 ml spoon/1 tablespoon chilli sauce

2 × 15 ml spoons/2 tablespoons dry sherry

150 ml/¼ pint clear broth (see page 15)

5 × 15 ml spoons/5 tablespoons oil

2 onions, thinly sliced

4 garlic cloves, crushed

3–4 spring onions (shallots), cut into 2.5 cm/1 inch pieces

1 egg, beaten

AMERICAN

2–3 crabs

2 teaspoons salt

4–5 slices ginger root, shredded

2 tablespoons soy sauce

1 tablespoon chili sauce

2 tablespoons pale dry sherry

⅔ cup clear broth (see page 15)

5 tablespoons oil

2 onions, thinly sliced

4 garlic cloves, minced

3–4 scallions, cut into 1 inch pieces

1 egg, beaten

Separate the claws from each crab and crack them open. Place each crab on its back and firmly pull the body, with the legs attached, away from the shell. Remove and discard the grey stomach sac and the grey feathered gills. Cut the body part into 4 pieces and sprinkle with the salt and ginger. Combine the soy sauce, chilli sauce, sherry and broth together. Heat the oil in a large pan over high heat. Add the onions and garlic. Stir-fry for 30 seconds. Add all the crab pieces, including the body shells, and the spring onions (shallots/scallions). Stir-fry for 3 to 4 minutes, until cooked through. Pour the soy sauce mixture over the crab pieces and bring to the boil, stirring constantly. Pour the egg into the pan in a thin stream and stir-fry for 30 seconds.

Turn the mixture onto a warmed serving dish. Eat by scraping the crab meat out of the main shells and claws. To eat the body, use the legs as handles, while extracting the meat.

Braised Chinese Sausage with Winter Melon

METRIC/IMPERIAL

1 × 15 ml spoon/1 tablespoon oil

2 Chinese sausages or 100 g/4 oz Virginia ham, diced

4 chicken wings, cut into 1 cm/½ inch pieces

4 small dried Chinese mushrooms, soaked for 20 minutes, drained, stemmed and quartered

1 spring onion (shallot), cut into 1 cm/½ inch pieces

1 × 15 ml spoon/1 tablespoon dry sherry

1 × 15 ml spoon/1 teaspoon salt

250 ml/8 fl oz water

1 × 225 g/8 oz can winter melon, peeled, seeded and cut into 2.5 cm/1 inch cubes

1 × 5 ml spoon/1 teaspoon cornflour, dissolved in 1 × 15 ml spoon/1 tablespoon water

AMERICAN

1 tablespoon oil

2 Chinese sausages, diced, or ½ cup diced Smithfield ham

4 chicken wings, cut into ½ inch pieces

4 small dried Chinese mushrooms, soaked for 20 minutes, drained, stemmed and quartered

1 scallion, cut into ½ inch pieces

1 tablespoon pale dry sherry

1 teaspoon salt

1 cup water

1 × ½ lb can winter melon, peeled, seeded and cut into 1 inch cubes

1 teaspoon cornstarch, dissolved in 1 tablespoon water

Heat the oil in a pan. Add the sausage or ham and fry for 2 seconds. Add the chicken wings and stir-fry until lightly coloured. Add the mushrooms and spring onion (shallot/scallion). Stir-fry for 1 minute. Add the sherry, salt and water. Bring to the boil, cover and simmer for 15 to 20 minutes or until the chicken is tender.

Add the winter melon. When the mixture returns to the boil, stir in the cornflour (cornstarch) paste and cook, stirring, until thickened. Serve hot.

Steamed Pork Spareribs with Black Beans

METRIC/IMPERIAL

1 × 15 ml spoon/1 tablespoon oil

2 × 15 ml spoons/2 tablespoons salted black beans, soaked for 10 minutes, drained and mashed

1 × 15 ml spoon/1 tablespoon dry sherry

1 × 5 ml spoon/1 teaspoon sugar

1 × 15 ml spoon/1 tablespoon soy sauce

0.5 kg/1 lb pork spareribs, cut into 2.5 cm/1 inch pieces

1 × 15 ml spoon/1 tablespoon cornflour, dissolved in 2 × 15 ml spoons/2 tablespoons water

2 red chilli peppers, cored, seeded and sliced

2 garlic cloves, chopped

AMERICAN

1 tablespoon oil

2 tablespoons salted black beans, soaked for 10 minutes, drained and mashed

1 tablespoon pale dry sherry

1 teaspoon sugar

1 tablespoon soy sauce

1 lb pork spareribs, cut into 1 inch pieces

1 tablespoon cornstarch, dissolved in 2 tablespoons water

2 red chili peppers, cored, seeded and sliced

2 garlic cloves, chopped

Heat the oil in a pan. Add the black beans and stir-fry for 1 second. Add the sherry, sugar and soy sauce and stir-fry for a few seconds. Remove from the heat and cool. Add the spareribs, cornflour (cornstarch) mixture, red chilli peppers and garlic. Stir well. Turn into a greased shallow heatproof dish. Steam for 30 minutes. Serve hot.

Braised Chinese Sausage with Winter Melon (left)
Steamed Pork Spareribs with Black Beans (centre)
Chicken in Soy Sauce (right)

Chicken in Soy Sauce

METRIC/IMPERIAL

600 ml/1 pint soy sauce

150 ml/¼ pint water

4 × 15 ml spoons/4 tablespoons dry sherry

225 g/8 oz sugar

3 whole star anise

1 × 5 ml spoon/1 teaspoon Szechuan or black peppercorns

1 × 5 ml spoon/1 teaspoon sesame seed oil

1 × 1.5 kg/3 lb chicken

1 spring onion (shallot), shredded, to garnish

AMERICAN

2½ cups soy sauce

⅔ cup water

¼ cup pale dry sherry

1 cup sugar

3 whole star anise

1 teaspoon Szechuan or black peppercorns

1 teaspoon sesame oil

1 × 3 lb frying chicken

1 scallion, shredded, to garnish

Place the soy sauce, water, sherry, sugar, star anise, peppercorns and sesame seed oil in a large pan. Bring to the boil, stirring. Place the chicken in the pan, breast side down. Reduce the heat, cover and simmer for 15 minutes.

Turn the chicken over and continue cooking for about 30 minutes, turning and basting with the pan juices occasionally. Remove from the heat and allow the chicken to cool in the cooking liquor. Drain and cut into serving pieces. Arrange on a plate and garnish with shredded spring onion (shallot/scallion).

Note: The cooking liquid provides excellent stock for future use.

Cantonese Roast Duck

METRIC/IMPERIAL

$1 \times 2\ kg/4\frac{1}{2}\ lb$ oven-ready duck

Stuffing

3 garlic cloves, crushed

10–12 spring onions (shallots), white part only

$1 \times 2.5\ ml\ spoon/\frac{1}{2}$ teaspoon 5-spice powder

$2 \times 5\ ml\ spoons/2$ teaspoons sugar

$5 \times 15\ ml\ spoons/5$ tablespoons clear broth (see page 15)

$1.5 \times 15\ ml\ spoons/1\frac{1}{2}$ tablespoons soy sauce

$1.5 \times 15\ ml\ spoons/1\frac{1}{2}$ tablespoons soy bean paste

$3 \times 15\ ml\ spoons/3$ tablespoons dry sherry

Coating

$300\ ml/\frac{1}{2}$ pint water

$4–5 \times 15\ ml\ spoons/4–5$ tablespoons clear honey

$5 \times 15\ ml\ spoons/5$ tablespoons wine vinegar

$2 \times 15\ ml\ spoons/2$ tablespoons soy sauce

AMERICAN

$1 \times 4\frac{1}{2}\ lb$ oven-ready duck

Stuffing

3 garlic cloves, minced

10–12 scallions, white part only

$\frac{1}{2}$ teaspoon 5-spice powder

2 teaspoons sugar

5 tablespoons clear broth (see page 15)

$1\frac{1}{2}$ tablespoons soy sauce

$1\frac{1}{2}$ tablespoons bean sauce

3 tablespoons pale dry sherry

Coating

$1\frac{1}{4}$ cups water

4–5 tablespoons clear honey

5 tablespoons wine vinegar

2 tablespoons soy sauce

Wipe the duck inside with a damp cloth. Combine the garlic, spring onions (shallots/scallions), 5-spice powder, sugar, broth, soy sauce, soy bean paste (sauce) and sherry together in a bowl. Spoon the mixture into the cavity of the duck. Close the neck opening and truss with skewers and string, or trussing needle and thread.

Cantonese Roast Duck

Pour boiling water over the duck skin then shake and pat dry with absorbent kitchen paper. Hang the duck up by the neck to dry in a well-ventilated place for 1 hour.

Combine the coating ingredients in a saucepan and heat until the honey has dissolved. Brush the duck with the coating mixture and hang up to dry overnight.

Put the duck on a wire rack in a roasting pan and roast in a preheated hot oven (220°C/425°F, Gas Mark 7) for 10 minutes. Turn the duck over and roast for a further 10 minutes. Reduce the temperature to moderately hot (190°C/375°F, Gas Mark 5). Turn the duck over once more and roast for 40 minutes. Increase the temperature to moderately hot (200°C/400°F, Gas Mark 6). Brush again with the coating mixture and roast for a final 10 minutes.

Chop the duck neatly into bite-size pieces and arrange on a serving platter with the stuffing. Serve hot or cold.

Fried Bean Sprouts with Meat

METRIC/IMPERIAL

0.5 kg/1 lb minced pork or beef

1 × 15 ml spoon/1 tablespoon dry sherry

1 × 15 ml spoon/1 tablespoon soy sauce

1 × 5 ml spoon/1 teaspoon cornflour

2 × 15 ml spoons/2 tablespoons oil

2 sping onions (shallots), chopped

0.5 kg/1 lb fresh or canned bean sprouts, drained and chopped

1 × 5 ml spoon/1 teaspoon salt

250 ml/8 fl oz water

AMERICAN

1 lb ground pork or beef

1 tablespoon pale dry sherry

1 tablespoon soy sauce

1 teaspoon cornstarch

2 tablespoons oil

2 scallions, chopped

1 lb fresh or canned bean sprouts, drained and chopped

1 teaspoon salt

1 cup water

Mix the pork or beef with the sherry, soy sauce and cornflour (cornstarch). Heat the oil in a pan. Add the meat mixture and stir-fry until the colour changes. Add the spring onions (shallots/scallions), bean sprouts and salt and stir-fry for 1 minute. Add the water. Bring to the boil, cover and cook for 15 minutes or until the meat and bean sprouts are tender. Serve hot.

Barbecued Pork

METRIC/IMPERIAL

2 × 15 ml spoons/2 tablespoons soy sauce

2 × 15 ml spoons/2 tablespoons yellow wine or dry sherry

2 × 5 ml spoons/2 teaspoons sesame seed oil

1 × 5 ml spoon/1 teaspoon salt

2 × 5 ml spoons/2 teaspoons ginger juice (see page 35)

2 × 15 ml spoons/2 tablespoons clear honey or golden syrup

50 g/2 oz sugar

1–2 cloves garlic, crushed

1 kg/2 lb pork shoulder, cut into 5 × 5 × 10 cm/ 2 × 2 × 4 inch chunks

AMERICAN

2 tablespoons soy sauce

2 tablespoons yellow wine or pale dry sherry

2 teaspoons sesame oil

1 teaspoon salt

2 teaspoons ginger juice (see page 35)

2 tablespoons clear honey or corn syrup

$\frac{1}{4}$ cup sugar

1–2 cloves garlic, minced

2 lb pork butt, cut into 2 × 2 × 4 inch chunks

Mix together the soy sauce, wine or sherry, oil, salt, ginger, honey or syrup, sugar and garlic in a dish. Add the pork and leave to marinate for at least 6 hours in the refrigerator, turning the meat occasionally.

Place the pork on a wire rack in a roasting pan. Roast in a preheated moderate oven (180°C/350°F, Gas Mark 4) for 40 to 45 minutes or until tender, basting with the pan juices frequently.

Cut into serving pieces and arrange on a plate. Serve hot or cold.

Note: This barbecued pork can be chopped and used as a filling for Barbecued Meat Buns, a favourite Chinese lunch or snack (see page 210).

Barbecued Pork (left)
Fried Bean Sprouts with Meat (right)

Beef with Broccoli

METRIC/IMPERIAL

0.5 kg/1 lb lean beef, thinly sliced across the grain into bite-size pieces

0.5 kg/1 lb broccoli

salt

3 × 15 ml spoons/3 tablespoons oil

2 garlic cloves, crushed

3–4 slices root ginger

2 × 5 ml spoons/2 teaspoons sugar

2 × 15 ml spoons/2 tablespoons soy sauce or oyster sauce

Marinade

2 × 5 ml spoons/2 teaspoons soy sauce

1 × 15 ml spoon/1 tablespoon dry sherry

1 × 15 ml spoon/1 tablespoon cornflour

1 × 15 ml spoon/1 tablespoon oil

AMERICAN

1 lb flank steak, thinly sliced across the grain into bite-size pieces

1 lb broccoli

salt

3 tablespoons oil

2 garlic cloves, minced

3–4 slices ginger root

2 teaspoons sugar

2 tablespoons soy sauce or oyster sauce

Marinade

2 teaspoons soy sauce

1 tablespoon pale dry sherry

1 tablespoon cornstarch

1 tablespoon oil

Mix together the ingredients for the marinade in a dish. Add the beef and leave to marinate while preparing the broccoli.
Separate the broccoli into florets and thinly slice the stem diagonally. Place in a pan of boiling salted water and cook for 1 minute. Drain and rinse with cold water.
Heat the oil in a pan. Add the garlic and ginger and stir-fry for a few seconds. Add the beef and stir-fry until the colour changes. Add the broccoli, sugar and soy sauce or oyster sauce. Stir-fry for 1 minute.
Serve hot.

Deep-Fried Crab Claws in Prawns (Shrimp)

METRIC/IMPERIAL

0.5 kg/1 lb large raw prawns, shelled and deveined

1 × 5 ml spoon/1 teaspoon salt

pinch of pepper

1 × 15 ml spoon/1 tablespoon dry sherry

1 egg white

6 × 15 ml spoons/6 tablespoons cornflour

10 cooked crab claws

oil for deep frying

tomato and lettuce to garnish

AMERICAN

1 lb large raw shrimp, shelled and deveined

1 teaspoon salt

pinch of pepper

1 tablespoon pale dry sherry

1 egg white

6 tablespoons cornstarch

10 cooked crab claws

oil for deep frying

tomato and lettuce to garnish

Crush the prawns (shrimp) with the side of a broad cleaver, then chop finely and place in a bowl. Add the salt, pepper, sherry, egg white and 2 × 15 ml spoons/2 tablespoons of the cornflour (cornstarch) and beat well until the mixture holds together.

Coat the crab claws with the prawn (shrimp) mixture, pressing it on firmly, then coat with the remaining cornflour (cornstarch).
Heat the oil to 180°C/350°F. Deep-fry the crab claws individually (otherwise they will stick together) until golden brown and crisp. Drain on absorbent kitchen paper and arrange on a serving plate. Garnish with tomato and lettuce. Serve hot with Peppercorn-Salt Dip (see page 191) and tomato ketchup (sauce), if liked.

Deep-Fried Bean Curd with Mushrooms

METRIC/IMPERIAL

4 cakes bean curd

1 × 15 ml spoon/1 tablespoon salt

oil for deep frying

cornflour for coating

2 × 15 ml spoons/2 tablespoons oil

1 garlic clove, crushed

4 spring onions (shallots), cut into 2.5 cm/1 inch pieces

225 g/8 oz pork fillet, thinly sliced into bite-size pieces

4 medium dried Chinese mushrooms, soaked for 20 minutes, drained, stemmed and quartered

1 × 15 ml spoon/1 tablespoon dry sherry

3 × 15 ml spoons/3 tablespoons soy sauce

1 × 5 ml spoon/1 teaspoon sugar

250 ml/8 fl oz water

AMERICAN

4 cakes bean curd

1 tablespoon salt

oil for deep frying

cornstarch for coating

2 tablespoons oil

1 garlic clove, minced

4 scallions, cut into 1 inch pices

½ lb pork tenderloin, thinly sliced into bite-size pieces

4 medium dried Chinese mushrooms, soaked for 20 minutes, drained, stemmed and quartered

1 tablespoon pale dry sherry

3 tablespoons soy sauce

1 teaspoon sugar

1 cup water

Put the bean curd on a plate and sprinkle with the salt. Leave for 1 minute, then drain the water from the plate.

Heat the oil to 180°C/350°F. Coat the bean curd cakes with cornflour (cornstarch) and deep-fry individually until light brown. Drain on absorbent kitchen paper.

Heat the 2 × 15 ml spoons/2 tablespoons oil in a pan. Add the garlic and stir-fry until brown. Add the spring onions (shallots/scallions), pork and mushrooms and stir-fry for 2 seconds. Add the bean curd, sherry, soy sauce, sugar and water. Cover and cook for 10 to 15 minutes or until the sauce has thickened. Serve hot

Deep-Fried Crab Claws in Prawns (Shrimp)
Beef with Broccoli (below left)
Deep-Fried Bean Curd with Mushrooms (below right)

Sweet Chicken Wings with Oyster Sauce

METRIC/IMPERIAL

0.5 kg/1 lb chicken wings

3 × 15 ml spoons/3 tablespoons oyster sauce

1 × 15 ml spoon/1 tablespoon soy sauce

300 ml/½ pint chicken stock

pinch of salt

1 × 5 ml spoon/1 teaspoon brown sugar

25 g/1 oz root ginger, finely chopped

pinch of black pepper

1 × 5 ml spoon/1 teaspoon coarse salt

AMERICAN

1 lb chicken wings

3 tablespoons oyster sauce

1 tablespoon soy sauce

1¼ cups chicken stock

pinch of salt

1 teaspoon brown sugar

2 tablespoons finely chopped ginger root

pinch of black pepper

1 teaspoon coarse salt

Put the chicken wings into a pan with just enough cold water to cover. Bring to the boil, cover and simmer for 10 minutes. Drain and discard the water.

Put the chicken wings back into the pan and add the oyster sauce, soy sauce, stock, salt and sugar. Bring slowly to the boil, cover and simmer for 20 minutes.

Sprinkle the ginger, pepper and coarse salt over the chicken and serve hot.

Chicken with Cashew Nuts

METRIC/IMPERIAL

1 egg white

2 × 15 ml spoons/2 tablespoons dry sherry

1 × 5 ml spoon/1 teaspoon salt

pinch of pepper

1 × 5 ml spoon/1 teaspoon cornflour

1 chicken breast, skinned, boned and cut into 2.5 cm/1 inch slices

9 × 15 ml spoons/9 tablespoons oil

100 g/4 oz cashew nuts

1 spring onion (shallot), chopped

1 green pepper, cored, seeded and cut into 1 cm/½ inch pieces

100 g/4 oz canned bamboo shoot, drained and sliced

1 × 15 ml spoon/1 tablespoon soy sauce

1 × 5 ml spoon/1 teaspoon sugar

1 × 5 ml spoon/1 teaspoon cornflour, dissolved in 1 × 15 ml spoon/1 tablespoon water

AMERICAN

1 egg white

2 tablespoons pale dry sherry

1 teaspoon salt

pinch of pepper

1 teaspoon cornstarch

1 chicken breast, skinned, boned and cut into 1 inch slices

9 tablespoons oil

Chicken with Cashew Nuts (left)
Triple Mushrooms Braised with Oyster Sauce

1 cup cashew nuts

1 scallion, chopped

1 green pepper, cored, seeded and cut into ½ inch pieces

1 cup canned sliced bamboo shoot

1 tablespoon soy sauce

1 teaspoon sugar

1 teaspoon cornstarch, dissolved in 1 tablespoon water

Mix together the egg white, 1 × 15 ml spoon/1 tablespoon of the sherry, the salt, pepper and cornflour (cornstarch). Add the chicken and turn to coat with the mixture. Heat 3 × 15 ml spoons/3 tablespoons of the oil in a pan. Add the chicken and stir-fry until golden. Remove from the heat.

Heat 5 × 15 ml spoons/5 tablespoons of the remaining oil in another pan. Add the cashew nuts and fry until lightly browned. Remove with a perforated spoon and drain on absorbent kitchen paper.

Heat the remaining oil in the pan. Add the spring onion (shallot/scallion), green pepper and bamboo shoot and stir-fry for 1 minute. Add the remaining sherry, the soy sauce, sugar and cornflour (cornstarch) mixture and cook, stirring, until thickened. Add the chicken, turn to coat in the sauce and heat through. Serve hot, sprinkled with the cashew nuts.

Triple Mushrooms Braised with Oyster Sauce

METRIC/IMPERIAL

2 × 15 ml spoons/2 tablespoons oil

100 g/4 oz small dried Chinese mushrooms, soaked for 20 minutes, drained and stemmed

250 ml/8 fl oz clear broth (see page 15)

1 × 225 g/8 oz can straw mushrooms, drained

100 g/4 oz button mushrooms

3 × 15 ml spoons/3 tablespoons oyster sauce

1 × 5 ml spoon/1 teaspoon sugar

1 × 5 ml spoon/1 teaspoon cornflour, dissolved in 2 × 5 ml spoons/2 teaspoons water

AMERICAN

2 tablespoons oil

¼ lb small dried Chinese mushrooms, soaked for 20 minutes, drained and stemmed

1 cup clear broth (see page 15)

1 × ½ lb can straw mushrooms, drained

¼ lb button mushrooms

3 tablespoons oyster sauce

1 teaspoon sugar

1 teaspoon cornstarch, dissolved in 2 teaspoons water

Heat the oil in a pan. Add the dried mushrooms and stir-fry for 1 minute. Add the broth and bring to the boil, then reduce the heat and cook for 15 to 20 minutes or until the dried mushrooms are tender.

Add the straw mushrooms and button mushrooms and cook, stirring, for 1 minute. Add the oyster sauce, sugar and cornflour (cornstarch) mixture. Cook, stirring, until thickened. Arrange the mushrooms on a serving dish and serve hot.

Sweet Chicken Wings with Oyster Sauce

Egg Fried Rice with Ham

METRIC/IMPERIAL

3 × 15 ml spoons/3 tablespoons oil

2 large eggs, beaten

350 g/12 oz cooked long-grain rice (see page 12)

1 × 2.5 ml spoon/½ teaspoon salt

50 g/2 oz cooked ham, diced

1 × 15 ml spoon/1 tablespoon chopped spring onion (shallot)

1–2 cooked carrots, finely chopped (optional)

coriander leaves to garnish

AMERICAN

3 tablespoons oil

2 large eggs, beaten

4 cups cooked long-grain rice (see page 12)

½ teaspoon salt

¼ cup diced cooked ham

1 tablespoon chopped scallion

1–2 cooked carrots, finely chopped (optional)

Chinese parsley leaves to garnish

Heat the oil in a pan over high heat. Pour in the beaten eggs and stir-fry for 1 second. Add the rice and salt and stir with the eggs until the rice grains are separated. Add the ham and spring onion (shallot/scallion). Stir-fry for 1 minute.

Add the carrot, if used, and stir-fry briefly. Transfer to a serving dish and garnish with coriander (Chinese parsley) leaves. Serve hot.

Deep-Fried Fresh Oysters

Deep-Fried Fresh Oysters (left)
Delicious Boiled Prawns (Shrimp)
Winter Melon Soup (right)

METRIC/IMPERIAL

12 large live oysters

1.5×5 ml spoons/$1\frac{1}{2}$ teaspoons salt

4×15 ml spoons/4 tablespoons cornflour

1×15 ml spoon/1 tablespoon dry sherry

1×5 ml spoon/1 teaspoon ginger juice (see page 35)

pinch of pepper

25 g/1 oz plain flour

1×5 ml spoon/1 teaspoon baking powder

2×15 ml spoons/2 tablespoons oil

120 ml/4 fl oz water

oil for deep frying

1 spring onion (shallot) and few strips of red pepper to garnish

AMERICAN

12 large live oysters

$1\frac{1}{2}$ teaspoons salt

4 tablespoons cornstarch

1 tablespoon pale dry sherry

1 teaspoon ginger juice (see page 35)

pinch of pepper

$\frac{1}{4}$ cup all-purpose flour

1 teaspoon baking powder

2 tablespoons oil

$\frac{1}{2}$ cup water

oil for deep frying

1 scallion and few strips of red pepper to garnish

Put the oysters into a bowl and clean off the slime with 1×5 ml spoon/1 teaspoon of the salt and 2×15 ml spoons/2 tablespoons of the cornflour (cornstarch). Scrub well, rinse under cold running water until clean. Parboil the oysters for 5 minutes, drain and shell. Mix together the sherry, ginger juice and pepper. Add the oysters and turn to coat. Mix the remaining cornflour (cornstarch) with the flour, baking powder and remaining salt in a bowl. Stir in the oil and water and beat to a smooth batter.

Heat oil to 180°C/350°F. Dip the oysters in the batter, then deep-fry until golden brown. Drain and serve hot, garnished with spring onion (shallot/scallion) and pepper strips.

Winter Melon Soup

METRIC/IMPERIAL

750 ml/$1\frac{1}{4}$ pints chicken stock

225 g/8 oz chicken meat, cut into 1 cm/$\frac{1}{2}$ inch cubes

6 small dried Chinese mushrooms, soaked for 20 minutes, drained, stemmed and cut into 1 cm/$\frac{1}{2}$ inch cubes

6 fresh or canned winter chestnuts, drained and cut into 1 cm/$\frac{1}{2}$ inch cubes

0.5 kg/1 lb winter melon, peeled, seeded and cut into 1 cm/$\frac{1}{2}$ inch cubes

50 g/2 oz Virginia ham, chopped (optional)

2–3 parsley sprigs, chopped

salt and pepper

AMERICAN

3 cups chicken stock

$\frac{1}{2}$ lb chicken meat, cut into $\frac{1}{2}$ inch cubes

6 small dried Chinese mushrooms, soaked for 20 minutes, drained, stemmed and cut into $\frac{1}{2}$ inch cubes

6 fresh or canned water chestnuts, drained and cut into $\frac{1}{2}$ inch cubes

1 lb winter melon, peeled, seeded and cut into $\frac{1}{2}$ inch cubes

$\frac{1}{4}$ cup chopped Smithfield ham (optional)

2–3 parsley sprigs, chopped

salt and pepper

Bring the stock to the boil in a saucepan. Add the chicken, mushrooms, water chestnuts and melon. Skim the scum from the surface of the soup. Lower the heat, cover and simmer for 15 to 20 minutes or until the melon is very tender and translucent. Serve hot, sprinkled with the ham, if used, parsley and salt and pepper to taste.

Note: If fresh winter melon is not available, substitute canned winter melon. Drain and use as above, but reduce the cooking time by 10 minutes.

Delicious Boiled Prawns (Shrimp)

METRIC/IMPERIAL

0.5 kg/1 lb raw prawns

1 × 5 ml spoon/1 teaspoon salt

2 × 5 ml spoons/2 teaspoons oil

6 × 15 ml spoons/6 tablespoons soy sauce

1 × 15 ml spoon/1 tablespoon sesame seed oil

AMERICAN

1 lb raw shrimp

1 teaspoon salt

2 teaspoons oil

6 tablespoons soy sauce

1 tablespoon sesame oil

Do not shell the prawns (shrimp), just devein, using a cocktail stick (toothpick), and cut off the legs if necessary.

Fill a saucepan with water and add the salt and oil. Bring to the boil and add the prawns (shrimp). Boil for 1½ minutes or until they turn pink. Drain and arrange on a warmed serving plate.

Mix together the soy sauce and sesame seed oil and serve as a dip with the prawns (shrimp).

Note: For an attractive garnish, serve the dip in a scooped-out tomato shell, as shown.

Stewed Oxtail with Tangerine Peel

METRIC/IMPERIAL

1 kg/2 lb oxtail, cut into 5 cm/2 inch pieces

1 × 15 ml spoon/1 tablespoon oil

6 cloves garlic, crushed

3 slices root ginger

dried peel of ¼ tangerine, soaked in water for 10 minutes, drained and shredded

1 × 5 ml spoon/1 teaspoon star anise

3 × 15 ml spoons/3 tablespoons 'chu hou' bean paste or brown bean paste

1 × 5 ml spoon/1 teaspoon Chinese rice wine

1.2 litres/2 pints water

oil for deep frying

75 g/3 oz dried bean curd, soaked in water for 20 minutes

1 × 2.5 ml spoon/½ teaspoon salt

1 × 15 ml spoon/1 tablespoon sugar

1 × 5 ml spoon/1 teaspoon soy sauce

1 × 15 ml spoon/1 tablespoon oyster sauce

1 × 5 ml spoon cornflour, dissolved in 1 × 15 ml spoon/1 tablespoon water

4 spring onions (shallots), cut into 5cm/2 inch pieces

AMERICAN

2 lb oxtail, cut into 2 inch pieces

1 tablespoon oil

6 cloves garlic, minced

3 slices ginger root

dried peel of ¼ tangerine, soaked in water for 10 minutes, drained and shredded

1 teaspoon star anise

3 tablespoons 'chu hou' bean paste or brown bean paste

1 teaspoon Chinese rice wine

5 cups water

oil for deep frying

3 oz dried bean curd, soaked in water for 20 minutes

½ teaspoon salt

1 tablespoon sugar

1 teaspoon soy sauce

1 tablespoon oyster sauce

1 teaspoon cornstarch, dissolved in 1 tablespoon water

4 scallions, cut into 2 inch pieces

Put the oxtail into a pan of boiling water and leave for 5 minutes; take out and drain. Heat the oil in a pan, add the garlic, ginger, tangerine peel, star anise, 'chu hou' bean or brown bean paste and stir-fry for 1 minute. Add the oxtail, Chinese rice wine and water. Bring to the boil, cover and simmer for 2 hours.

Meanwhile heat the oil to 180°C/350°F and fry the dried bean curd sticks until golden brown. Drain on absorbent kitchen paper.

Add the salt, sugar, soy sauce, oyster sauce and dried bean curd to the oxtail. Simmer for 30 minutes. Add the cornflour (cornstarch) mixture and cook, stirring, until the sauce has thickened. Sprinkle in the spring onions (shallots/scallions) and serve hot.

Fried Wonton

METRIC/IMPERIAL

0.5 kg/1 lb wonton paste

0.5 kg/1 lb minced streaky pork

2 × 15 ml spoons/2 tablespoons soy sauce

1 × 5 ml spoon/1 teaspoon brown sugar

1 × 5 ml spoon/1 teaspoon salt

350 g/12 oz frozen leaf spinach, thawed

oil for deep frying

AMERICAN

1 lb wonton skins

1 lb ground streaky pork

2 tablespoons soy sauce

1 teaspoon brown sugar

1 teaspoon salt

¾ lb frozen leaf spinach, thawed

oil for deep frying

Fried Wonton

Cut out 5 cm/2 inch rounds from the wonton paste (skins). Put the pork, soy sauce, sugar and salt in a bowl and mix well. Leave for 10 minutes. Squeeze the spinach in a clean, dry cloth to remove excess moisture. Add to the pork mixture and mix thoroughly.

Place a little of the pork and spinach mixture in the centre of each wonton paste round. Dampen the edges, fold over the filling and press together to seal. Heat the oil to 180°C/350°F. Deep-fry the wonton for about 5 minutes until golden brown. Drain on absorbent kitchen paper. Serve hot, with tomato ketchup (sauce).

Note: Wonton paste, or wonton skin as it is sometimes called, is available from most Chinese stores.

Oyster Sauce Abalone with Lettuce

METRIC/IMPERIAL

450 ml/¾ pint clear broth (see page 15)

0.5 kg/1 lb lettuce, quartered lengthwise

2 × 15 ml spoons/2 tablespoons oil

1 × 15 ml spoon/1 tablespoon dry sherry

3 × 15 ml spoons/3 tablespoons oyster sauce

1 × 5 ml spoon/1 teaspoon salt

1 × 5 ml spoon/1 teaspoon sugar

1 × 425 g/15 oz can abalone (whole), drained and thinly sliced

1 × 15 ml spoon/1 tablespoon cornflour, dissolved in 2 × 15 ml spoons/2 tablespoons water

AMERICAN

2 cups clear broth (see page 15)

1 lb head lettuce, quartered lengthwise

2 tablespoons oil

1 tablespoon pale dry sherry

3 tablespoons oyster sauce

1 teaspoon salt

1 teaspoon sugar

1 × 15 oz can abalone (whole), drained and thinly sliced

1 tablespoon cornstarch, dissolved in 2 tablespoons water

Pour 250 ml/8 fl oz (1 cup) of the broth into a saucepan. Bring to the boil and add the lettuce. Cook for 10 seconds, then drain and arrange on a serving plate. Keep warm. Heat the oil in a pan. Add the sherry, remaining broth, the oyster sauce, salt and sugar and bring to the boil. Add the abalone and cook for about 2 minutes or until tender. Add the cornflour (cornstarch) mixture and cook, stirring, until the sauce has thickened.

Arrange the abalone on the lettuce and pour over the sauce. Serve hot.

Oyster Sauce Abalone with Lettuce

Fried Crab with Black Beans

METRIC/IMPERIAL

1 large crab, parboiled and cleaned

2 × 15 ml spoons/2 tablespoons oil

1 × 5 ml spoon/1 teaspoon grated root ginger

2 garlic cloves, crushed

2–3 spring onions (shallots), chopped

1.5 × 15 ml spoons/1½ tablespoons salted black beans, soaked for 10 minutes and drained

2 × 15 ml spoons/2 tablespoons dry sherry

2 × 15 ml spoons/2 tablespoons soy sauce

1 × 15 ml spoon/1 tablespoon sugar

1 × 15 ml spoon/1 tablespoon cornflour, dissolved in 1 × 15 ml spoon/1 tablespoon water

AMERICAN

1 large crab, parboiled and cleaned

2 tablespoons oil

1 teaspoon minced ginger root

2 garlic cloves, minced

2–3 scallions, chopped

1½ tablespoons salted black beans, soaked for 10 minutes and drained

2 tablespoons pale dry sherry

2 tablespoons soy sauce

1 tablespoon sugar

1 tablespoon cornstarch, dissolved in 1 tablespoon water

Remove the legs from the crab and set aside. Extract the meat from the body and claws. Heat the oil in a pan. Add the ginger, garlic, spring onion (shallot/scallion) and the black beans and stir-fry for 1 minute. Add the crab meat, sherry, soy sauce and sugar. Cover and cook for 10 minutes or until the crab meat turns red. Add the cornflour (cornstarch) mixture and cook, stirring, until thickened. Serve hot, garnished with the crab legs.

Barbecued Meat Buns

METRIC/IMPERIAL

Wrapping

2 × 5 ml spoons/2 teaspoons dried yeast

300 ml/½ pint warm water

1 × 15 ml spoon/1 tablespoon sugar

0.5 kg/1 lb plain flour

Filling

1 × 15 ml spoon/1 tablespoon oil

2 garlic cloves, crushed

1 small spring onion (shallot), chopped

1 × 15 ml spoon/1 tablespoon dry sherry

1 × 5 ml spoon/1 teaspoon soy sauce

1 × 5 ml spoon/1 teaspoon oyster sauce

2 × 5 ml spoons/2 teaspoons sugar

120 ml/4 fl oz water

225 g/8 oz Barbecued Pork (see page 201)

1 × 5 ml spoon/1 teaspoon cornflour, dissolved in 1 × 15 ml spoon/1 tablespoon water

AMERICAN

Wrapping

1 package active dry yeast

1¼ cups warm water

1 tablespoon sugar

4 cups all-purpose flour

Filling

1 tablespoon oil

2 garlic cloves, minced

1 small scallion, chopped

1 tablespoon pale dry sherry

1 teaspoon soy sauce

1 teaspoon oyster sauce

2 teaspoons sugar

⅓ cup water

½ lb Barbecued Pork (see page 201)

1 teaspoon cornstarch, dissolved in 1 tablespoon water

For the wrapping, dissolve the yeast in the warm water, with 1 × 5 ml spoon/1 teaspoon of the sugar added. Leave in a warm place for 15 minutes or until frothy. Sift flour and remaining sugar into a bowl. Add the yeast mixture and mix to a firm dough. Knead on a lightly floured board until the dough is smooth and elastic. Place in a large bowl, cover and leave in a warm place to rise for about 2 hours.

To make the filling, heat the oil in a pan. Add the garlic and spring onion (shallot/scallion) and stir-fry for 1 second. Add the sherry, soy sauce, oyster sauce and sugar and stir-fry for 20 seconds. Pour in the water and bring to the boil. Chop the pork, add to the pan and cook for 1 minute. Add the cornflour (cornstarch) mixture and cook, stirring, until thickened. Remove from the heat and allow to cool.

Divide the dough in half and shape each piece into a roll. Cut each roll into 10 slices. With the palm of the hand, shape each slice to a circle, about 7.5 cm/3 inches in diameter. Place 1 × 5 ml spoon/1 teaspoon of the pork filling in the centre of each circle. Bring up the sides of the dough, pleat and pinch the edges together to seal tightly.

Place the meat buns on a damp cloth in a steamer and steam for 15 minutes. Serve hot. **Note:** These steamed buns will keep in the refrigerator for up to 1 week and can be reheated by steaming.

Barbecued Meat Buns (top left)
Stewed Duck with Onion (right)
Fried Crab with Black Beans (bottom)

Stewed Duck with Onion

METRIC/IMPERIAL

oil for deep frying

1×1.5 kg/$3\frac{1}{2}$ lb duckling

2×15 ml spoons/2 tablespoons oil

1 kg/2 lb onions

3×15 ml spoons/3 tablespoons dry sherry

3×15 ml spoons/3 tablespoons soy sauce

1×5 ml spoon/1 teaspoon salt

pinch of pepper

1×15 ml spoon/1 tablespoon sugar

parsley sprigs and strips of red pepper to garnish

AMERICAN

oil for deep frying

$1 \times 3\frac{1}{2}$ lb duckling

2 tablespoons oil

2 lb onions

3 tablespoons pale dry sherry

3 tablespoons soy sauce

1 teaspoon salt

pinch of pepper

1 tablespoon sugar

parsley sprigs and strips of red pepper to garnish

Heat the oil to 180°C/350°F. Deep-fry the duckling until lightly browned. Drain and place in a saucepan.

Heat the 2×15 ml spoons/2 tablespoons oil in a pan. Add the onions and fry, turning, until brown on all sides. Add to the duck with the sherry, soy sauce, salt, pepper, sugar and water to cover. Bring to the boil, cover and simmer for about 30 minutes. Turn the duck over and simmer for another 30 minutes or until tender. Serve hot, garnished with parsley and strips of red pepper.

Egg Flower Soup

METRIC/IMPERIAL

1 × 5 ml spoon/1 teaspoon lard

4 dried Chinese mushrooms, soaked in water
for 20 minutes, drained, stemmed and
shredded

900 ml/1½ pints chicken stock

1 × 5 ml spoon/1 teaspoon soy sauce

3 × 15 ml spoons/3 tablespoons coriander
leaves

1 spring onion (shallot)

3 eggs, whisked until frothy

salt

freshly ground black pepper

Egg Flower Soup (above)
Corn and Fish Soup (below)

Fried Pork with Baby Corn (below)

Corn and Fish Soup

METRIC/IMPERIAL

0.5 kg/1 lb filleted white fish (cod or sea
bass)

1 × 5 ml spoon/1 teaspoon ginger juice (see
page 35)

1 × 5 ml spoon/1 teaspoon sherry

salt

900 ml/1½ pints water

1 × 225 g/8 oz can sweetcorn, drained

1 × 5 ml spoon/1 teaspoon oil

1.5 × 5 ml spoons/1½ teaspoons cornflour,
dissolved in 1 × 15 ml spoon/1 tablespoon
water

1 spring onion (shallot), chopped

AMERICAN

1 lb fileted white fish (cod or sea bass)

1 teaspoon ginger juice (see page 35)

1 teaspoon sherry

salt

3¾ cups water

1 × ½ lb can kernel corn, drained

1 teaspoon oil

1½ teaspoons cornstarch, dissolved in 1
tablespoon water

1 scallion, chopped

Place the fish in a shallow heatproof dish
with the ginger juice, sherry and a generous
pinch of salt. Leave to marinate for 10
minutes. Place in a steamer and steam for 5
to 6 minutes. Remove from the heat and
mash the fish with a fork. Set aside.
Pour the water into a large saucepan and
bring to the boil. Add the sweetcorn, oil and
1 × 5 ml spoon/1 teaspoon salt. Simmer for 2
minutes. Add the cornflour (cornstarch) mixture and cook, stirring, until the soup thickens. Add the fish and cook for 1 minute.
Pour into soup bowls, sprinkle with spring
onion (shallot/scallion) and serve hot.

1 teaspoon lard

4 dried Chinese mushrooms, soaked in water for 20 minutes, drained, stemmed and shredded

3¾ cups chicken stock

1 teaspoon soy sauce

3 tablespoons Chinese parsley leaves

1 scallion

3 eggs, whisked until frothy

salt

freshly ground black pepper

Heat the lard in a saucepan, add the Chinese mushrooms and stir-fry for 1 minute. Pour in the stock and bring to the boil. Simmer for 1 minute. Add the soy sauce, coriander (Chinese parsley) leaves and spring onion (shallot/scallion). Pour in the eggs in a steady stream; do not stir. Remove from the heat. Add salt and pepper to taste.

Divide between individual soup bowls and serve immediately.

Fried Pork with Baby Corn

METRIC/IMPERIAL

1 × 15 ml spoon/1 tablespoon dry sherry

1 × 15 ml spoon/1 tablespoon soy sauce

1.5 × 5 ml spoons/1½ teaspoons cornflour

0.5 kg/1 lb pork fillet, sliced as thinly as possible

1 × 15 ml spoon/1 tablespoon oil

50 g/2 oz mange-tout

1 × 5 ml spoon/1 teaspoon salt

1 × 425 g/15 oz can baby corn, drained

1 × 425 g/15 oz can straw mushrooms, drained

2 × 5 ml spoons/2 teaspoons sugar

AMERICAN

1 tablespoon pale dry sherry

1 tablespoon soy sauce

1½ teaspoons cornstarch

1 lb pork tenderloin, sliced as thinly as possible

1 tablespoon oil

2 oz snow peas

1 teaspoon salt

1 × 15 oz can baby corn, drained

1 × 15 oz can straw mushrooms, drained

2 teaspoons sugar

Mix the sherry and soy sauce with 1 × 5 ml spoon/1 teaspoon of the cornflour (cornstarch). Add the pork and toss to coat thoroughly. Heat the oil in a pan. Add the pork and stir-fry until lightly browned. Add the mange-tout (snow-peas) and salt and stir-fry for 30 seconds. Add the baby corn and straw mushrooms and stir-fry for 1 minute. Sprinkle in the sugar. Mix the remaining cornflour (cornstarch) with 2 × 5 ml spoons/2 teaspoons water and stir into the pan. Cook, stirring continuously, until thickened.

Transfer to a serving dish and serve hot.

Cantonese Sweet and Sour Pork

METRIC/IMPERIAL

0.5 kg/1 lb pork fillet, cut into 2.5 cm/1 inch cubes

1 × 5 ml spoon/1 teaspoon salt

pinch of pepper

1 × 2.5 ml spoon/½ teaspoon 5-spice powder

2 × 15 ml spoons/2 tablespoons dry sherry

1 egg

3 × 15 ml spoons/3 tablespoons cornflour

oil for deep frying

2 × 15 ml spoons/2 tablespoons oil

1 garlic clove, crushed

1 onion, roughly chopped

1–2 green peppers, cored, seeded and diced

1 × 225 g/8 oz can pineapple chunks, with juice

3 × 15 ml spoons/3 tablespoons wine vinegar

50 g/2 oz sugar

4 × 15 ml spoons/4 tablespoons tomato ketchup (sauce)

pineapple and cherries to garnish

AMERICAN

1 lb pork tenderloin, cut into 1 inch cubes

1 teaspoon salt

pinch of pepper

½ teaspoon 5-spice powder

2 tablespoons pale dry sherry

1 egg

3 tablespoons cornstarch

oil for deep frying

2 tablespoons oil

1 garlic clove, minced

1 onion, roughly chopped

1–2 green peppers, cored, seeded and diced

1 × ½ lb can pineapple chunks with juice

3 tablespoons wine vinegar

¼ cup sugar

¼ cup tomato ketchup

pineapple and cherries to garnish

Fill a saucepan with water and bring to the boil. Add the pork and boil until it changes colour. Drain the pork, cool and pat dry with absorbent kitchen paper. Mix together the salt, pepper, 5-spice powder, sherry, egg, and cornflour (cornstarch). Add the pork and turn to coat well. Heat the oil to 180°C/350°F. Deep-fry the pork until brown. Drain on absorbent kitchen paper. Heat the 2 × 15 ml spoons/2 tablespoons oil in a pan. Add the garlic and fry until brown. Add the onion and green pepper and stir-fry for 1 minute. Stir in the pineapple juice with the vinegar, sugar and tomato ketchup (sauce). Cook, stirring, until thickened. Add the pineapple and stir until heated through. Serve hot, garnished with pineapple and cherries.

Braised Pork with Bamboo Shoots

METRIC/IMPERIAL

2 × 15 ml spoons/2 tablespoons oil

3 slices root ginger

1 spring onion (shallot), cut into 2.5 cm/1 inch pieces

0.75 kg/1½ lb pork shoulder, cut into 2.5 cm/1 inch pieces

2 × 15 ml spoons/2 tablespoons dry sherry

2 × 15 ml spoons/2 tablespoons soy sauce

1 × 225 g/8 oz can bamboo shoot, drained and chopped

4 medium dried Chinese mushrooms, soaked for 20 minutes, drained, stemmed and quartered

2 × 5 ml spoons/2 teaspoons garlic salt

1 × 5 ml spoon/1 teaspoon sugar

300 ml/½ pint water

Cantonese Sweet and Sour Pork (left)
Poached Fresh Fish (centre)
Briased Pork with Bamboo Shoots (right)

AMERICAN

2 tablespoons oil
3 slices ginger root
1 scallion, cut into 1 inch pieces
1½ lb pork butt, cut into 1 inch pieces
2 tablespoons pale dry sherry
2 tablespoons soy sauce
1 × ½ lb can bamboo shoot, drained and chopped
4 medium dried Chinese mushrooms, soaked for 20 minutes, drained, stemmed and quartered
2 teaspoons garlic salt
1 teaspoon sugar
1¼ cups water

Heat the oil in a pan. Add the ginger and spring onion (shallot/scallion) and stir-fry for 30 seconds. Add the pork and stir-fry for 2 minutes or until lightly browned. Add the sherry and soy sauce and stir for 1 minute, then add the bamboo shoots and mushrooms. Stir-fry for 30 seconds. Add the garlic salt, sugar and water. Bring to the boil, cover and simmer for about 20 minutes or until the meat is tender. Serve hot.

Poached Fresh Fish

METRIC/IMPERIAL

4 slices root ginger
2 spring onions (shallots)
1 × 0.75 kg/1½ lb whole fish (cod, sea bass, snapper or John Dory), cleaned
2 coriander sprigs, chopped
4 × 15 ml spoons/4 tablespoons oil
2 × 15 ml spoons/2 tablespoons soy sauce

AMERICAN

4 slices ginger root
2 scallions
1 × 1½ lb whole fish (cod or sea bass), cleaned
2 Chinese parsley sprigs, chopped
¼ cup oil
2 tablespoons soy sauce

Fill a large oval saucepan or fish kettle to a depth of 5 cm/2 inches with water. Add 2 of the ginger slices and 1 of the spring onions (shallots/scallions) and bring to the boil. Place the fish in the boiling water. Cover and cook for 1 minute, then turn off the heat. Leave, covered, on the top of the cooker for 8 to 10 minutes.

Meanwhile, cut the remaining spring onion (shallot/scallion) into 2.5 cm/1 inch pieces and shred the remaining 2 slices of ginger. Drain the fish and place on a serving plate. Sprinkle with the chopped spring onion (shallot/scallion), shredded ginger and the coriander (Chinese parsley).

Heat the oil in a small pan. When it is very hot, pour over the fish. Sprinkle the soy sauce on top and serve immediately.

Egg Rolls

METRIC/IMPERIAL

225 g/8 oz minced lean pork

100 g/4 oz shelled prawns

1 × 15 ml spoon/1 tablespoon oil

2 spring onions (shallots), finely chopped

225 g/8 oz fresh or canned bean sprouts, drained

1 × 15 ml spoon/1 tablespoon soy sauce

1 × 5 ml spoon/1 teaspoon salt

pinch of brown sugar

75 g/3 oz plain flour

300 ml/½ pint water

6 eggs, beaten

oil for deep frying

AMERICAN

½ lb ground lean pork

⅓ cup shelled shrimp

1 tablespoon oil

2 scallions, finely chopped

½ lb fresh or canned bean sprouts, drained

1 tablespoon soy sauce

1 teaspoon salt

pinch of brown sugar

1 cup all-purpose flour

1¼ cups water

6 eggs, beaten

oil for deep frying

Fried Crab with Egg (above right)
Crab Meat with Straw Mushrooms (below right)

Egg Rolls (below)

Mix the pork and prawns (shrimp) together. Heat the oil in a pan. Add the pork mixture and fry for 2 minutes. Add the spring onions (shallots/scallions) and bean sprouts and cook for a further 2 minutes or until the bean sprouts are tender. Stir in the soy sauce, salt and sugar and remove from the heat.

Sift the flour into a bowl. Add the water and eggs and beat to a smooth batter. Heat a greased heavy-based frying pan (skillet). Pour in enough batter to make a thin pancake and cook on one side only. Transfer to a plate. Repeat with the remaining batter. Place some of the pork mixture in the centre of the cooked side of each pancake. Fold the nearest edge over the filling, fold both sides in to the centre, then roll up, sealing the last edge with a little water. Repeat with the remaining pancakes.

Heat oil to 180°C/350°F. Deep-fry the rolls for about 10 minutes. Drain on absorbent kitchen paper. Serve hot with tomato ketchup (sauce).

Fried Crab with Egg

METRIC/IMPERIAL

225 g/½ lb fresh or canned crab meat

1 × 15 ml spoon/1 tablespoon dry sherry

1 × 5 ml spoon/1 teaspoon grated root ginger

5 large eggs, beaten

1 × 5 ml spoon/1 teaspoon salt

pinch of pepper

5 × 15 ml spoons/5 tablespoons oil

2 × 15 ml spoons/2 tablespoons chopped spring onion (shallot)

100 g/4 oz canned bamboo shoot, drained and chopped

100 g/4 oz canned straw mushrooms, drained

2 × 15 ml spoons/2 tablespoons peas

2 × 15 ml spoons/2 tablespoons soy sauce

1 × 5 ml spoon/1 teaspoon cornflour, dissolved in 120 ml/4 fl oz water

parsley sprig to garnish

AMERICAN

½ lb fresh or canned crab meat

1 tablespoon pale dry sherry

1 teaspoon minced ginger root

5 large eggs, beaten

1 teaspoon salt

pinch of pepper

5 tablespoons oil

2 tablespoons chopped scallion

½ cup chopped canned bamboo shoot

1 cup canned straw mushrooms

2 tablespoons peas

2 tablespoons soy sauce

1 teaspoon cornstarch, dissolved in ½ cup water

parsley sprig to garnish

Combine the crab meat, sherry and ginger in a bowl. Add the eggs, salt and pepper and mix well.

Heat 3 × 15 ml spoons/3 tablespoons oil in a pan. Add the egg mixture and fry until set and golden brown underneath. Turn over and cook the other side. Transfer to a serving plate and keep warm.

Heat the remaining oil in the pan. Add the spring onion (shallot/scallion), bamboo shoot, mushrooms and peas and stir-fry for 1 minute. Add the soy sauce and cornflour (cornstarch) mixture and cook, stirring, until thickened. Arrange the mixture on top of the egg and serve hot, garnished with parsley.

Crab Meat with Straw Mushrooms

METRIC/IMPERIAL

3 × 15 ml spoons/3 tablespoons oil

2 slices root ginger

1 spring onion (shallot), cut into 5 cm/2 inch pieces

1 × 15 ml spoon/1 tablespoon dry sherry

1 × 2.5 ml spoon/½ teaspoon salt

pinch of pepper

225 g/8 oz fresh or canned crab meat

1 × 225 g/8 oz can straw mushrooms, drained

120 ml/4 fl oz clear broth (see page 15) or water

1 × 5 ml spoon/1 teaspoon cornflour, dissolved in 1 × 15 ml spoon/1 tablespoon water

AMERICAN

3 tablespoons oil

2 slices ginger root

1 scallion, cut into 2 inch pieces

1 tablespoon pale dry sherry

½ teaspoon salt

pinch of pepper

½ lb fresh or canned crab meat

1 × ½ lb can straw mushrooms, drained

¼ cup clear broth (see page 15) or water

1 teaspoon cornstarch, dissolved in 1 tablespoon water

Heat the oil in a pan. Add the ginger and spring onion (shallot/scallion) and stir-fry for 1 second. Add the sherry, salt, pepper and crab meat and stir-fry for 1 minute. Add the mushrooms and broth or water. Bring to the boil, cover and simmer for 5 to 10 minutes.

Remove the ginger and onion. Add the cornflour (cornstarch) mixture and cook, stirring, until thickened.

Serve hot, sprinkled with chopped spring onion (shallot/scallion), if liked.

217

International list of top Chinese Restaurants

U.S.A.

Chef Ma's *Shanghai*
10 Pell St.,
New York
Tel: (212) 964 5842

Chung Kuo Yuan
Peking, Szechuan, Hunan
1115 3rd Ave.,
New York
Tel: (212) 371 9090

Foo Joy *Fukien*
13 Division St.,
New York
Tel: (212) 431 4931

Hee Seung Fung *Cantonese*
46 Bowery,
New York
Tel: (212) 374 1319

Hong Gung *Cantonese*
30 Pell St.,
New York
Tel: (212) 571 0545

Shun Lee Palace
Peking, Szechuan, Hunan
155 East 55th St.,
New York
Tel: (212) 371 8844

Silver Palace Restaurant
52 Bowery,
New York
Tel: (212) 964 1204

Szechuan Cuisine
Hunan & Szechuan
30 East Broadway,
New York
Tel: (212) 966 2326

Uncle Tai's Hunan Yuan
Hunan & Szechuan
1059 Third Ave.,
New York
Tel: (212) TE 8-0850

Yun Luck Rice Shoppe
Cantonese
17 Doyers St.,
New York
Tel: (212) 571 1375

King Wah Restaurant
25–29 Beach St.,
Boston, Massachusetts
Tel: (617) 426 2705

'70' Restaurant
70 Beach St.,
Boston, Massachusetts
Tel: (617) 542 7136

Chinese Dumpling House
7647 N. Pauline St.,
Chicago, Illinois

Peking Palace
4119 Lomo Alto,
Dallas, Texas
Tel: (214) 522 1830

Miriwa Restaurant
750 North Hill St.,
Los Angeles, California
Tel: (213) 687 3088

Tai Hong Restaurant
845 N. Broadway,
Los Angeles, California
Tel: (213) 485 1052

Asia House
2310 E. McDowell Rd.,
Phoenix, Arizona
Tel: (602) 267 7461

Empress of China
838 Grant Ave.,
San Francisco, California
Tel: (415) 434 1345

Kan's
708 Grant Ave.,
San Francisco, California
Tel: (415) 982 2388

Ku Soon's Penthouse
433 Airport Blvd.,
Burlingame, San Francisco,
California

GREAT BRITAIN

China Town *Cantonese*
7–14 Coventry St.,
London W.1.
Tel: (01) 437 6419

Chuen-Cheng Ku *Cantonese*
17 Wardour St.,
London W.1.
Tel: (01) 437 1398

Dragon Gate *Szechuan*
7 Gerrard St.,
London W.1.
Tel: (01) 734 5154

Gallery Rendezvous *Peking*
53/55 Beak St.,
London W.1.
Tel: (01) 437 4446

Uncle Pang *Cantonese*
30 Temple Fortune Parade,
London N.W.11.
Tel: (01) 455 9444

**The Riverside Chinese
Restaurant** *Cantonese*
Tudor Rd.,
Riverside, Cardiff
Tel: (0222) 37 2163

Edinburgh Rendezvous *Peking*
10a Queensbury St.,
Edinburgh
Tel: (031) 225 3777

Lau's *Peking*
358 Prescott Rd.,
Liverpool
Tel: (051) 228 6447

Woo Sang *Cantonese*
19–21 George St.,
Manchester
Tel: (061) 236 3697

AUSTRIA

China-Pavillon
XV, Winckelmannstrasse 38,
Vienna
Tel: 83 32 25

Lotus
1, Jasomirgottstrasse 3,
Vienna
Tel: 63 13 92

Zum Mandarin
1, Singerstrasse 11a,
Vienna
Tel: 52 28 04

Zum Drachen
Bayerhamerstrasse 33,
Salzburg
Tel: 72642

BELGIUM

Fontaine De Jade
Avenue Tervuren 5,
Brussels
Tel: 736 32 10

Grande Muraille *Cantonese*
Avenue de Woluwe St. Lambert
34,
Brussels
Tel: 736 84 74

Kam Seng *Cantonese*
12 rue du Pepin,
Brussels
Tel: 512 27 57

Lido
Rue Marie-Thérèse 106,
Brussels
Tel: 218 72 24

China Garden
De Keyserlei 17,
Antwerp
Tel: 32 85 81

Y-Sing
50 Boulevard de la Sauvenière,
Liège
Tel: 23 35 78

DENMARK

Bamboo
Rädhuspladen 77,
Copenhagen
Tel: 14 40 77

China House
Favergade 17,
Copenhagen
Tel: 12 99 59

Shanghai
Nygade 6 (Strøget),
Copenhagen
Tel: 12 10 01

FRANCE

Le Doyen Chinois
6, Avenue New York,
16ᵉ, Paris
Tel: 723 98 21

La P'tite Tonkinoise
56 fg Poissonnière,
10ᵉ, Paris
Tel: 246 85 98

Pagoda
50 rue Provence,
9ᵉ, Paris
Tel: 874 81 48

GERMANY

Hongkong
Kurfürstendamm 220,
West Berlin
Tel: 8 81 70 50

Tai-Tung
Budapesterstrasse 50,
West Berlin
Tel: 2 61 30 91

Mandarin
Steinstrasse 23,
Düsseldorf
Tel: 32 81 96

Peking
Kaiserstrasse 7,
Frankfurt
Tel: 28 85 72

Princess Garden
Leopoldstrasse 25,
Munich
Tel: 34 38 37

ITALY

La Pagoda
Via Filzi 2,
Milan
Tel: 65 47 00

Wan Tong
Via Paola Sarpi,
Milan
Tel: 34 36 33

THE NETHERLANDS

China
Rokin 20,
Amsterdam
Tel: 26 35 64

Lotus
Binnen Bantammerstraat 5–7,
Amsterdam
Tel: 24 26 14

De Grote Muur
Stadhuisplein 2,
Rotterdam
Tel: 12 35 81

De Lange Muur
West Kruiskade 1,
Rotterdam
Tel: 14 74 70

Kota Radja
Steenweg 37,
Utrecht
Tel: 31 94 68

NORWAY

Chung Ming House
Arbeidersamf, plasse 1,
Oslo 1
Tel: 20 03 54

Ming Wah Kro
Parkveien 13,
Oslo 1
Tel: 46 80 96

Peking House
Vikatorget, Ruseløkkveien 26,
Oslo 1
Tel: 41 05 76

Yang Tse Kiang
Torget 3,
Bergen 5000
Tel: 21 06 10

SPAIN

China
Valverde 9,
Madrid
Tel: 232 31 15

Nankin
Avenue Alberto Alcocer 27,
Madrid
Tel: 457 75 23

La Pagoda
Leganitos 22,
Madrid
Tel: 247 51 06

Chino Cathay
Santalo 86,
Barcelona
Tel: 212 56 73

SWEDEN

Berns Chinese Restaurant
Kornhamnstorg 55,
Stockholm
Tel: 20 53 40

China Garden
Karlavägen 15,
Stockholm
Tel: 21 55 34

Ming Garden
Götgatan 41,
Stockholm
Tel: 44 42 76

Shangri-La
Morra Bantorget,
Stockholm
Tel: 23 50 93

SWITZERLAND

Hong Kong Restaurant
Seefeldstrasse 60,
8008 Zurich
Tel: 32 82 02

Shanghai
Baeckerstrasse 62,
8004 Zurich
Tel: 242 40 39

Zum Gelben Schnabel
Zinnengasse 7/9,
8001 Zurich
Tel: 211 06 20

Hong Kong
Sempacherstrasse 7,
4053 Basel
Tel: 35 38 65

AUSTRALIA

Emperors Court Restaurant,
Rundle Mass,
Adelaide
Tel: 212 4076

Cathay Restaurant
Wickham Street,
Fortitude Valley,
Brisbane
Tel: 52 2765

Flower Drum
Little Bourke Street,
City,
Melbourne
Tel: 663 2531

Tientsin
175 Acland Street,
St. Kilda,
Melbourne
Tel: 534 2425/6

Golden Eagle
130 James Street,
Perth
Tel: 328 5420

Ming's Court Restaurant
New South Head Road,
Double Bay,
Sydney
Tel: 326 2266

Tai Ping Restaurant
Elizabeth Street,
Redfern, Sydney
Tel: 699 2133

NEW ZEALAND

Dynasty Restaurant
Customs Street East,
City,
Auckland
Tel: 372421

The Orient
Basement Strand Arcade,
Queen Street,
City,
Auckland
Tel: 797793

The Mayflower Eating House
George Street,
Dunedin
Tel: 76263

The Mandarin
23 Rostrevor Street,
Hamilton
Tel: 86349

HONG KONG

Hoover Restaurant
2 Wah Fu Road,
Aberdeen
Tel: 5-514151

Pearl City Restaurant
22 Paterson Street
Causeway Bay
Tel: 5-778226

Jade Garden Restaurant
Star House,
Kowloon
Tel: 3-675655

Oceania Restaurant
Ocean Terminal,
Kowloon
Tel: 3-670181

JAPAN

Chateau Mita
3-7-1 Mita,
Mintoku,
Tokyo
Tel: 453 7092

Chinese Restaurant
10th Floor,
Hanshin Department Store,
1 Umedacho,
Osaka
Tel: (06) 345 1201

Suppliers of Chinese Foodstuffs and Cooking Equipment

*The New Frontier Trading Corporation,
2394 Broadway,
New York
Tel: (212) 799 9338

*Kam Kuo Food Corporation,
7–9 Mott St.,
New York
Tel: (212) 349 3097

Kam Man Food Products Inc.,
200 Canal St.,
New York
Tel: (212) 571 0171

Chung Wah Hong Co.,
53–55 Beach St.,
Boston, Massachusetts
Tel: (617) 426 3619

*Shing Chong & Company,
800 Grand Avenue,
San Francisco, California
Tel: (415) YU 2-0949

*Star Market,
3349 North Clark St.,
Chicago, Illinois
Tel: (312) GR 2-0599

Kowloon Market,
755 North Hill St.,
Los Angeles, California
Tel: (213) 488 0264

Kwan Lee Lung Co.,
801 North Hill St.,
Los Angeles, California
Tel: (213) 628 5735

*International Supermarket,
117 North 10th St.,
Philadelphia, Pennsylvania
Tel: (215) 922 6062

*Ginn Wall Company Inc.,
1016 Grant Ave.,
San Francisco, California
Tel: (415) 982 6307

*The Wok Shop,
804 Grant Avenue,
San Francisco, California
Tel: (415) 989 3797

*Oriental Import-Export Co.,
2009 Plok St.,
Houston, Texas
Tel: (713) 233 5621

* Denotes that they will fill mail orders

Index

Special photography by Robert Golden and Melvin Gray.

The publishers would like to thank the following individuals and organisations for their kind permission to reproduce the other photographs in this book:—

Bryce Attwell: 66, 134, 135, 177, 205; Brown & Polson: 168; Barry Bullough: 115; S. & R. Greenhill: 100–1; John Hillelson Agency: Marc Riboud/Magnum 138–9; Paul Kemp: 126, 130; Paolo Koch: 60–1; John Lee: 62, 110, 148; Neil Lorrimer: 70, 164; Zefa: Dr. H. Kramarz 178–9.

The publishers would also like to express their gratitude to Liberty & Co. Ltd. and The New Neal Street Shop for the loan of accessories for photography, and to China Town Restaurant, Piccadilly, in particular for help with location photography.

PDO 78/466